All Around Mesquite

History, Trails, & Destinations

Dustin Charles Berg

Disclaimer: Liability Waiver and Release of Claims for "All Around Mesquite: History, Trails, and Destinations"

This Disclaimer is a legally binding agreement between you, the reader, and Desert Covenant Books, LLC ("Publisher"), regarding your use and reliance on the publication titled "All Around Mesquite: History, Trails, and Destinations," authored by Dustin Berg ("Author"). By accessing or using any part of the publication, you acknowledge and agree to the terms outlined below. If you disagree with these terms, do not use the publication.

1. Assumption of Risk
1.1. The publication contains historical, anecdotal, and informational content about the Mesquite region. It is for general informational purposes only and does not constitute professional or expert advice.

1.2. Engaging in activities or visiting places mentioned may involve risks, such as physical injury or property damage. Deciding to partake in such activities is voluntary and at your own risk. If planning to visit or engage in activities, consider consulting local authorities or experts.

2. Accuracy and Completeness
2.1. Although the Publisher and Author have made diligent efforts, there are no guarantees regarding the accuracy, reliability, or suitability of the content.
2.2. Information may become outdated due to changes in local conditions and other factors. Always verify information from reliable and current sources.

3. Release and Waiver of Liability
3.1. To the fullest extent permitted by law, you release Desert Covenant Books, LLC, Dustin Berg, and their affiliates from any claims or liabilities related to your use of the publication or any activities undertaken based on its content.
3.2. You agree not to hold any of the aforementioned parties liable for any injuries, losses, or damages resulting from or related to the publication.

4. Indemnification
4.1. You agree to indemnify and hold harmless all parties associated with the publication from any claims or liabilities arising from your use or any breach of this Disclaimer.

5. Contact
5.1. For questions, concerns, or to report errors, contact Desert Covenant Books, LLC at:

Email: allaroundmesquite@gmail.com
Address: #256 550 W Pioneer Blvd, Ste 140, Mesquite, NV 89027 US.

6. Governing Law
6.1. This Disclaimer is governed by the laws of the State of Nevada.

7. Entire Agreement
7.1. This Disclaimer supersedes all previous agreements and understandings regarding its subject matter.

Defamation and Accuracy
8.1. The content within the publication is presented in good faith and with the intention of providing historical and current information about the Mesquite region.
8.2. All statements and depictions within the publication are either based on research, historical records, and interviews, or are expressly stated as the opinions of the Author.
8.3. The Publisher and Author disclaim any intent to defame, malign, or unjustly portray any individual, organization, or entity. If any content is found to be factually incorrect or potentially defamatory, it is unintentional, and the Publisher and Author commit to correcting such information in subsequent editions.

Content Disclaimer

9.1. This publication includes a variety of content that reflects the diverse history and culture of the Mesquite region. It is not the intent of the Publisher or Author to offend, but rather to inform and provide a comprehensive view of the region.
9.2. Readers are advised that the publication may include historical or cultural references that are sensitive or controversial. Such content is included for the sake of historical accuracy and is not intended to offend or propagate outdated or offensive views.

Fair Use and Copyright
10.1. This publication may include material such as quotes, excerpts, or images that are covered under fair use for educational or informational purposes.
10.2. The Publisher and Author respect the intellectual property rights of others and have sought to ensure that all such material is properly credited and used within the bounds of fair use.

Updates and Corrections
11.1. The Publisher and Author are committed to accuracy and transparency. Readers are encouraged to report any errors or concerns regarding the content to the Publisher for review and potential correction in future editions.

No Endorsement
12.1. Mention of any businesses, services, or locations within the publication does not constitute an endorsement by the Publisher or Author, nor any possible Contributors.
12.2. Readers should exercise their own judgment and due diligence regarding the quality, safety, and suitability of any businesses, services, or locations mentioned.

By using the publication, you acknowledge your agreement to these terms. If you disagree, your sole remedy is to discontinue its use.

Note: This publication does not offer professional advice. While advertising is present, it has had no influence on the content, narrative, or integrity of the book. There has been no endorsement, influence, or modification based on sponsors' opinions. Should you find any errors, please bring them to our attention immediately for rectification.

Publication Details:
First Published: November, 2023. Edition: 1st.

Copyright & Credits:
Front cover design, photographs, text, and map: © Desert Covenant Books, LLC.
Some images within this book are available for licensing.

Photography Credits:
All photographs in this book are the work of Dustin Berg, except as noted below in the special acknowledgments.

Special Photography Acknowledgments:
We express our gratitude to the Virgin Valley Heritage Museum for allowing the use of 7 images from their collection. Their contribution has significantly enhanced the historical and visual narrative of this book.

We also acknowledge the artistic contributions of the following iStockphoto.com photographers, whose images have been included in this publication:
Hannah Mathews
whammer121736
GiorgioMorara
Different_Brian
kojihirano
J Gillispie
Lightguard
lucky-photographer
Bobbushphoto
Jeremy Christensen
travelview

Printing:
Desert Covenant Books, LLC. For More Info: www.mesquitebook.com

Layout by Desert Covenant Books, LLC & Mesquite Branding LTD.
Special Layout Acknowledgment: Trenton Robison.

Thank you to everyone who shared insights, advice, and stories.
Individual contributors are acknowledged at the end of the publication.

© 2023 Desert Covenant Books, LLC. All Rights Reserved.

Table of Contents

I. Preface..1

II. Introduction..3
- Timeline of the Tri State Area
- The Good, The Bad, and the Ugly: A Detailed Portrait of the City
- Navigating the Nuances: Top 5 Things I Wish I Knew Before I Moved Here

III. Historical Overview of the Region
- Part 1: Setting the Scene..15
  - The Mojave Desert: An Arid Canvas
  - Echoes of Ancient: The Lost City
  - The Virgin River: A Winding Lifeline through the Desert
  - The 1776 Connection: A Patriotic Pilgrimage
  - Gold Butte: A Geological Marvel in the Southwest
  - Unyielding Spirits: Life on the Muddy River (1865-1871)
  - The Davidson Tragedy
  - St. Thomas: A Journey Through Time
  - Mesquite Flats: The Founding Footsteps
  - Fractured Frontiers: The Territorial Disputes of Lake Mead
  - The Mormon Pioneer Pathway
  - Verdant Valley and Paiute Roots: The Tri-State's Botanical Tapestry
  - The Wild Burros of Gold Butte: Mesquite's Silent Builders
- Part 2: The Making of Modern Mesquite 36
  - Mesquite's Link to Treasure & the Old Spanish Trail
  - Settler's Division & The Lost Boys
  - The Hoover Dam Chronicles: A Meld of Ambition, Controversy, and Sacrifice
  - Mesquite Arrows: The Guiding Giants of Airmail History
  - Mesquite's Storied Past: From Pioneer Struggles to Pandemics
  - Civilian Conservation Corps: A Legacy Cast in Sand & Stone
  - Mafia Mysteries in the Desert
  - Embracing the Call of the Wild: Mesquite's Natural Tapestry
  - Mesquite Amidst the Mushroom Clouds: Echoes from Bunkerville's Past
  - A Ribbon Through the Desert: The I-15's Legacy in the Tri-State Area
  - Farmer's Tenacity: An Emblem of Mesquite
  - Rural Robberies & Crime Chronicles: From a Bank to a Casino
  - Takeaways from Mesquite's "Battle for Decency"
  - The Confluence of Time Zones: The Tri-State Experience
  - The Oasis Casino: A Beacon in the Desert
- Part 3: Booms, Busts, and Resurgence..65
  - The Fastest Growing City in the USA: The Rise of Mesquite
  - The Evolving Frontier: Arizona Strip in the Modern Era
  - Mesquite's Underbelly: Murder, Mystery, & History
  - The Great Recession - Boom or Bust: Weathering the Economic Storm
  - Mesquite's Trails and Parks: Promoting an Active Lifestyle
  - Mojave Mavericks: Rugged Ingenuity Amidst the Desert Sands
  - Long Drive, Rodeo, and All Stars: Mesquite's Spectacular Showcase
  - On the Rocks: Golf Resorts & Recreation

Table of Contents

- Federal Influence: Protection & Restriction
- Mesquite in Popular Culture: Echoes of Gold Butte's Whispers
- Nature's Wonders: State & National Parks Around Mesquite
- A Line in the Sand: Bunkerville & the Struggle for Sovereignty
- A Spiritual Oasis: God's Work & the Flourishing Faith of Mesquite
- Exploring Modern Mesquite: Safety, Natural Resources, & Future Prospects
- The Current State of the Tri State Region
- Interconnected Dreams and Shared Futures

IV. Urban Information & Events 86

V. OHV Information & Trails and Destinations by Region 93

A. Mesquite 104
- Introduction and Significance of the Region
- Downtown: Urban Destinations & Historical Markers
- Trails & Scenic Destinations

B. Moapa Valley 120
- Introduction and Significance of the Region
- Downtown: Urban Destinations & Historical Markers
- Trails & Scenic Destinations

C. Lincoln County 130
- Introduction and Significance of the Region
- Downtown: Urban Destinations & Historical Markers
- Trails & Scenic Destinations

D. Arizona Strip 137
- Introduction and Significance of the Region
- Downtown: Urban Destinations & Historical Markers
- Trails & Scenic Destinations

E. Southern Utah 152
- Introduction and Significance of the Region
- Downtown: Urban Destinations & Historical Markers
- Trails & Scenic Destinations

VI. Epilogue 172

VII. Acknowledgments 177

VIII. About the Author 181

IX. Index 182

DID YOU KNOW?
Mesquite Fact Sheet

To whet your appetite for the adventure ahead, here are some mesmerizing tidbits about Mesquite. Each revelation invites you to explore why this city is beloved by both thrill-seekers and tranquility-lovers.

Did You Know?

Mesquite ranks consistently among the top two safest cities in Nevada.

Mesquite, once among the fastest-growing cities in the country, conveniently positions itself between two significant markets: St George, Utah and Las Vegas, Nevada.

Mesquite is home to 7 championship golf courses & 3 upscale casino resorts, offering a blend of relaxation and excitement.

The city has thousands of acres of public land available for exploration, perfect for adventurous souls.

The Virgin River & various mountain aquifers not only ensure a sufficient water supply but support a vibrant & diverse ecosystem.

Mesquite is an OHV/ATV-friendly city, with its city roads open to street-legal off-road vehicles, making it ideal for enthusiasts who enjoy thrilling off-road adventures.

The city boasts beautiful parks and miles of scenic city trails, promoting an active and healthy lifestyle within its community.

Mesquite has six state and national parks within a 3-hour drive, making it a key tourism generator.

DID YOU KNOW?
Mesquite Fact Sheet

Mesquite is a hotspot for intriguing rumors and wild tales, encompassing everything from Bigfoot sightings, and UFO encounters, to a series of bizarre crimes.

Mesquite is famous for being home to the world's longest non-union strike.

Uniquely, you can experience three states and three different time zones within a 30-minute drive from the city.

Nearby Pakoon Springs, just 30 miles south of the city once held not only 500 ostriches, but a real-life alligator in the desert.

Mesquite is located in Clark County, which is by far the most populous county in Nevada, and the 11th most populous county in the United States. Whereas the nearby bordering area of Mohave County (Northwest Arizona) is even larger - the fifth largest county in the United States by area.

Mesquite and surrounding area has a long history of what may be considered controversial and extremist positions on government, religion, and politics.

The nearby Arizona Strip has 3.2 million acres of land north of Grand Canyon, is landlocked by the rest of the state of Arizona and Southern Utah. The region is home to a half dozen communities including the famous and controversial FLDS home of Colorado City.

As you turn the pages of "All Around Mesquite: History, Trails, & Destinations," we encourage you to keep an open heart and a keen eye. For Mesquite, with its layers of intrigue and charm, is ready to reveal itself to those who dare to explore.

PREFACE

Welcome to **"All Around Mesquite: History, Trails, & Destinations"** - a detailed and captivating exploration of Mesquite, Nevada and the surrounding area. By exploring this distinct locale, we gain valuable insights that deepen our appreciation for the small town and its neighboring communities. We strived to paint a comprehensive portrait of the region, but given the rich tapestry of its history, landscape, and charm, some stories inevitably fell beyond the scope of this volume. Our narrative remains firmly rooted in accuracy and factual representation, with a sprinkle of engaging tales.

Our hope is with enough interest, the book will lend itself to revisions or even a second edition soon. We will update our e-edition regularly with new information, references, graphic updates and resource links.

For ease of navigation, the book's structure is crafted with utmost clarity and simplicity. It's divided into three areas:

1. History: Divided into three periods, this section unravels the chronicles of Mesquite's past. We included captivating information about the city's history from the Paiute tribe to the settling pioneers, to its modern developments.

2. Trails: Throughout the book, you will encounter guides and descriptions of the area's breathtaking landscape. We organized the content by region integrating trail information into the narrative for a more intuitive exploration experience.

3. Destinations: The section serves as a visual index, listing notable locations alphabetically and linking them to historical data and maps in other parts of the book.

This division allows you to explore the city's history, geography, and landmarks, providing a clear understanding of Mesquite and the surrounding area.

To enhance your reading experience, we included photographs, infographics, bullet points, checklists, and more in the guide, making it visually appealing and user-friendly.

Are you ready to unravel the fascinating mysteries of Mesquite? Venture into its captivating landscapes and unearth the stories hidden beneath its sands. Be enthralled by the allure of its lush golf courses, set against a backdrop of intriguing folklore and rich history. This journey is an invitation to both seasoned adventurers and those curious at heart, to discover the unique blend of nature and culture in the heart of Mesquite.

Whether you are a seasoned local or a curious visitor, "All Around Mesquite, Nevada" is crafted for you - the explorers, hikers, treasure hunters, ghost town aficionados, and those who are simply intrigued by the unknown. This book invites you to dive deep into the heart of the American Southwest, uncovering the hidden gems and untold stories of Mesquite, Nevada, and the expansive Tri-State area.

Discover the ingenuity and resilience of its people, who have shaped this land through time. Experience the unique blend of natural beauty and cultural heritage that makes this region so captivating. Dive into this guide and let the adventure unfold.

"All Around Mesquite: History, Trails, & Destinations" is our labor of love - a chronicle, a guide, and an homage to the resilient and intriguing corner of the world, Mesquite, & the Tri-State area. As you turn these pages, you're set to embark on a journey that seamlessly weaves the past into the present, celebrates the natural wonders of the landscape, and explores the city's slightly eccentric past. Get ready for an exhilarating ride through history, geology, and the undeniable spirit of Mesquite. Welcome to our narrative. Welcome to Mesquite, Nevada!

INTRODUCTION

Mesquite, Nevada—a city that defies convention to craft an experience as distinct as it is indelible. Nestled within the rugged splendor of the Mojave Desert, creating a vivid tableau of a place that continues to astonish and captivate. As we embark on this detailed expedition, prepare to be taken by surprise and immersed in the unusual. Fascinatingly complex and surprisingly rich in history, Mesquite is like a canvas painted with hidden treasures and captivating tales.

Positioned at the juncture of beauty, enigma, and history, Mesquite offers a safe haven in the heart of the desert. Located halfway between Salt Lake City and Los Angeles, it's a popular stop for travelers and truckers traveling 350 miles in either direction.

In "All Around Mesquite, Nevada: Your Guide to Trails, Destinations, and Discoveries," we'll delve into the hidden attractions and vibrant spirit of this captivating city. Mesquite is the ultimate destination for both relaxation and adventure, boasting seven championship golf courses, three casino resorts, and vast public land just waiting to be explored. The presence of the Virgin River creates a diverse ecosystem, with mountain aquifers supplying ample water. Mesquite's terrain welcomes off-roaders, promising endless adventure on OHVs and ATVs.

Mesquite's family-friendly atmosphere and unique qualities make it a popular destination for residents and tourists year after year. Energetic entrepreneurs are creating thriving business districts, while residents enjoy the charm of our beautiful neighborhoods adorning the desert landscape.

Recognized as a prime retirement destination, Mesquite is the perfect choice for those seeking a serene Nevada retirement away from the hustle and bustle of Las Vegas.

Just 80 miles from the biggest city in Nevada (Las Vegas), Mesquite rests on the Nevada-Arizona border and is also a mere 40 miles away from St. George, Utah. Currently home to fewer than 25,000 residents, the city is experiencing rapid growth.

Mesquite is a true desert oasis that masterfully combines the comforts of small-town living with the allure of big-city attractions. Nestled in the scenic Virgin Valley, the city boasts breathtaking mountain backdrops and sunsets that defy reality. But Mesquite's appeal extends beyond aesthetics.

Centrally located and blessed with over 300 days of sunshine annually, Mesquite's desert setting offers endless opportunities for walking, hiking, biking, and more.

Golf enthusiasts will find a true haven in Mesquite, which is heralded as a golfer's paradise. Championship courses grace the landscape, consistently earning national acclaim. However, Mesquite is not just for golfers—off-road enthusiasts are finding Mesquite to be a perfect destination to pursue their passion in solitude.

Mesquite is the gateway to exploring over 1500 square miles of some of the world's most awe-inspiring landscapes and archaeological sites. This is why many claim this area is truly God's Country.

Within a day's drive, you can visit nine national parks, twelve national monuments, six national forests, three national recreation areas, and countless state parks. Mesquite serves as the ideal base for excursions to Bryce, Zion, and Grand Canyon National Parks, along with Lake Mead, Snow Canyon, and Valley of Fire State Park.

Whether you're seeking a brief escape or a new place to call home, Mesquite is the destination of choice. We're always thrilled to welcome new friends and community members. Come and acquaint yourself with our city—you'll undoubtedly be glad you did.

But beyond the leisure and luxury, there's a deeper narrative. Mesquite's story is one of perseverance, of challenges met and overcome. It's about a community that faced adversity head-on and emerged stronger.

The town of Mesquite was not always the thriving hub it is today. Of all the settlements in the Virgin Valley, Mesquite faced some of the most daunting challenges. Imagine a settlement wiped out, not once, but twice by flash floods, only to rebuild and stand firm. The town's residents didn't just rebuild homes; they carved out the now historic Interstate 15 through the breathtaking Virgin River Gorge. The determination of Mesquite's settlers is epitomized by that age-old adage—the third time's the charm.

Diving into the annals of Mesquite's history, the settler's journey becomes clear. The Virgin Valley, comprising Littlefield and Beaver Dam in Arizona, and Bunkerville and Mesquite in Nevada, is defined by its connection to the Virgin River. This river, flowing through three states before joining the mighty Colorado, has both sustained and tested the settlements on its banks.

A glance at the past reveals the initial euphoria of Mesquite's first settlers. Successful cotton crops, bountiful barley harvests, and a growing community hinted at a promising future. But nature had other plans. In 1882, heavy rain caused flash floods, prompting cries of alarm in neighboring Bunkerville and bringing devastation to Mesquite. With houses damaged and canals destroyed, the community pulled together in an awe-inspiring display of unity and grit.

In Mesquite, the community faced challenges beyond environmental adversities. The Edmunds Act of 1882, a federal law aimed at curtailing polygamy in territories such as Utah, introduced complex social and legal dynamics. This legislation significantly impacted some local families who maintained such practices, compelling them to adopt a more discreet way of life. The community's response to this federal intervention was nuanced, with many balancing their private customs and traditions against the need for compliance with national laws. This period in Mesquite's history is characterized by a delicate interplay of public conformity and private adherence to personal beliefs.

With the invention of automobiles, Mesquite saw a new opportunity. The town became a hub for travelers and entrepreneurs alike. Cotton from Mesquite traveled all the way to mills in Washington, Utah funding community projects like the Relief Society Building. As years passed, the Virgin Valley Heritage Museum took shape, with local youths playing a pivotal role in its construction, a true testament to Mesquite's community spirit.

Photo Courtesy of Virgin Valley Heritage Museum

Each page of "Mesquite: Trails, History and Destinations," uncovers captivating tales, adding to the seasoned medley of this exceptional city. Welcome to Mesquite, a place where the past meets the present, and every corner holds a story waiting to be told.

Unbelievable rumors, breathtaking landscapes, folklore, coincidences, and beyond await. Ready to unravel the mysteries? Let's begin.

Your voyage into the heart of Mesquite begins now.

Timeline of MESQUITE

START — 1776
Spanish settlers first encounter Southern Paiute tribes

1829
Antonio Armijo passes through Mesquite, establishing Old Spanish Trail

1850s
Mormon Pioneers attempt to settle the area, initially failing

1861
Utah divided; western part called Nevada

1864
Nevada becomes a state

1865
Moapa Valley and St. Thomas first settled by Mormons

1866
Lincoln County created

1871
LDS Church members abandon St. Thomas in February

1877
Bunkerville Settled

1880
Permanent Settlement established by Mormon Pioneers, farming begins

1880
Post office named; first settled as Mesquit, changed to Mesquite in 1897

1882
Flood in Mesquite washed canal away in 58 places

1883
Mesquite becomes a branch of Bunkerville

1894
3rd and final attempt to settle Mesquite

1894
Mesquite Flats Post Office is established

1896
First voting precinct and post office in Mesquite

1901
Smallpox & typhoid epidemic

1905
Virgin Valley Railroad is built, boosting local economy

1906
Mesquite takes 1st place in Pomegranates & Thompson seedless grapes at World's Fair in San Francisco

- **1909** — Clark County created
- **1911** — Virgin Valley High School is established
- **1911** — Circus in Moapa
- **1913** — January - cold weather; river freezes over
- **1914** — Virgin Valley Railroad is abandoned
- **1916** — Virgin Valley takes first state title in basketball
- **1918** — Flu outbreak; schools and meetings closed
- **1920** — Grand opening for Zion National Park
- **1921** — First airplane passes over Littlefield
- **1922** — Hail as big as bird's eggs in June
- **1927** — Red measles epidemic; Scarlet fever epidemic
- **1928** — Swamps drained in Mesquite to get rid of mosquito problem
- **1929** — 3 inches of snow in Virgin Valley; Smallpox epidemic; no public meetings; Great Depression begins; Windstorm, many trees uprooted
- **1930-31** — Gypsum Cave excavated
- **1931** — Nevada legalizes gambling
- **1932** — Record 11.97 inches of rain in St. George
- **1933** — Nevada adopts official "Home Means Nevada" song
- **1934** — CCC helps construct dam at ditch head
- **1935** — The filling of Lake Mead starts, inundating St. Thomas
- **1938** — One of the last residents to leave St. Thomas was Hugh Lord, who paddled away from his home when the rising water lapped at his front door
- **1939** — Mesquite & Bunkerville get electricity
- **1940** — Boundaries of Mesquite extended, fixed, and defined
- **1941** — Virgin Valley takes home the first state title in football
- **1944** — Clark County holds 2nd annual county fair in Mesquite
- **1945** — 3 sailors from New York caught in a flash flood near Mesquite
- **1948** — Littlefield gets electricity from Beaver Dam Lodge
- **1949** — Petition to prohibit liquor in Mesquite rejected

1954 — Mesquite Bunkerville Highway 91 contract was at the time the 3rd largest in the state, eliminated 2 crossings of the Virgin River

1955 — Permanent dam completed

1958 — Mesquite Post Office opens

1963 — Supreme Court settles a 40-year dispute between Arizona, California, & Nevada regarding water rights from the Colorado River

1967 — 30' x 50' concrete slab installed at White Rock

1969 — Government nuclear testing goes underground

1970 — Baneberry test in Nevada sends radioactive cloud 10,000 feet into the sky

1972 — Mesquite Community center construction; First casino, Peppermill Casino opens

1973 — Gasoline shortage in Mesquite; tourism on decline

1980 — Tornado-strength storm hits Virgin Valley, resulting in millions in damage; Population exceeds 800 residents

1982 — Virgin Valley takes first in Girls' volleyball and Girls' basketball

1984 — Mesquite incorporates as a town

1985 — First Mesquite Days Celebration

1989 — Police department established; Virgin Valley girls take the first state title in Track; Peppermill/Palms golf course opens

1990 — Virgin River Casino opens; Welcome Center opens; Mesquite Airport dedicated

1992 — Mesquite "Master Plan" development complete

1993-96 — Longest-running non-union picket line held against the Pure Pleasure Adult Book and Video store in Mesquite, ultimately leading to City policy changes and closure of the store

1994 — Mesquite City Centennial; Mesquite, Nevada Stake created

Timeline

1995 — First RE/MAX World Long Drive Championship held

1989-99 — The first Running of the Bulls Festival in the USA is held in Mesquite

2000 — Population grows to over 10,000

2006 — Mesquite and Southern Utah are named among the fastest growing areas in the United States

2007 — Mesquite Fine Arts Center opens

2009 — Closure of the Oasis (formerly the Peppermill) due to recession

2011 — First Mesquite Hot Air Balloon Festival held

2022 — City recovers from COVID-19 economic strain

2022 — St. George ranked as the fastest growing metro area in America, again

2023 — Present day, with tourism & hospitality dominating the market

Let's Get Started!

The Good, the Bad, and the Ugly: A Detailed Portrait of the City

The Good: A Tapestry of Community and Nature

The resilient community in our city has flourished despite challenges in the environment and economy. The small-town charm that wraps around its residents provides a warmth that's hard to find elsewhere. As a rapidly growing city, it has managed to offer a cost of living that is both reasonable and enticing to those looking for retirement, or even just a fresh start.

The environment is stunning in its beauty and beckons outdoor enthusiasts, with each season (save for the scorching summer) offering its own blend of adventures. From hiking trails adorned with fall's golden hues to winter's occasional snow-capped vistas, there's an activity for every spirit. Woven into the city's fabric is its unique history, a narrative that's both interesting and intriguing, shaping its identity with every passing chapter.

The Bad: Facing the Challenges of Growth

But like every city, there are shadows that play amidst its sunlit avenues. The heat, intense and unrelenting, defines the very rhythm of life, compelling residents to seek solace during its peak.

With the town rapidly expanding we're feeling the pressure on infrastructure, resulting in occasional inconveniences. While the city has a thriving community of retirees, it's clear there's a need for activities for junior residents and families. The challenge is finding a balance as the city grows, meeting the needs of its residents and appealing to visitors.

The Ugly: Shadows of the Past and Present

Delving deeper, there are chapters in the story of Mesquite that many would rather forget but are essential in understanding its character. Significantly, the city finds itself linked to a tragic chapter in modern American history, having once been the second home of the individual behind the deadliest mass shooting in the United States. This harrowing event in Las Vegas stands as a stark reminder of the unpredictability of human nature, etching a somber note in the annals of history.

The Bundy standoff is another controversial moment, with arguments that the federal government overstepped its boundaries. Although the standoff is a subject of national attention, it also underscores local tensions over land use and federal governance.

A group among the local population values seclusion and reduced government intervention, sometimes to the extent of organizing militias. These actions are often driven by a belief in the importance of safeguarding against a potential bureaucratic overreach. The assortment of perspectives on governance and autonomy in this local area adds another to the distinct atmosphere of this unique part of the world.

Less publicized incidents, such as the creation and demolition of Temple Bar in the 1990's, add another layer of complexity. This short-lived private township raised important questions about freedom, law, and sovereignty that continue to rumble beneath the surface. Local politics further amplify this tension, especially when election cycles roll around, offering a portrait of a community grappling with its evolving identity. The troubling history of suicides and unexplained murders emphasizes the need for reflection and community unity in these stories.

In Conclusion: A City of Contrasts

The city exemplifies a striking contrast, balancing its strong sense of tight-knit community against the backdrop of its stunning natural beauty. Its rich history is dotted with notable figures, including a well-known stuntman whose life ended tragically in a jump across the Oasis "air walk." The city's narrative, weaving past and present, poses challenging questions, especially in governance. Issues surrounding elections and local sovereignty movements bring to light complex matters of taxation and federal rights.

Navigating this city's story is akin to a journey through a labyrinth, filled with moral and social complexities. The citizens, while sometimes on the periphery, find themselves at the heart of broader discussions about values and identity. As the city grows, it retains a unique sense of belonging, a witness to its diverse character.

Embracing its entire spectrum—the good, the bad, and the unexpected—this city transcends mere geography. It is a vibrant, evolving community, a place of joy for many who call it home.

Navigating the Nuances: Top 5 Things I Wish I Knew Before I Moved Here
From the Author's Perspective

Bug Battles: The Unseen War Beneath Mesquite Homes

In the vast landscape of Mesquite, there's a challenge that's often overlooked: the small creatures that have claimed this region for centuries. Bark scorpions with their menacing venom, are but one facet of this microcosm. Swarming termites, in particular, are a sight to behold, blanketing areas in a whirl of activity. Their presence isn't just a fleeting spectacle; many of the area's foundations are under siege by these relentless pests.

Since a small portion of Mesquite's development stands upon old landfills, the soil composition, primarily dirt, can easily become infested. Further complicating matters, some construction teams have historically sidestepped rigorous geological surveys. As a result, a handful of structures in the region have suffered, literally sinking into the challenges that lie beneath their foundations. The history of Mesquite is shaped by its inhabitants, landscapes, and by nature's enduring hold.

Meanwhile, the sting of the red fire ant is painful and can cause a raised welt. The early days taught me to be vigilant and to appreciate the intricacies of the local ecosystem.

The Charms and Challenges of Rural America

Ah, the serenity of rural life—a dream I eagerly chased. However, I quickly realized that this dream comes with its own set of realities. The vast stretches, while picturesque, sometimes translate to limited access to resources. Spontaneous late-night ice cream runs or quick hops to a large grocery store become calculated endeavors. Yet, with every sunset over the open fields, I'm reminded of the peace that drew me here. Learn to be efficient and plan your trips to Costco and you'll do just fine.

The Ever Evolving I-15: Roads, Ruins, and Revelations

Interstate 15 (I-15), winding its way through Mesquite, is more than just asphalt and traffic signs. It stands as a testament to the region's growth and relentless spirit. As travelers often note, the regular hum of construction speaks to progress, yet also hints at Mesquite's deeper layers.

Many a traveler has encountered detours on the I-15, leading them to discover Mesquite's hidden scenic byways. These diversions, while sometimes inconvenient, also guide visitors to the region's tucked-away beauties.

But beneath the modern upgrades, whispers circulate about ancient histories. Rumor suggests that construction projects on I-15 may have uncovered, or even buried over, ancient Indigenous ruins. While these tales remain unconfirmed, they add a layer of intrigue to the journey, hinting that every mile might hold centuries of stories.

The I-15 isn't merely a highway; it's a narrative of Mesquite's balance between the past and future. As you travel its length, you're traversing more than just a road—you're journeying through Mesquite's rich tapestry.

Whispers in the Wind: The Small-Town Rumor Mill

Small towns have their own rhythm, a tapestry woven with tales, truths, and the somewhere in between. Word travels fast in rural America, and before you know it, you're part of a narrative you didn't even know existed. Embracing community life means understanding its heartbeat - and sometimes its penchant for gossip. As a cowboy learns to bridle his horse, you too, will learn to bridle your tongue, at least here in the suburbs. In recent times, social media has played a new role in this phenomenon and Facebook groups have become a harbor ground of negative coverage and reviews. Occasionally, though, you will see positivity shine through. If you are a good service provider or business owner that goes the extra mile, your suburban neighbors will be your biggest cheerleaders.

Dry Heat: A Deceptive Embrace

Everyone talks about the dry heat as if it's a soft caress—a contrast to the oppressive stickiness of humid climates. And while it's true you won't feel you've stepped into a sauna, the sun's intensity is no joke. It's a searing kind of hot, one that teaches respect for shade and the value of a well-timed cold beverage. Drink lots of water and service your AC regularly. And yes, things slow down significantly in the summer here.

Finding Home Amidst Surprises

Every place has its quirks, its challenges, and its unexpected moments. While I've been taken by surprise more than once, these experiences have enriched my journey, adding depth to my understanding of this unique corner of the world. Despite the initial hurdles, my heart has found its rhythm here, dancing to the tune of desert winds and starlit nights. Embracing a new home often means navigating its surprises and quirks. From unexpected wildlife encounters to the realities of rural life, each experience teaches and enriches. Mesquite's I-15 not only signifies progress, but whispers of deep-rooted histories.

In small towns, community connections run deep, both in person and on digital platforms, magnifying both challenges and support. The deceptive embrace of dry heat underscores the importance of adaptation. Through it all, these experiences weave a rich tapestry of life in this unique corner of the world. As challenges turned into cherished memories, I've found not just a house, but a true home amidst the desert winds and starlit nights. There's a profound sense of belonging here. I've always felt I was led here for a reason and there's no place I'd rather be.

In Summary

As I ponder the unexpected turns my own journey has taken since moving here, I'm reminded of a story that perfectly encapsulates the essence of life's unpredictability. In her book, "A River and a Road" by Dorothy Dawn Frehner Thurston, a compelling legend is recounted. Set in 1945, it tells of three New York sailors who unexpectedly faced a flash flood near Mesquite. Amid this tragic event, one sailor perished. Capturing the irony of their situation, a surviving sailor remarked, "We've been on every water in the world and have come to the desert to drown." This story reflects the unpredictability of Mesquite, a place where the extraordinary often unfolds. Expect the unexpected.

HISTORIC OVERVIEW OF THE REGION

Part 1: Setting the Scene
The Mojave Desert: An Arid Canvas

Amidst the vast landscapes of the American Southwest, the Mojave Desert stretches its arms, presenting a terrain that is as intriguing as it is formidable. Mesquite, Nevada, is a gem in the desert, and the layers of the Mojave reveal it's the character.

Desert Extreme and Subtle Nuances

Characterized by minimal rainfall, extreme temperatures, and sweeping sand dunes, the Mojave Desert is North America's driest desert. This may paint a picture of desolation, but it's far from accurate. In this stark environment, a variety of hardy plants and animals have not just survived but thrived.

The Joshua Tree, with its peculiar twisted shape, emerges as a desert icon. It's believed that pioneers named this tree after the biblical figure Joshua, seeing its outstretched limbs as guiding hands, beckoning travelers westward through the vast, harsh terrain.

As you venture deeper into Mesquite's surrounding desert, the dance of shadows under a crescent moon or the golden hue of the sun on red sandstones reveals the Mojave's poetic side.

Geological Marvels and Mysteries

While the Mojave Desert is known for its share of remarkable geological formations, the tri-state area near Mesquite unveils a variety of distinctive natural wonders. From the expansive mesas of the Virgin River Gorge to the captivating rock formations of the Arizona Strip, this region offers a tapestry of geological treasures that extend beyond the traditional notions of sand and barren landscapes. Each rock, hill, and crevice narrates a tale waiting for curious explorers to uncover.

Man and Mojave: A Relationship Etched in Sand

The allure of the Mojave isn't just its natural beauty. Human civilizations have called this desert home for millennia. Indigenous tribes, Spanish explorers, and American pioneers all understood the potential of this inhospitable land. They recognized its charm, challenges, and promise.

But why Mesquite?

Nestled between grand geological formations and significant cultural sites, Mesquite's location is a blend of ancient history and natural wonders. And as we'll discover in the chapters to come, this is a place where history and geography converse in the most unexpected ways.

The Mojave Desert is not just an 'arid canvas'; it's a living, breathing entity with tales as old as time. Its stark landscapes serve as the backdrop for countless stories, including that of Mesquite. As we journey through Mesquite's history and attractions, remember that this city's story is deeply intertwined with the mysteries and wonders of the Mojave.

In the following pages, we'll explore ancient civilizations, pioneers on the Spanish Trail, and the challenges of taming the desert land. And at the heart of it all lies Mesquite, a testament to human tenacity and the magic that happens when man and nature come together in harmony.

Echoes of Ancient: The Lost City

Nestled amid the vast expanse of the Mojave Desert lies an enigma that has puzzled archaeologists and fascinated visitors for years: the remnants of a mysterious place called The Lost City. Bathed in the morning sun, Mesquite becomes a backdrop for a journey through time. Revealing tales of an ancient civilization; their sophisticated way of life, and its eventual collapse, leaving only traces behind.

The First Settlers: Ancestral Puebloans

Long before the neon lights of Las Vegas or the founding steps at Mesquite Flats, the Ancestral Puebloans (formerly known as the Anasazi) inhabited this region. These settlers constructed intricate, multi-storied dwellings using the region's abundant clay, developing a sophisticated culture in the arid expanse of the Mojave.

Intricate Architecture and Ingenious Adaptations

The Ancestral Puebloans' architectural designs were remarkable considering the challenging environment and scarce resources. Utilizing cliffs or constructing standalone structures, their dwellings ingeniously used shade and water resources, demonstrating a profound understanding of their environment.

Visitors today can see remnants of kivas (ceremonial chambers) and petroglyphs, revealing a deeply spiritual society. These rock arts portray animals, hunting scenes, and celestial patterns, giving us a glimpse into their world—one of rituals, stories, and survival.

Trade, Culture, and Decline

Evidence suggests that this region wasn't just an isolated outpost. Archaeological discoveries, such as shells from the Pacific and artifacts from Central America, suggest that Mesquite's ancient residents were connected to a vast prehistoric world through extensive trade routes.

However, around the 12th century, something shifted. Dwellings were abandoned, pots left mid-use, and fields untilled. Was it a prolonged drought? Societal conflict? Or perhaps both? The exact reasons remain a mystery, turning the once-thriving region into what we now refer to as 'The Lost City.'

A Modern Rediscovery

The Lost City, a testament to the resilience of the past, lay hidden in the embrace of time until the early 20th century. As the sands of time gradually shifted, this enigmatic archaeological marvel regained its place in the limelight. Careful excavations and detailed studies uncovered the untold stories of the people who lived there, giving us a clear understanding of their lives and dreams. Today, reconstructed sites invite curious tourists and historians to explore the mysteries of the past. The Lost City links the present to the distant past, encouraging us to appreciate the diverse tapestry of human existence that once prospered within its walls.

A Living Heritage

For the people of Southern Nevada, The Lost City is not merely an archaeological site; it's a testament to human resilience and innovation. It serves as a reminder that, in the heart of the Mojave, civilizations once thrived, cultures blossomed, and stories were born.

The Lost City is an important chapter in the area's history, with the whispers of ancient spirits in the desert winds. As you walk the trails or visit the remnants, pause for a moment. Listen. You might just hear tales of a time long gone, tales that Southern Nevada proudly embraces as part of its tapestry.

The Virgin River: A Winding Lifeline through the Desert

Meandering gracefully across the desolate landscape of the Mojave, the Virgin River emerges as an emblem of life, sustenance, and hope. For millennia, this river has been both a witness to the Mojave's evolutionary tale and a vital participant in its unfolding drama. The Virgin River's journey from Utah's mountains to Mesquite and beyond is a tale of resilience and unwavering spirit.

The Oasis Maker: Source of Life in the Desert

In a region as arid as the Mojave, water is nothing short of a miracle. The Virgin River, with its refreshing presence, has provided much-needed sustenance to a myriad of life forms. Cottonwood and willow trees border the river, offering a green escape from the sandy landscape and providing a cool oasis for desert animals.

Early Inhabitants and the River's Bounty

The river's fertile banks have attracted human settlement for centuries. The Ancestral Puebloans, the ancient denizens of the region, relied heavily on the river. They crafted ingenious irrigation systems, making agriculture possible in an otherwise unforgiving landscape. Corn, beans, and squash flourished, laying the foundation for a society that would thrive against all odds.

The Pathfinding River: Guiding Pioneers to Prosperity

As pioneers traversed the vast American West, the Virgin River served as a beacon, guiding them through the treacherous desert terrain. Mesquite owes its genesis to this river. Early settlers recognized the river's potential, using the river's resources to build the bustling town.

Mesquite's Special Bond: A Lifelong Partnership

For the people of Mesquite, the Virgin River is more than just a water body. It's a cherished partner, a constant companion. The town has grown in its embrace, and many local tales, festivities, and traditions find their roots in the river's winding paths.

However, this partnership hasn't been without challenges. Flash floods, a common occurrence, have often tested Mesquite's resolve. The town has shown resilience and adaptability, turning challenges into opportunities for growth.

Recreational Paradise: More Than Just a Lifeline

Today, the Virgin River isn't just a historical marvel; it's a hub of recreational activities. Kayaking, fishing, and serene riverside picnics are just a few of the joys it offers to residents and tourists alike. The winding trails attract adventurers for hiking and exploration, offering both excitement and tranquility.

The Virgin River is a great example of nature's contradictions-gentle yet powerful, persistent yet adaptable. As you explore Mesquite and its many tales, let the river be your guide, reminding you of the enduring spirit of nature and humanity's eternal bond with it. In the heart of the Mojave, the Virgin River flows, singing songs of the past, present, and future, awaiting those eager to listen.

The 1776 Connection: A Patriotic Pilgrimage

1776 – the year reverberates through the annals of history as one of the most transformative. The eastern coast of North America was filled with revolutionary energy and the desire for freedom, while thousands of miles away in the southwest, a parallel journey was taking place, driven by exploration, faith, and the same unyielding pioneering spirit.

Parallel Paths of Destiny

As the American Revolution unfolded, Spanish explorers in the southwest embarked on their own expedition. Their goal was to link Mexico's northernmost colonial outposts by establishing routes through the challenging Mojave and surrounding deserts.

The cries for freedom and the sounds of guns marked a significant period of change in the east, as colonists stood up against British control. Their struggle was a symbol of hope, showing resistance to oppression and the dream of self-determination. Town meetings, passionate speeches, and clandestine plans became the daily rhythm for those seeking independence. The birth of the United States transformed global politics, inspiring democratic principles, and self-governance worldwide.

Meanwhile, in the rugged landscapes of the southwest, Spanish explorers faced challenges of a different kind. The vast expanses of sand and sun held secrets and dangers in equal measure. Each day was an adventure, encountering new wildlife, weather, and negotiating with native tribes. Often, it was the wisdom of these indigenous inhabitants that guided the explorers through the most hostile stretches of their journey. By connecting outposts and charting miles, they created a network that enabled trade, communication, and cultural exchange. The combination of these two important movements represent the diverse elements that have shaped North American history.

Silvestre Vélez de Escalante and the Quest for Unity

Led by Silvestre Vélez de Escalante, these Spanish explorers had a shared destiny with their revolutionary counterparts in the east. They both ventured into uncharted territories – one for freedom from colonial oppression, and the other for religious evangelism.

The Mojave's Welcoming Arms

Despite Mojave's harsh appearance, it offered opportunities for Spanish settlers. The Virgin River and the lush banks of the Colorado became their guiding stars, similar to how the eastern settlers relied on the Atlantic for sustenance and guidance.

Shared Challenges and Triumphs

The challenges faced by these pioneers were immense. Be it the unyielding British forces or the vast unknown desert terrain, the spirit of determination was a common thread. Yet, both persevered, driven by a shared faith in a brighter future and an unwavering commitment to their respective causes. In Mesquite and its surroundings, remnants of this Spanish expedition are still palpable. Local place names, culture, and legends carry whispers of these early pilgrims, connecting the region to a broader story of American evolution.

Patriotism Beyond Borders

This dual journey, unfolding simultaneously in 1776, brings forth an intriguing perspective on patriotism. It wasn't just about battles and declarations; it was about forging ahead, driven by conviction. The Spanish explorers, in their quest to chart the unknown, mirrored the same fervor and courage as the revolutionaries in the east.

Legacy in Mesquite

Mesquite, with its unique position in the southwest, became a confluence of these histories. The values of perseverance, exploration, and unity that defined 1776 are deeply embedded in the town's ethos. It serves as a living testament to the interconnected destinies of diverse groups of pioneers.

1776 was not just a year; it was a statement, a proclamation of hope, and a beacon for all who dared to dream. In the vast landscapes of the Mojave, amidst the sand dunes and river bends, the echoes of this shared journey are still alive. The 1776 connection in Mesquite serves as a patriotic pilgrimage honoring individuals who, regardless of their origins or destinations, were united in spirit and purpose.

Gold Butte: A Geological Marvel in the Southwest

Amidst the sun-soaked vistas and the sweeping sands of the Mojave Desert, Gold Butte emerges as a captivating geological masterpiece. This region near Mesquite serves as a canvas showcasing an array of rock formations that tell the Earth's story in vivid detail.

In this dry and rugged wilderness, a diverse group of people driven by their individual passions gather as the sun shines its golden light upon them. The remnants of the past lure mining enthusiasts as echoes of historical mining activities reverberate through the canyons, sparking a sense of adventure and a yearning to uncover hidden treasure from the earth.

For the nature explorers, Gold Butte is a realm of endless fascination, a realm where every twist and turn reveals a new marvel of nature's craftsmanship. Whether it's the intricate sandstone patterns etched by wind and or the resilient desert flora, every facet of this landscape invites exploration into the mysteries of the Mojave.

The number of environmental activists is increasing in this land of contrasts, where both delicate ecosystems and traces of human civilization coexist. With a strong dedication to safeguarding the fragile ecosystem, these desert guardians emphasize the need to preserve the delicate balance between nature and human activity.

The trails that weave through Gold Butte invite side-by-side enthusiasts to explore the rugged terrains and bond with fellow adventure seekers, while hikers enjoy discovering new panoramic vistas.

In the vastness of Gold Butte, birdwatchers find their haven, as a kaleidoscope of winged residents paint the skies above. The melodies of avian choruses blend with the rustling of leaves, creating a symphony that echoes the harmony of the desert.

Gold Butte, with its rich tapestry of interests and pursuits, mirrors the dynamic mosaic of the desert's spirit. It's a place where mining history meets modern exploration, where environmental consciousness blends with adventure, and where the ancient whispers harmonize with the calls of its winged inhabitants. Gold Butte stands as a geological marvel that unites the passions of a community captivated by its timeless allure.

The Palette of the Earth: Vibrant and Varied

Upon first glance, Gold Butte in the Mojave Desert might be mistaken for just another rugged outcrop. However, a closer look reveals its true splendor as a geological wonder. This natural canvas is adorned with a rich palette, featuring deep reds and tranquil blues. The landscape, embellished with ancient petroglyphs and winding rock layers, tells a story of its rich history.

The array of colors and formations at Gold Butte is more than a mere coincidence of nature. For many, it signifies the presence of a grand design, what can only be described as the work of the creator. Shaped by volcanic activity, erosion, tectonic shifts, and flooding, Gold Butte stands as a vibrant example of the Earth's dynamic past. For those who witness its varied hues and intricate features, Gold Butte presents a profound illustration of the beauty and complexity inherent in the natural world.

Petroglyphs: Echoes of Ancient Voices

Gold Butte isn't just a geological wonder; it's an archaeological treasure trove. The region is dotted with petroglyphs – ancient rock art that provides glimpses into the lives of its earliest inhabitants. These symbols, painstakingly carved by native tribes, provide valuable insights into their beliefs and way of life.

For centuries, these petroglyphs have withstood the ravages of time, weather, and human interference. Their resilience is a testament to the expertise of their creators and the importance of the messages they sought to convey. The drawings depict animals, such as bighorn sheep and reptiles, implying a strong connection between the tribes and their surroundings. The reverence for nature and its creatures reflects the symbiotic relationship the tribes had with the land, depending on it for sustenance, shelter, and spiritual nourishment.

The patterns and symbols are not just mere drawings; they are the language of a bygone era, speaking of ceremonies, migrations, hunts, and possibly even celestial events. Some scholars believe petroglyphs might represent maps or markers of tribal boundaries, while others might indicate seasonal changes, for planting or harvesting. Interpreting these ancient symbols is a complex task, akin to deciphering a lost language. Yet, with each interpretation, we come a step closer to understanding the aspirations, fears, and the immense wisdom of the people who once called Gold Butte their home, ensuring that their voices, though distant, are never truly silent.

An Ecosystem: Thriving Against the Odds
Amidst this rugged terrain, life finds a way. Gold Butte is home to a variety of flora and fauna uniquely adapted to its harsh environment. From the Joshua tree, standing tall against the azure sky, to the elusive desert tortoise, each organism adds to Gold Butte's multifaceted charm.

Modern Day Guardians: Preservation and Appreciation
Recognizing its unparalleled value, efforts have been made to preserve Gold Butte, resulting in its designation as a National Monument, ensuring its preservation for future generations. Mesquite has played a crucial role in conservation efforts, serving as a gateway for those who want to explore this geological marvel.

Unyielding Spirits: Life on the Muddy River (1865-1871)

The American West in the 19th century is known as the last frontier, and the Muddy River settlements exemplify the spirit of exploration during that era. L. A. Fleming's book, "The Settlements on the Muddy 1865 to 1871: A God Forsaken place," offers a comprehensive portrayal of the challenges faced by settlers in this harsh terrain.

Moapa Valley in Southeastern Nevada, just a stone's throw from the majestic landscapes of Mesquite and Gold Butte, is home to the Muddy River, a part of a vast and treacherous landscape. Covering 30 miles but rarely expanding past two and a half miles, this stretch of Moapa was crucial for early settlers who, despite the valley's abundance, had to travel 60 miles for timber.

Origins in Naming
Renowned figures such as Kit Carson and Orville C. Pratt named the river 'Muddy' due to the terrain, while Joseph W. Young offered a different explanation, linking the name to an adjacent alkali swamp. The swamp, located on the east side of the creek near the California Road, is challenging to cross in wet weather. However, the creek itself has clean water, albeit too warm for pleasant drinking.

Mormon Motivations
The Latter-day Saint movement settled along the muddy River for three reasons.
- The meandering Colorado River offered a safer route to Salt Lake City, reducing the dangerous journey of 1000-miles to a more manageable 450 miles.
- Economic prosperity was pivotal for Brigham Young's envisioned inland empire. After realizing cotton's potential at the Santa Clara Indian Mission, the church began searching for valleys suitable for growing cotton. Moapa Valley, near Mesquite, emerged as a primary contender.

• The need to protect these fertile lands from non-Mormon settlers became urgent as nearby mines in Pioche, El Dorado Canyon, and the Arizona Territory started to prosper. A natural path emerged from these mines through the Meadow Valley Wash and the rivers of Muddy, Virgin, and Colorado, which became essential to control.

Terrain's Testimony

The Muddy River region in North America was arguably one of the most challenging areas to colonize in all the expansion of the West. The environment was inhospitable due to its remoteness, lack of proper roads, scorching summer heat, and persistent winds. Sandstorms frequently disrupted daily life, filling homes, food, and water sources. Besides these natural hardships, settlers had to contend with theft and disruptions from local Indian tribes.

Despite these challenges, a group of Latter-day Saints established settlements in the region as directed by their church's supposed prophetic calls. These pioneers believed their mission was divinely inspired, and this deep faith drove their perseverance and tenacity.

The settlers faced immense challenges in their first year. Besides building their community from scratch, they faced health crises like malaria and dysentery. Many lost hope and left; of the initial 40 families, only 25 remained by the end of the year.

Tensions with the local Native populations escalated. Stock thefts, murders, and retaliation acts made coexistence challenging. Concerned about the deteriorating situation, Brigham Young wrote to the local Mormon leadership, proposing the abandonment of smaller, vulnerable settlements in favor of more defensible locations.

War, Cotton, and Trade

With the Civil War disrupting cotton supplies, the Mormons pivoted to self-reliance in textile production. News of potential river freighting routes reached Hardy's Landing, prompting William H. Hardy to extend a trade olive branch to the Mormons. This spurred a new expedition led by luminaries like Jacob Hamblin, James M. Whitmore, and Anson Call who was particularly taken by the Colorado River's resemblance to the Illinois River. While his enthusiasm was palpable, challenges remained — the projected cost for a road to the chosen landing was a staggering $60,000.00.

Trials and Triumphs

The stories of the settlements near the Muddy River, particularly Mesquite and Gold Butte, were tales of overcoming challenges and achieving victory. With Thomas S. Smith helming the initial settlement in 1865, settlers were subjected to nature's wrath, battling ailments, hostile terrains, and frequent skirmishes with the indigenous populations.

Legacy Unfolded

Fleming's detailed account goes beyond the mere retelling of events. It breathes life in the past, capturing the essence of the pioneers' undying spirit.

As they adapted to the harsh environment, the challenging terrain intertwined with their choices, triumphs, and tribulations. Every contour of the land, every gust of wind, and every hardship they faced molded their journey. Their unwavering determination in the wild American West showcases a rich tapestry of human resilience. In their story, we find a reflection of our own capacity to persevere, adapt, and carve out a place for ourselves in the vast theater of history.

The Davidson Tragedy: A Tale of Lost Pioneers

The American Southwest's vast and mysterious landscapes have inspired stories of adventure, hope, and discovery. However, intertwined with these narratives of triumph are poignant tales of tragedy and loss. The Davidson Tragedy serves as a somber reminder of the sacrifices pioneers made in their quest for a new life and the often unforgiving nature of the desert they dared to cross.

The Quest for a New Horizon:
The Davidson's Family's Journey

The late 1800s were a time of movement and change. The promise of uncharted territories, fertile lands, and a brighter future beckoned many to the West. The Davidsons, a hopeful family dreamed of prosperity and a life away from the crowded cities of the East. They were called to serve as LDS missionaries.

Like many pioneers, they embarked on their journey with optimism. The Mojave Desert, with its challenging terrains and unpredictable climate, would prove to be a formidable adversary.

The Ill-Fated Day: When Hope Turned to Despair

On what started as a typical day, the Davidson family, driven by their pioneering spirit, ventured deeper into the desert. Guided by rudimentary maps and spurred by tales of oases and thriving settlements, they believed they were on the right path. As the sun climbed higher and their water supplies dwindled, the Mojave's vastness and isolation became terrifyingly clear.

Despite their determination, the merciless sun and the deceptive mirages of the desert took their toll. The Davidsons, tragically, never reached their intended destination.

Echoes in the Sands: The Legacy of the Tragedy

The Davidson Tragedy reverberated throughout the region. It served as a cautionary tale for future travelers, emphasizing the importance of preparation and respect for the desert's might. Local communities, including Mesquite, made improvements to routes, rest stops, and support systems in response to the tragedy.

Today, a modest monument stands in honor of the Davidson family. It's not just a tribute to them but to all pioneers who faced immense challenges in their pursuit of dreams. This marker, in the vast Mojave, is a poignant reminder of human vulnerability, nature's unpredictability, and the sacrifices made in shaping the American West.

The Davidson Tragedy is a tale of dreams, determination, and ultimate sacrifice. While exploring the Southwest, it's important to honor those who came before us, their hopes, their struggles, and their indomitable spirit. In the silence of the Mojave, whispers of their tales linger, urging us to remember and learn.

St. Thomas: A Journey Through Time

Pioneering Beginnings

St. Thomas was founded in 1865 by members LDS Church under Thomas Smith's leadership. St. Thomas emerged as a testament to human tenacity in the face of harsh desert conditions. With a population reaching 500 at its zenith, the town thrived as a hub of farms and businesses. Notably, St. Thomas played a role in history as the final destination of explorer John Wesley Powell's inaugural Colorado River expedition in 1869.

Shifts and Setbacks

The story of St. Thomas took a surprising turn in 1871 when a land survey shifted the Nevada state line, moving the LDS settlements in the Muddy Mission under Nevada's jurisdiction. In order to escape the state's gold-backed tax demands, the LDS Church members abandoned the town and established new settlements in Long

Valley, Utah. Despite the challenges, Daniel Bonelli and a few others remained in St. Thomas, and persisted in farming, mining, and commerce.

The Waters Rise

The construction of Hoover Dam marked the beginning of the end of St. Thomas. As the Colorado River's waters surged because of the dam's completion, the town faced its ultimate challenge. They completed the exodus of residents on June 11, 1938, with Hugh Lord becoming the last to depart, leaving behind a town submerged beneath the rising tide of history.

Rediscovery and Legacy

St. Thomas's story wasn't lost beneath the waters of Lake Mead. As the lake's levels receded, the ruins of the town resurfaced, offering a window into the past. Recognizing its historical significance, the town's remains were protected by the National Park Service. Overton, Nevada has an interpretive center that delves into its rich history and settlement patterns.

Stories Carved in Ink

St. Thomas's narrative has found its way into literature, cementing its place in cultural memory. Books like "Lords of St. Thomas" by Jackson Ellis, "Muddy: Where Faith and Polygamy Collide" by Dean Hughes, and "The Desert Between Us" by Phyllis Barber preserve the stories of early pioneers, and their influence on this desert settlement.

St. Thomas, a town that once thrived against all odds, now serves as a poignant reminder of human resilience and the connection between nature, history, and the pursuit of a lasting legacy in even the harshest of landscapes.

Mesquite Flats: The Founding Footsteps

Nestled in the heart of the Mojave Desert lies Mesquite Flats, a testament to human tenacity, resilience, and the will to carve out an oasis amidst the desert. Like other pioneering settlements, Mesquite Flats' history is a tale of both triumph and adversity, notably the challenges posed by the region's unpredictable waterways.

Emergence of a Settlement: The Early Days

Pioneers explored the Mojave in search of new horizons. The fertile plains near the Virgin River, called Mesquite Flats, seemed promising. Here, the soil was rich, nourished by the river's periodic deposits, making it an attractive prospect for farming and settlement.

The Virgin River: A Double-Edged Sword

The same river that brought life to Mesquite Flats, also pose challenges for the settlement. The tranquil appearance of the Virgin River masked its unpredictable nature.

The Floods: Nature's Unyielding Force

With little warning, the river would swell, breaking its banks and inundating Mesquite Flats. Floods, triggered by rainstorms or melting snow, would destroy crops, damage properties, and change the settler's landscape

Such events were not merely physical disruptions but emotional trials, testing the mettle and resolve of the community. Every flood washed away the dreams and hard work of many, yet the spirit of Mesquite Flats remained unbroken.

Adapting to the Inevitable: Resilience and Innovation

Recognizing the recurrent threat, the settlers of Mesquite Flats showcased remarkable adaptability. They developed early warning systems, built elevated homes, and designed ingenious irrigation methods that they could quickly adjust during flood events. The community's response to the floods influenced Mesquite's modern disaster management and preparedness strategies.

From Adversity to Unity: The Spirit of Mesquite Flats

Every flood, while a moment of crisis, also became an event that tightened the bonds of the community. Neighbors supporting one another, and working together to rebuild and adapt, became the defining characteristic of Mesquite Flats' identity.

Mesquite Flats, with its tale of founding footsteps, stands as a beacon of human spirit and perseverance. The floods highlighted the importance of unity, adaptability, and respect for nature's power. As we explore modern Mesquite, it's important to remember the early settlers who persevered to create a thriving community in the heart of the desert.

Photo Courtesy of Virgin Valley Heritage Museum

Fractured Frontiers: The Territorial Disputes of Lake Mead

Lake Mead has been a point of contention for a long time, even before the construction of the Hoover Dam. The territorial disputes surrounding this crucial water source are deeply rooted in a history that combines ancient indigenous lifestyles, colonial ambitions, and modern statehood aspirations.

Ephemeral Boundaries: Indigenous Tribes and Vital Waterways

Centuries before state lines or modern treaties, indigenous tribes such as the Mojave, Hopi, and Navajo held the Colorado River in reverence. The river was essential for their survival and their connection to it was flexible, determined by seasonal patterns and needs rather than rigid borders. Despite resource conflicts, many tribes had complex trade systems and mutual respect.

Spanish Footprints and the Dawn of European Claims

The Southwest attracted Spanish explorers in the 16th and 17th centuries, who staked the first European claims to the territory. The Spaniards' quest for legendary cities of gold led to conflicts with indigenous communities and rival European powers.

The Mexican Epoch and America's Manifest Destiny

After Mexico's emancipation from Spain in 1821, the vast landscapes of the American Southwest came under Mexican control. But, the strong desire to expand westward and the relentless efforts of American pioneers soon challenged this control. This led to the Mexican-American War and the eventual cession of massive territories to the U.S. through the Treaty of Guadalupe Hidalgo in 1848.

Carving the Modern Southwest: The Birth of States

In the war's wake, the U.S. began organizing these newly acquired lands, sowing the seeds for modern-day states like Arizona, Nevada, and Utah. Even as these proto-boundaries crystallized, they became subjects of contention, evolving with growing populations, newfound resources, and the ambitions of communities seeking statehood.

The Colorado Compact and the Emergence of Lake Mead

Amidst these territorial evolutions, the significance of the Colorado River remained unchallenged. In the early 20th century they drafted the Colorado River Compact to attempt a distribution of its waters among seven states. The construction of Lake Mead and the Hoover Dam in the 1930s transformed the river into a vital reservoir, leading to conflicts and diplomatic efforts.

Lake Mead, reflecting the skies of the Mojave, is more than just a water reservoir. It encapsulates centuries of dreams, challenges, and endeavors of diverse peoples. The shores have been witness to a rich history of collaboration, understanding, and mutual respect among different communities.

The Mormon Pioneer Pathway: An Intriguing Tale

The American West, with its vast stretches of arid desert and towering mesas, may seem an unlikely location for a religious pilgrimage. Yet, in the mid-19th century, it became the backdrop for one of the most remarkable migrations in American history: the journey of the Mormon pioneers.

Divine Desperation: A Quest for Sanctuary

In the early 1830s, the Mormon Church was established, in upstate New York. Joseph Smith led a religious community that faced intense persecution for their beliefs and practices. Their search for a sanctuary drove them from New York to Ohio, then Missouri, and later to Illinois.

The Call Westward

Following the assassination of Joseph Smith in 1844, Brigham Young assumed leadership of most Mormons. Recognizing the need for a fresh start, Young set his sights on the Great Basin region, a vast expanse of the American West yet to be claimed by any state or territory. He envisioned a new "Zion" where his people could practice their faith free from external threats and interference.

The Harrowing Journey

In 1846, the initial group of Mormon pioneers embarked on their journey from Nauvoo, Illinois. They faced challenges that tested their faith and strength, braving difficult terrains, battling illnesses, and enduring extreme weather conditions. The pioneers built roads, established ferries across difficult river crossings, and established supply posts along the way.

The Floods: Nature's Unyielding Force

With little warning, the river would swell, breaking its banks and inundating Mesquite Flats. Floods, often triggered by rain storms or melting snow in the uplands, would destroy crops, damage properties, and change the settler's landscape. Such events were not merely physical disruptions but emotional trials, testing the mettle and resolve of the community. Every flood washed away the dreams and hard work of many, yet the spirit of Mesquite Flats remained unbroken.

Adapting to the Inevitable: Resilience and Innovation

Recognizing the recurrent threat, the settlers of Mesquite Flats showcased remarkable adaptability. They developed early warning systems, built elevated homes, and designed ingenious irrigation methods that could be quickly adjusted during flood events. The community's response to the floods laid the groundwork for modern-day Mesquite's disaster management and preparedness strategies.

From Adversity to Unity: The Spirit of Mesquite Flats

Every flood, while a moment of crisis, also became an event that tightened the bonds of the community. Neighbors helped neighbors, and collective efforts to rebuild and adapt became the cornerstone of Mesquite Flats' identity.

Mesquite Flats, with its tale of founding footsteps, stands as a beacon of human spirit and perseverance. The floods highlighted the importance of unity, adaptability, and respect for nature's power. As we explore modern Mesquite, it's important to remember the early settlers who persevered to create a thriving community in the heart of the desert.

Verdant Valleys and Pauite Roots: The Tri-State's Botanical Tapestry
An Agricultural & Historical Overview

The Tri-State area, encompassing parts of Arizona, Nevada, and Utah, is characterized by a rich agricultural tapestry and holds deep historical roots. The Virgin River nourishes the Virgin and Moapa Valleys and the Arizona Strip, rendering them fertile for diverse crops, flora, and fauna.

Mesquite's Agricultural Legacy

• Diverse Cultivation: Mesquite stands as a testament to the agricultural variety of the region. Cotton, grapes, alfalfa, wheat, cane, pomegranates, and figs became foundational in establishing its economic foothold.

• Key Cash Crops: Cotton and raisins became the primary crops in Mesquite, transforming agricultural practices.

• Dairy Dominance: With time, dairies spread across Mesquite. Beyond serving locals, these dairies catered to the expanding tastes of Las Vegas.

• Signature Produce: Moapa Valley's watermelons achieved legendary status. The region's honey became a highly sought-after delicacy, and the annual county festival celebrated the pomegranate.

Hafen Dairy, Photo Courtesy of Virgin Valley Heritage Museum

The Paiute Influence on the Moapa Valley

• Harmony with Nature: In the region's high-country, the Southern Paiute lived in symbiosis with the environment. They collected berries and plants, hunted mule deer, elk, bighorn sheep, antelope, woodchucks, and rabbits. They transformed the agate they collected into essential stone tools, reflecting their deep understanding of their surroundings.

• Adaptable Lifestyle: The Paiute were flexible in their lifestyle, changing their hunting and gathering practices depending on the season. Winter saw them collecting seeds and berries; the gathering bulbs and roots marked spring; the fall pinion crop was another resource. They augmented their diet with insects, and hunted smaller animals like ground squirrels and trapped rabbits in the absence of abundant large game.

Historical Roots of Agriculture in the Moapa Valley

- Indigenous Cultivation: Before the Mormon settlers came, indigenous tribes like the Paiute cultivated crops such as corn, beans, and squash in the valley.
- Mormon Settlers' Contributions: The early Mormons found a valley brimming with vineyards, grain fields, and trees. They further enriched this tradition.
- Later Additions: Subsequent settlers diversified the botanical offering:
- Orchards: Produced peaches, figs, apples, apricots, and pears.
- Ground Crops: Featured cantaloupes, watermelons, pomegranates, carrots, potatoes, celery, lettuce, and more.

The Joshua tree, like other yuccas, has edible fruits, seeds, flowers, and young flower stalks that were eaten by native peoples of the southwest, like the Death Valley Shoshone.

Wildlife and Ecosystem

The Tri-State region's agriculture coexists harmoniously with the native wildlife. The produced crops not only cater to human consumption but also sustain the local fauna, ensuring a biodiverse and balanced ecosystem.

The Mojave Desert may seem dry and barren, but there are pockets of thriving life. At the heart of this fertility lies the Virgin River, a life-giving vein that threads through the Virgin and Moapa Valleys and spills into the Arizona Strip. It's a waterway that has, for generations, transformed the landscape, making it conducive for the varied crops and a haven for diverse species.

The land here doesn't just yield produce for tables; it's a living breathing system where flora and fauna have a symbiotic relationship. The farmers grow grains, fruits, and vegetables that are essential for both people and local animals. Birds, small mammals, and even larger fauna find sustenance in the agricultural abundance.

But beyond mere sustenance, the crops and native plants provide habitats, nesting grounds, and protective cover. Fields may have roadrunners chasing insects, or a desert tortoise slowly navigating its way. At night, bobcats might prowl the peripheries, and the soft hum of insects pollinating under the moonlit sky becomes a common nocturnal melody.

The symbiosis ensures the region's ecological balance. Wildlife play important roles in agriculture by aiding in pollination, pest control, and soil aeration.

The Tri-State region represents more than a simple geographical convergence; it's a place where farming and nature come together, creating a diverse and vibrant environment in the desert.

The Wild Burros of Gold Butte: Mesquite Silent Builders

When you think of Mesquite's Gold Butte area, the mind often wanders toward its beautiful landscapes and rich history. But there's a lesser-known, yet equally important, aspect to this region: the Wild Burros.

A Tale as Old as Time: Donkeys and Their Stalwart Service

Among the rugged landscapes and echoing canyons of Gold Butte, you'll often find the gentle gaze of donkeys, or 'burros' as they're affectionately known locally. But to regard them merely as part of the region's wildlife would be an oversight; these creatures are a bridge to a time gone by, bearing tales of tenacity and service.

Long before the hum of engines echoes through the valleys, it was the steady footfall of these hardy animals that marked the progression of pioneers. Tracing their origin back to early settlers, burros played a quintessential role in shaping the history of the region. The adventurers depended on the steadfastness of these animals to brave the challenges of the Spanish Trail; carrying heavy loads, navigating rocky terrains, and enduring extreme temperatures. Their importance wasn't just logistical. Beyond carrying goods and people, they carried dreams, aspirations, and the spirit of a pioneering age. They symbolized hope in the face of adversity, perseverance in challenging times, and the relentless drive of those who dared to tread the unknown.

Today, we observe these animals freely grazing and roaming the lands they once helped settle, reminding us of their significant contribution. The burros of Gold Butte are more than just residents. They're guardians of a rich legacy, silent storytellers of an time when humans and animals worked together to overcome challenges and envision a better future.

When the Mormon settlers began their journey westward, the burros were always by their side. Their resilience and skill in navigating tough terrains made them extremely valuable. As settlements grew, the burros played a crucial role in connecting communities, transporting supplies, and aiding in farming.

Their significance was such that they became synonymous with the idea of frontier life.

Preserving the Legacy: Nevada's Museums and Rescues

Today, places like Nevada's history museum celebrate and preserve the history and impact of these burros. Here, visitors can learn about the deep-rooted connection between Mesquite's development and these animals. Artifacts, stories, and interactive displays paint a vivid picture of their contributions.

But it's not just about the past; it's about the present too. The large donkey rescue in Nevada stands as a monument to the regions commitment to these animals and what contributed to our early settlements. The rescue ensures that we give the wild burros, who once served the settlers so selflessly, the care and protection they deserve.

A Nod to the Unsung Heroes

As you walk the trails of Gold Butte or take a stroll in Mesquite, remember the silent footprints of the wild burros. Although not in the spotlight often, their legacy is woven into the essence of this town. They're the unsung heroes of Mesquite's colorful tapestry of history. And for that, they deserve a nod, a smile, and our deepest respect.

For a more detailed understanding of their role in our past, a visit to the Donkey History Museum, a part of Peaceful Valley Donkey Rescue, the world's leading donkey rescue organization, is highly recommended. Located in downtown Mesquite, the museum offers insights into the historical significance of these creatures in our community, as well as a variety of memorabilia, collectibles and relics.

In addition to learning about their past, consider supporting the efforts of donkey sanctuaries, such as Donkey Dreams Sanctuary in Scenic, AZ. This sanctuary is dedicated to providing a safe and nurturing environment for donkeys that have been rescued or displaced. By supporting these sanctuaries, either through visits or donations, we can help ensure that these noble animals continue to thrive and receive the care they deserve, honoring their legacy in our community.

Part 2: The Making of Modern Mesquite
Mesquite's Link to Hidden Treasure and the Old Spanish Trail

Mesquite's Connection to a Historic Route

In downtown Mesquite, Nevada, there's a reminder of a significant chapter in history – the Old Spanish Trail. This path, once a lifeline from Santa Fe to Los Angeles, included what's now Mesquite in its route. The Nevada State Historical Marker No. 31, located just outside the Virgin Valley Heritage Museum in downtown Mesquite. This historical site marks this important piece of the past, dating back to 1829.

Mesquite's Role in the Trail's History

The Old Spanish Trail, initially a route with a singular purpose to lead its followers to the fabled Cibola and its immense treasures of silver and gold, was more than just a pathway; it evolved into a bustling corridor of commerce and migration. 'Lost Treasures of the Spanish Trail' delves into the trail's rich history, from the era of Spanish conquistadors and the treasures of Montezuma, through its northward expansion. This history is etched into the land, with traces of the trail still visible today, worn deeply into the soft sandstone, possibly still leading to hidden treasures that fuel legends.

Following 1848, as Mormon settlers began establishing communities in Utah, Nevada, and California, the trail's significance was further heightened. These settlers, residing along the trail, introduced new dynamics to trade and significantly influenced perceptions of Native American slavery, reshaping the trail's legacy in profound ways.

Unearthing Hidden Treasures and Forgotten Tales

The Old Spanish Trail, winding through the American Southwest, holds countless tales of concealed riches and historical intrigue. It's believed that the Knights of the Golden Circle secreted away parts of their vast treasures along this route, igniting the curiosity of treasure seekers. These tales, entwined with the trail's history, captivate those in search of the Golden Circle's lost gold, Montezuma's fabled treasure, and the relics of Spanish conquistadors.

Adjacent to this historic trail is Pottery Hill, a site abundant in native pottery and rumored to house an ancient Indian tomahawk near the Virgin Mountain. Its proximity to the Old Spanish Trail enriches the area with added historical significance, suggesting a past where diverse cultures and histories converged along this crucial path.

The Old Spanish Trail is more than a historical route; it's a portal to a world where every discovery, from ancient fragments to forgotten artifacts, opens a window into a vibrant past. The allure of these finds lies not just in their material value but in the narratives they carry, linking us to a time when the Southwest was a crucible of diverse cultures and tales. For modern explorers, this trail offers an unparalleled opportunity to uncover stories and legends embedded in the landscape for centuries.

Mesquite's Strategic Importance

Mesquite's location on this trail put it at the heart of significant historical events. It became a crossroads where different cultures intersected, economies expanded, and new communities emerged. The Mormon settlement along the trail played a key role in shaping the region's development.

The path of the Old Spanish Trail near Mesquite wasn't easy. Heading west to Pipe Spring, it followed the Virgin River up near today's St. George, Utah. It then wound its way over the challenging terrain of the Beaver Dam Mountains. This section was critical for travelers of the era, facilitating movement, trade, and cultural connections.

Preserving Mesquite's Heritage

Today, Mesquite proudly preserves its historical ties to the Old Spanish Trail. Through landmarks like the historical marker and educational efforts at the Virgin Valley Heritage Museum, the city keeps the memory of this trail alive. These places link the present to the past, highlighting how the journeys and experiences of early travelers influenced Mesquite's evolution.

The Bigger Picture

The Old Spanish Trail, winding through the rugged landscape of the American Southwest, is more than just a historic route near Mesquite. It encapsulates a rich narrative of exploration and cultural exchange, deeply embedded in the history of the American West. This trail, marked by stories of migration and hidden treasures, is an integral part of the complex tapestry that forms Mesquite's heritage.

The trail is shrouded in legends of hidden treasures, from the gold of the Knights of the Golden Circle to the elusive wealth of Spanish conquistadors. These tales, intertwined with the history of the trail, capture the enduring human fascination with discovery and the mysteries of yesteryears. Today, as a historical landmark in Mesquite, the Old Spanish Trail connects us to the stories of its past travelers. It's a journey that goes beyond geography, linking the present to the adventurous spirits who once traversed its paths and to the future that continues to unfold.

Settler's Division & The Lost Boys

The Southwest's intricate tapestry weaves together stories of faith, power, and survival. The stories of the Latter-day Saint movements intertwine with unexpected connections to politics and the law.

The Great Schism: LDS and FLDS

The LDS Church transformed from being persecuted to an established religion by the mid-twentieth century. As it grew, they renounced some of its earlier practices, including polygamy, in 1890 to align with U.S. law and to gain statehood for Utah.

However, splinter groups who believed in the original tenets, including polygamy, broke away. Among the most prominent of these groups was the Fundamentalist Church of Jesus Christ of Latter-Day Saints (FLDS). The FLDS settled in isolated communities in this region and continued practicing polygamy, leading to future conflicts.

The Tragedy of the Lost Boys

In the Arizona Strip, the historical issue of "Lost Boys" highlights a complex facet of community life, particularly within certain polygamous Mormon fundamentalist groups. These young men, usually aged between 13 and 21, were often excommunicated or pressured to leave their communities. This practice, primarily aimed at reducing competition for wives, left many unprepared for life outside their familiar environment, leading to significant challenges in adapting to broader society.

Colorado City, Arizona, became a focal point for these practices in the past, with local authorities actively working to maintain the community's polygamous structure.

While these practices have since been scrutinized and challenged, their legacy remains. Efforts by former community members and support groups have been crucial in aiding these young men as they transition into new lives. Legal actions have also been pursued against certain groups for the economic and psychological impact on the "Lost Boys."

The situation in the Arizona Strip and Colorado City area reflects the intricate balance between communal beliefs and individual rights. It serves as a reminder of the profound effects that community dynamics can have on the lives of individuals, particularly in closed societies.

Unexpected Alliances

As the LDS Church grew, it developed ties with various influential individuals, drawing on its strong community focus, business expertise, and emphasis on education. A significant connection was with billionaire Howard Hughes, whose extensive business endeavors in Las Vegas included hiring Mormons for their reputed work ethic and dependability. This association, particularly in the Las Vegas casino sector—a realm with mafia ties—might have inadvertently linked the church with other notable figures in the city. The legacy of Hughes' enterprises is enduring, with his impact evident even in places like Mesquite today.

In addition to business, the church's reach extended into the political realm and, as conjectured, potentially into different intelligence circles, showcasing its comprehensive integration into the fabric of American society.

A Study on Power and Influence

These tales serve as a poignant reminder of the complexities inherent in various religious movements. The LDS Church sought acceptance forming powerful alliances over shared values, while the FLDS faced consequences for its most vulnerable members.

Mormonism's impact in the American West goes beyond the intricacies of internal community dynamics. The LDS Church has had a significant impact on both the physical and cultural landscapes of Utah, Mesquite, and other parts of the Southwest. We can see their pioneering spirit, which originated from their early exodus to escape persecution, reflected in the meticulous grid layout of Salt Lake City, various historical sites, and even in the names of towns and landmarks.

This influence goes beyond architecture and town planning. The LDS Church's emphasis on community, family, and a strict moral code has significantly shaped the cultural fabric of the region. In towns like Mesquite, the rhythms of life often revolve around family gatherings, and community service. Local celebrations, festivals, and even business ethics carry the undertones of Mormon values. Over the years, these values have intermingled with broader Western ideals, creating a unique cultural blend. This fusion is clear in everything from local art and music to culinary traditions.

However, the Mormon Church's influential role has had both positive and negative effects. While it has provided a sense of unity and purpose, it has also been a source of contention, as seen by the Lost Boys and other controversies. The church's historical stance on issues like polygamy has caused conflicts with societal norms, both internally and externally. Some LDS groups have adopted more worldly aspects over time, profoundly impacting various communities in the United States and beyond.

The Hoover Dam Chronicles:
A Meld of Ambition, Controversy, and Sacrifice

The Hoover Dam is located in the rugged American Southwest, where the Black Canyon and the Colorado River converge. An emblem of the 20th-century ambition, this colossal structure isn't merely an engineering marvel. Its history is steeped in controversy, sacrifice, tales of human spirit, and whispers of the supernatural.

In the 20th century, with the American Southwest's urgent need for water storage and hydroelectric power, the idea of the Hoover Dam emerged. Yet political and water rights challenges hindered its realization among the seven states of the Colorado River basin. Herbert Hoover, familiar with the region's potential and challenges, championed the dam's cause. In 1921, as Secretary of Commerce, he proposed building the dam for flood control, tom provide water for irrigation, and ensure a reliable water source for Los Angeles and Southern California. Beyond the practicalities, the dam promised economic revitalization through the sale of hydroelectric power.

The journey to consensus wasn't easy. Interstate disagreements and the concerns of upstream states were significant barriers. Hoover's diplomacy led to the Colorado River Compact in 1922, which divided the river basin and laid the groundwork for water distribution, culminating in the dam's construction beginning in 1930.

Echoes of the Ancestral Past

Among the more haunting tales tied to the dam's construction is the claim that they built atop Native American burial grounds. Though not well documented, local stories suggest the dam's construction disturbed ancestral spirits, and cast a somber mood over the project. Such accounts have become part of the region's folklore, adding a layer of mystique to the dam's storied past.

Dark Mysteries and Occult Theories of the Hoover Dam

The Hoover Dam, beyond its role as an engineering marvel and a beacon of progress, has not been without its share of mysteries and intrigue. One particularly chilling theory, popularized by shows like 'Ghost Adventures', is that the dam's design was intended to mirror Satan's throne. Supporters of this theory carefully study the dam's art deco designs, suggesting they contain symbols and motifs reminiscent of dark occult practices. Critics and conspiracy theorists believe the dam's architectural details area connected to esoteric symbols. Some believe these interpretations, ranging from the dam's statues to its ornate engravings, to be deliberate nods to the underworld. Those interested in the supernatural or the arcane find such claims tantalizing, but skeptics largely meet them with skepticism.

Mainstream historians and architects often disregard these theories, emphasizing the artistic movements of the time and the desire for grandeur as the major influences behind the dam's design. However, despite the dismissal, these tales have found a place in popular culture. That such an emblem of human achievement could be tied, even in myth, to darker narratives offers a rich tapestry of juxtaposition that captivates audiences. Therefore, as the Hoover Dam fulfills its functional roles in hydroelectric power and water storage, it simultaneously embodies the human intrigue with the mysterious and the captivating narratives of forbidden lore, including strange and unexplained deaths.

Lake Mead's Grim Record

Lake Mead, birthed by the construction of the Hoover Dam, stands as the nation's largest reservoir. While it offers a vast playground for recreation and natural beauty, its waters hide a distressing reality. Statistically, this reservoir has the highest number of deaths in the U.S. because of its dangerous undercurrents and deceptive depths. The lake's unpredictable nature has caused numerous tragedies, even for experienced swimmers and boaters.

Besides its perilous waters, Lake Mead has become a repository for remnants of the past. One particularly haunting artifact is a sunken B-52 bomber. The wreckage is a popular destination for divers, enhancing its reputation as a dangerous yet exciting place for underwater exploration. The plane's underwater resting place is a symbol of the past and also sparks conspiracy theories and paranormal tales.

Locals and visitors have experienced ghostly apparitions, eerie underwater sounds and unexplained phenomena around the lake. These tales, combined with the lake's tragic record and sunken relics, lend Lake Mead a mystique that is both captivating and chilling. To some, it's a place of adventure and natural beauty, but others view it with a mix of awe and apprehension, mindful of the tales and truths that coexist beneath the surface.

The Price of Progress

The dam's construction phase, from 1931 to 1936, was fraught with peril. Official records state that 112 individuals lost their lives directly because of the construction processes. These brave individuals faced treacherous conditions, from extreme heat to high altitudes, and their sacrifices show the human cost of such massive endeavors.

Conclusion

The Hoover Dam in the American Southwest is a remarkable display of engineering and a symbol of human ambition, sacrifice, and resilience. The dam represents the nation's determination for progress during the Great Depression.

However, the dam's construction was not without its shadows. The promise of employment drew thousands to the site, but the harsh conditions and the complicated construction of the massive structure resulted in the loss of over a hundred lives. The workers, often unsung, are an integral part of the dam's story. Rumors of the dam being constructed on indigenous burial grounds have made its history more complex. While these tales are hard to validate, they underline the uneasy balance between advancement and reverence for the sacred.

Amidst the gleaming turbines and vast reservoirs, the Hoover Dam's true essence lies in its layers of narratives. Its serves as a mirror reflecting both the brilliance and the blind spots of its era. Today, as visitors walk its expansive corridors and gaze upon Lake Mead, they're not just witnessing a marvel of engineering; they're stepping into a rich tapestry of history, where ambition, controversy, and sacrifice are etched into the bedrock of the American Southwest.

Mesquite Arrows: The Guiding Giants of Airmail History

Landmark Overview

In the vast, quiet stretches of the American desert, remnants of a past age whisper tales of early aviation triumphs and the dawn of aerial communication. Here, the Navigation Arrows, immense concrete markers, stand as silent guardians of history, narrating the story of air mail's pioneering days. These monumental arrows, rooted in places like Mesquite, Moapa, and St. George, were essential in the 1920s and '30s, guiding pilots as they navigated the nascent air mail routes across the nation. Known as Beacon Stations, they were the guiding stars for those early aviators, a testament to human ingenuity and the spirit of exploration. Their significance and intriguing history were even illuminated in a popular TV series, bringing their legacy to the forefront of American aviation folklore. These stoic arrows, set against the backdrop of the desert, serve as enduring symbols of a time when air mail began to connect distant communities, forever altering the landscape of communication.

An Era Takes Flight

The airmail concept was revolutionary. It promised to shrink the vast distances of the country and bring people closer. While the aircraft of that time were feats of engineering, the pilots faced the Herculean task of navigating vast, unmarked terrains.

The 20th century's early years brought with it not just technological marvels but also dreams as vast as the American landscapes. The desert regions of Mesquite, Moapa, and St. George played silent witnesses to one such dream: an interconnected United States via airmail.

The Luminous Path

In 1924, a solution took shape. They constructed large concrete arrows every 10 miles, accompanied by light towers. These markers acted as a visual guide during the day, while their beacons served as lighthouses at night, ensuring airmail's promise was kept 24/7.

Desert Sentinels: Mesquite, Moapa, and St. George

In the vast desert landscape, these arrows had a unique role. Mesquite's markers were critical, guiding pilots safely across challenging terrains. Moapa, bridging the expanse between Mesquite and St. George, added another layer of connectivity. And in St. George, Utah, the St. George Airmail Beacon on the Black Hill further underscored the importance of this route. These three cities, and their arrows, played pivotal roles, making airmail work seamlessly across challenging terrains.

Sun Sets on the Arrows

By the late 1930s, radio navigation and improved aviation infrastructure started replacing these concrete guardians. Their era, though short-lived, was intense and impactful.

Innovation and exploration marked the dawn of the aviation age in the early 20th century. Pilots and engineers sought to push the boundaries of what was possible. The arrows, acting as guiding lights, symbolizing hope, adventure, and the human spirit's desire to conquer the skies. Each arrow symbolized the ambition of an era, aiming to connect the vast American landscape and make the dream of coast-to-coast travel possible.

As with many pioneering methods, new technology eventually rendered them obsolete. The rapid pace of innovation in aviation during the inter-war years was nothing short of phenomenal. The shift from visual to radio navigation was a significant leap, representing changes happening globally. Radios made cross-country fights safer and more efficient for pilots. As planes flew higher and at longer ranges, ground-based visual cues like the arrows became less relevant.

Although they may have faded from aviation history, these concrete arrows remain an enduring symbol of a transformative era in air travel. They symbolize the challenges and ingenious solutions of early pilots, when the skies were the newest frontier and bravery and innovation were the keys to unlocking its potential.

Today, as you explore the terrains of Mesquite, Moapa, and St. George, these silent arrows have tales to tell. Stories of brave pilots, of dreams as vast as the horizon, and of a nation's relentless march towards progress.

The desert of Mesquite, Moapa, and St. George holds more than just natural beauty. Each arrow, each beacon, is a testament to human perseverance and the dreams of a nation ready to embrace the skies.

Flying Legends & Mesquite Mysteries

Amelia's Grounded Dreams in Moapa Valley

Amelia Earhart, the world-renowned aviator, had other passions beyond airborne adventures. In the 1920s, an unexpected chapter of her story unfolded in the shadows of Mesquite, specifically in the Moapa Valley. She owned a gypsum mine here, recognizing it as more than just a business opportunity, but as a potential lifeline for her family's financial future.

However, the unpredictable desert landscape had other plans. One fateful day, Amelia and her father found themselves trapped in the rage of a sudden flash flood while inspecting the mine. This natural disaster not only ravaged the mine, but also tragically claimed the life of a close friend. As the waters receded, so did Amelia's hopes tied to the mine. Facing the financial aftermath, she made the tough decision to sell her cherished plane.

But even in these trying times, Amelia's spirit was unbroken. Her correspondence with Clinton Averett, a resident of Moapa Valley, provides a window into her resilience. They exchanged letters, ranging from brief notes to detailed narratives, painting a picture of a woman undeterred by setbacks, passionate about flight, and connected to this unique corner of Nevada.

Mysteries of the Desert Skies

The vast desert skies of Mesquite have silently witnessed countless stories. Many aircraft, from private planes to military jets, and even some that were not officially documented, have met their end in this region. There are rumors among the locals that these crashes could be tied to covert military operations, specifically near Area 15. Such tales add an aura of mystery, making one ponder the untold stories that the desert skies might conceal.

The Shah's Plane & Bounsall's Magic Touch

Among these stories, one episode stands out for its international significance and its sheer unexpectedness. The tranquility of Old Highway 91 was disrupted when it transformed into an emergency landing strip. A desert-camouflaged plane, carrying tales of political upheaval, touched down. This wasn't just any aircraft; it was the very plane that had whisked the Shah of Iran away into exile during his nation's tumultuous times.

Enter Eddie Bounsall of Mesquite. Known locally not just for his own aircraft, the Bounsall Super Prospector, but also for his uncanny knack with planes. Eddie took this historical artifact, a plane laden with machine guns and tales of political escape, and gave it a Mesquite makeover. He discarded the heavy armor, tuned the engine, and adorned it with fresh paint. The plane quickly transformed and took to the skies, leaving the town buzzing with excitement and a legacy of Mesquite's connection to aviation and the world at large.

Mesquite's Storied Past: From Pioneer Struggles to Pandemics

Mesquite's rich history dates back to its early settlement days. Today, it's known for bustling casinos and a thriving tourism industry. The Covid pandemic serves as a reminder of previous challenges the town has faced.

Disease and Quarantine: Then and Now

Geraldine White Zarate's book, "Mesquite and the Virgin Valley" offers valuable insights into Mesquite's vulnerability to diseases. The 1918 influenza pandemic swept across the globe, and Mesquite felt its effects deeply. When the schools in the Virgin Valley were closed, the community showed their innovative spirit by quarantining the young girls from the normal school in the mountains, ensuring that their education continued without interruption. This episode reflects our recent experiences with quarantines and lockdowns.

A Decade of Health Crises

The 1920s saw Mesquite grappling with successive health crises. After recovering from the influenza outbreak, red measles and scarlet fever emerged in 1927. In 1928, a mosquito infestation intensified the threat of disease. By 1929, the town had to contend with the threat of smallpox.

Photo Courtesy of Virgin Valley Heritage Museum

Economic and Environmental Strains

Along with health challenges, the Great Depression brought financial struggles to an already beleaguered community. Nature, too, wasn't kind. The town faced severe weather challenges, including both flooding and droughts.

Pioneering Hardships

Similar to our recent "pandemic", the early settlers faced common challenges of pioneer life and unexpected disasters while trying to settle in this part of the Virgin Valley. The land was both beautiful and unforgiving, with challenges including scorching heat, scarcity of food and water, diseases, and occasional threats from indigenous communities.

Conclusion: The Indomitable Spirit of Mesquite

Through all these challenges, Mesquite's resilience has shone through. The community rallied, shared resources, and stood united. The tales from the early days serve not only as historical accounts but as enduring symbols of hope and determination. No matter the challenge, Mesquite's spirit remains unbroken, and continues to adapt and thrive.

Civilian Conservation Corps: A Legacy Cast in Sand & Stone

Amidst the daunting challenges of the 1930s, an organization emerged, casting hope across the American landscape. The Civilian Conservation Corps (CCC) left a lasting impact on Mesquite, Nevada, and taught its people enduring values and resilience.

The Great Depression's shadow was both deep and widespread, darkening America's hopes. But with President Franklin D. Roosevelt's New Deal, the CCC rose like a beacon. It gave hope to young men in Mesquite and surrounding areas through environmental and infrastructural projects.

A Desert Transformed

The vast and challenging plains of Mesquite, crisscrossed by the Virgin River, became the canvas for the CCC's endeavors. Crafting roadways across this desolate expanse, they rewrote Mesquite's narrative. These pathways, many still connecting hearts and homes today, ignited economic resurgence and an unparalleled spirit of community.

More Than Just Physical Footprints

The CCC's legacy in Mesquite is extends beyond its visible imprints. It's the camaraderie forged among men from diverse origins, unified by a shared mission. Their hard work not only respected the beauty of Nevada desert but also became an important part of Mesquite's culture.

Conserving the Desert's Lifeblood

Recognizing the desert's precious elixir, water, the CCC pioneers implemented seminal conservation projects. Their tireless efforts in creating erosion control and rainwater retention boosted Mesquite's agriculture and economy.

Challenging the arid embrace of the desert, the CCC undertook ventures in revegetation. Their efforts painted the sand in shades of green, offering pockets of solace for wildlife and adorning the landscape with an oasis-like charm.

Mesquite's horizon is peppered with tangible legacies of the CCC. Structures, trails, and a museum in St. George honor their tireless spirit and work.

Moapa Valley's New Deal Legacy

Nestled in Moapa Valley, The Lost City Museum showcases a blend of ancient and modern influences. As visitors cross its threshold, they step into the 1935 Gallery, a space reminiscent of an era gone by. Yet, this gallery isn't just an ode to the past; it's also a celebration of the future forged during one of America's most challenging epochs.

The Civilian Conservation Corps (CCC), created during the Great Depression, helped shape America's landscape. Their legacy is deeply etched into the Moapa Valley and is best captured by the very walls of the 1935 Gallery. The gallery was built with adobe brick and represents the CCC's dedication to sustainable development and conservation. The CCC's mission went beyond job creation. In Moapa Valley, the goal was to build with a purpose and to preserve history.

Linking Eras: From Ancestral Puebloans to the CCC

The Pueblo Grande de Nevada, colloquially known as the Lost City, stands as a testament to the thriving civilization of the Ancestral Puebloans. The 1935 Gallery exhibits artifacts that reveal the history, culture, and craftsmanship of the ancient community. These artifacts reveal the CCC's involvement in the exploration, excavation, and preservation efforts. The Corps men did more than just build structures; they safeguarded the legacy of the Ancestral Puebloans.

National Recognition and The Journey Ahead

The efforts of the CCC in the Moapa Valley culminated in the 1935 Gallery being listed on the National Register of Historic Places. This recognition demonstrates their unwavering commitment to conservation and community-building. The gallery now stands restored to its 1930s glory, showcasing the legacy of the Ancestral Puebloans and the efforts of the CCC.

The Heartbeat Continues

The story of the CCC in Mesquite extends beyond the confines of history. It's an enduring ethos marrying hard work, community unity, and reverence for the environment. The principles of the CCC can be felt in every corner of Mesquite, through its resources, community spirit, and tribute to past heroes. In Mesquite, the echoes of CCC's accomplishments remind us of what we can achieve when people and nature come together. The trees they planted have now grown tall, offering shade to weary travelers and serving as living memorials to the men who once toiled under the sun. The infrastructure they built is strong, enduring the time and elements, echoing dedication and commitment.

The CCC's influence isn't just physical; it's a deeply admired ethos here in Mesquite. The CCC's commitment to community collaboration has shaped the town's identity. Today, Mesquite residents continue to build on the collective effort and inspiration the CCC. Annual events, local stories, and school curriculum's recognize the CCC's impact, teaching future generations to understand and appreciate their important contributions.

The wisdom of the CCC, their profound respect for the environment, and the lessons of sustainable development they championed are now more relevant than ever. Mesquite is a shining example of balancing progress and preservation in an age of rapid urbanization and environmental changes. With its roots firmly anchored in CCC values, the city moves forward with purpose, integrity, and a respect for the land.

Mafia Mysteries in the Desert

The vast stretches of the American Southwest, with its intricate canyons, haunting landscapes, and endless skies, has always been veiled in a cloak of mystery. But beyond the natural enigma of the desert lie tales of human intrigue, spanning faith, crime, and the allure of the clandestine. The stories set in this corner of the country, spanning parts of Nevada, Utah, and Arizona, are as contrasting as the landscapes themselves; the devout journey of Mormons, the secretive exploits of the Mafia, and the allure of celebrities seeking solace from the public eye.

Mesquite's Mysterious Getaways: Of Stars, Secrets, and Shadows

Nestled a stone's throw away from the radiant nightlife of Las Vegas, Mesquite and its surroundings have borne witness to tales less told. The vast desert terrains, with their silent allure, have attracted a diverse range of visitors, each leaving an imprint on its sandy canvas

When the Mob Met Mesquite

While Vegas boomed with the hum of slot machines and the dazzle of its neon lights, the nearby desert, known for its quiet expanses, caught the fancy of the Mafia. In places where the desert whispers its secrets, criminals sought sanctuary in the desert to escape from the law and rival factions. Locations like Beaver Dam, Arizona, and Gold Butte, Nevada, provided them with the ideal blend: isolated yet close to bustling urban areas. These tranquil spots in the desert, served as the backdrop for hushed meetings, secret exchanges, and occasionally makeshift burial plots.

Locals in Beaver Dam have reported sightings of individuals that resemble mobsters, standing guard in black suits and hats. It's said that these guarded figures carried an aura of authority, intensifying the region's mystique.

The desert drew not only those seeking discretion from illegal dealings. The desert's beauty, a stark contrast to the relentless pace of urban life, was a magnet for Hollywood's finest. Celebrities went to the Southwest to escape the paparazzi and the demands of fame.

Among these retreats was the renowned Beaver Dam Lodge. Before its fame as a starry sanctuary, the Beaver Dam Wash served as an oasis for travelers during the 1849 gold rush. Located conveniently along the trail set by John C. Freemont, it was the much-needed respite for both man and animal.

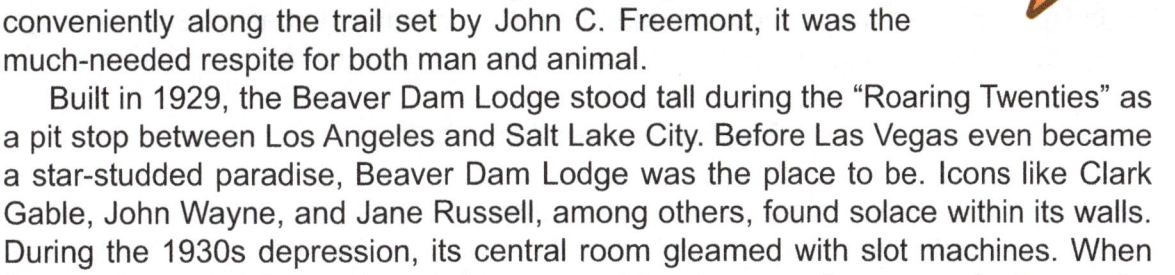

Built in 1929, the Beaver Dam Lodge stood tall during the "Roaring Twenties" as a pit stop between Los Angeles and Salt Lake City. Before Las Vegas even became a star-studded paradise, Beaver Dam Lodge was the place to be. Icons like Clark Gable, John Wayne, and Jane Russell, among others, found solace within its walls. During the 1930s depression, its central room gleamed with slot machines. When times got even harder, penny machines saved the day, ensuring wages for those who worked there.

The lodge still stands, proud of its legacy, beautifully restored and keeping its historic charm. The very rooms where golden age celebrities rested continue to invite guests, whispering tales of the glamorous past.

But history isn't the lodge's only tale. Beneath it lies a mysterious tunnel. At its heart, a safe that once concealed secrets. It's now opened and empty, contributing to the area's allure. There's also the talk of spectral residents. Whispered conversations speak of ghostly encounters, giving the lodge an ethereal aura.

When you set foot in the Beaver Dam Lodge, take in the ambiance, and remember the infamous guests who have stayed there, including Clark Gable!

Desert Deeds: The Mafia's Mark on Nevada

A mosaic where diverse narratives converge shaped the Southwest's mystique. In this landscape, places like Mesquite (remove Nevada) stand out, bridging stories from spiritual realms to secretive Mafia dealings.

Particularly intriguing is the term "86," used in Mafia circles, which possibly alludes to "80 miles out and 6 feet under." This takes on a speculative significance given Mesquite's location, almost exactly 80 miles away from Las Vegas, a known Mafia hub. While not central to its history, this connection adds a layer of intrigue to the Southwest desert, hinting at a hidden chapter where organized crime might have intersected with the remote tranquility of Mesquite.

Embracing the Call of the Wild: Mesquite's Natural Tapestry

Beyond the bustling heart of Mesquite, the call of the wild beckons; echoing through the vast stretches of the Arizona Strip and reverberating through the rugged landscape. Join us on a journey through Mesquite's captivating natural surroundings, where every rock, plant, and creature has a tale of endurance, and enchantment.

The Flora's Resilient Ballet

Beyond the iconic vistas of the Arizona Strip and Mesquite, Nevada, the native plants tell a captivating story of survival and revival. The Joshua tree, with its iconic spiky silhouette, dominates the landscape, serving as a sentinel of the southern desert ecosystem. The Blackbrush's ability to flourish in nutrient-poor soils highlights nature's resourcefulness.

As you venture nearer to water sources or washes, the vegetation transitions. Cottonwood and willow trees, with their tall, swaying forms, provide vital shade and shelter for desert wildlife. The palo verde tree defies traditional tree norms with its green bark capable of photosynthesis, demonstrating nature's adaptability in harsh conditions.

The flora of the surrounding landscapes is a testament to nature's tenacity and adaptability. Amidst the arid expanse, plants like the Mojave yucca, creosote bush, and various species of cacti stand tall, painting the land with hues of green. These plants have evolved to not merely survive but to thrive, their deep roots seeking scarce water and their leaves adapted to minimize moisture loss. Each season brings a burst of colors as desert wildflowers like the Indian paintbrush, desert marigold, and globe mallow adorn the terrain, reminding us of nature's relentless urge to celebrate life.

The Virgin River supports a diverse riparian ecosystem with flourishing reeds, sedges, and rushes providing a biodiverse sanctuary for desert wildlife. The region's flora is a testament to adaptability, transforming with the seasons. After rare rains, the desert blooms vibrantly with flowers like desert lily, evening primrose, and purple mat. The plant life in this landlocked region is both an ecological wonder and a testament to nature's resilience.

A Symphony of Fauna

In the expansive landscapes of Mesquite, a diverse tapestry of creatures thrives, painting the desert with life and movement. Big horn sheep skillfully navigate the rugged peaks and deep valleys, demonstrating their mastery of the terrain. Vibrant geckos traverse the sands, while roadrunners dart with sudden bursts of speed, their distinct calls reverberating in the air.

Wild horses and burros, symbols of freedom and endurance, graze and gallop freely, leaving behind trails in the dust. The slower-paced desert tortoise takes its time, carrying its home on its back, embodying patience and resilience. Tufted-eared bobcats prowl in the shadows, while lizards scurry across the hot surface, seeking shade and sustenance. Tarantulas make nightly appearances, while golden eagles survey the land from above. From the mesmerizing dance of the Gila monster to the coexistence of playful black-tailed jackrabbits and nocturnal coyotes, Mesquite's desert is a symphony of creatures, contributing to the grand composition.

Unexpected Guests in Mesquite's Landscape

Mesquite, with its blend of unique terrains and microclimates, has always been more than just home to its native creatures. At one point, a nearby zoo introduced an eclectic mix of exotic animals to the area. Although the zoo is no longer open, its legacy lives on through memories of energetic kangaroos, curious lemurs, playful otters, scurrying coatis.

Mesquite's Camel Safari has carved a niche for itself, transitioning from the old zoo days. It's a surreal experience to ride a camel through Mesquite's desert landscape.

But the surprises don't just end there. For those who relish local tales and mysteries, whispers of a "Bigfoot" creature have often made the rounds. Though some might dismiss it as mere folklore, a handful of credible eyewitness accounts keep the legend alive, leaving us to wonder what else might lurk in the hidden corners of Mesquite. Here, the lines between the ordinary and the extraordinary blur, ensuring that there's always something new to discover.

Mesquite Amidst the Mushroom Clouds: Echoes from Bunkerville's Past

In the vast Nevada desert, Mesquite's narrative intertwines with that of Bunkerville—a town that stood unwittingly on the frontline of the atomic age. Here, history and humanity intersect, casting long shadows and inspiring tales of resilience.

The Nevada Test Site: Ground Zero of the Atomic Era

Only 65 miles from the vibrant hum of Las Vegas, the Nevada Test Site (NTS) stood in stark contrast—a silent ground for over a thousand nuclear tests. These detonations, powerful and haunting, reverberated far beyond their immediate epicenter.

Bunkerville's Unexpected and Unintended Consequences

The quiet town of Bunkerville, located only 25 miles southeast of the Nevada Test Site (NTS), became the center of a radioactive controversy. The once serene community was now entangled in the tension and fear of the Cold War.

The 1950s were a tumultuous time for this unsuspecting town. As nuclear tests were routinely carried out in the neighboring desert, the contrast between life's daily rhythms and the nearby atomic explosions disturbed the town's residents. Each detonation would light up the horizon in a blinding flash, only to give way to the haunting silhouette of a mushroom cloud.

Children, in their innocence, played in the nuclear fallout, mistaking it for snow, unaware of the dangers it posed. Such instances deeply ingrained a lasting skepticism towards government assurances. Increasing reports of childhood leukemia and other cancers fueled the growing mistrust.

For many in the Tri-State area, witnessing these tests became a bittersweet experience. On one hand, there was pride knowing that their homeland was at the forefront of scientific prowess. On the other, the looming specter of the bomb's destructive capabilities instilled a deep-seated unease. The terrifying beauty of the mushroom clouds symbolized humanity's potential for progress and self-destruction.

As decades rolled on, recognition of the trials faced by Bunkerville and similar communities grew. The government acknowledged the health and environmental impacts and began compensating affected families, launching cleanup projects, and implementing preventative measures.

The imprint of this era on Bunkerville's history serves as a poignant reminder of the price of ambition and the necessity for ethical foresight.

Radiant Roentgens: An Invisible Adversary

Amidst the shifting shadows of atomic clouds, a mysterious force began a fateful journey beyond the confines of the Nevada Test Site. In a twist of fate, this secret journey had a lasting impact on the unsuspecting town of Bunkerville. The residents were unaware the air they breathed posed health and environmental risks that would impact their lives.

In 1951, as the world grappled with the repercussions of nuclear experimentation, a disturbing truth came to light Bunkerville had unknowingly become part of a somber record. In a shocking disclosure, they revealed that the town had the unfortunate distinction of having the highest level of detectable radioactive fallout outside of the Nevada Test Site. Uncertainty filled the community as the news spread. The convergence of elements resulted in an air of mystery upon the land, air, and life itself.

Despite the gravity of this revelation, they made efforts to downplay the potential dangers that loomed. In 1957, the Nevada Test Organization published a carefully orchestrated press release, demonstrating the art of managing perceptions. To quell the rising tide of concern, the release sought to depict the radioactive exposure as relatively safe. The mysterious forces created this dangerous situation were no crafting a narrative where the shadows held no menace, and where they could brush aside the legacy of radioactive whispers like desert dust.

The residents of Bunkerville felt uneasy, knowing the once familiar landscape had changed, morphed by forces beyond human control. The once fertile land now posed potential danger, while the skies whispered of the mysteries that the desert held close.

As time went on, the echoes of atomic experimentation continued in Bunkerville showing the complex dance between progress and its unintended consequences. The community's journey continued, shaped not only by its past but also by the resolute spirit of its residents—a spirit that vowed to navigate the labyrinth of challenges, to unravel the mysteries that lingered, and to forge a future where the legacy of uncertainty could be met with the unwavering strength of resolve.

Economic Tremors: The Tie that Frayed

Beyond the health implications, the fallout cast ripples across Bunkerville's once-steady agrarian economy. Farms faced uncertainty, and families grappled with decisions that could redefine their futures.

From Recognition to Redress: The Path to Healing

The federal response, though late, sought to mend the fissures. The 1990 Radiation Exposure Compensation Act acknowledged the problem and began cleanup projects in the damaged desert.

Stories of Strength: Bunkerville's Unyielding Spirit

Today, Bunkerville stands resilient, its tales of the atomic age shared with a mix of reverence and resolve. The town's spirit is a powerful reminder of humanity's capacity to endure, recover, and look forward to brighter tomorrows.

Photo Courtesy of Virgin Valley Heritage Museum

A Ribbon Through the Desert: The I-15's Legacy in the Tri-State Area

The American Southwest is famous for its sprawling deserts and rugged terrains, and rich stories of ancient civilizations, courageous explorers, and modern marvels. One marvel is Interstate 15, an impressive symbol of human ambition and engineering skill that goes through challenging Virgin Gorge. The construction and decisions regarding it have had significant impact for the region, particularly the Arizona Strip.

Carving a Path: The Virgin Gorge Odyssey

The section of I-15 that traverses the Virgin Gorge is more than just a stretch of highway; it's a testament to engineering audacity. Winding its way through the steep cliffs and rocky terrains of the gorge, this section was one of the most expensive highway endeavors in US history. It stands as a physical embodiment of the challenge of taming the wild desert for the sake of connectivity.

Economic Implications: A Missed Opportunity?

With over 30,000 vehicles passing through the Virgin Gorge daily, the potential for revenue generation through tolling is immense. However, Arizona's decision not to toll this highway section has sparked debate over the years. While travelers are granted free passage through one of the most scenic and challenging sections of the national interstate system, it also means forgone revenue that could be used for infrastructure development, conservation projects, or other state initiatives.

The Tri-State Area: Beyond Borders and Boundaries

The I-15 doesn't just serve Arizona; it's a lifeline for the Tri-State area, connecting Nevada, Utah, and Arizona. This connectivity has facilitated trade, tourism, and mutual economic growth. Towns and cities along this interstate, including those in the Arizona Strip, have seen an uptick in visitors, leading to local business growth and increased regional collaboration.

Ecological Balance: Progress Meets Preservation

Building the I-15, in environmentally sensitive areas like the Virgin Gorge raised concerns about preserving the environment. The region, abundant in unique flora and fauna, requires conscientious efforts to maintain ecological balance. Over the years, they have taken measure to mitigate the environmental impact of the highway and ensure the region's natural beauty remains unspoiled.

Forward Momentum: The I-15's Role in the Tri-State's Future

As the Tri-State area looks ahead, the I-15, with the iconic Virgin Gorge section at its heart, will continue to play a pivotal role in shaping its destiny. The stakeholders in the region recognize the highway's potential for sustainable growth and regional integration, going beyond its role as a transport route.

The I-15 is not just a roadway; it's the Tri-State area's artery, pulsating with promise and potential. The Virgin Gorge, with its awe-inspiring beauty and engineering challenges, symbolizes the harmony between nature's grandeur and human endeavor.

Farmer's Tenacity: An Emblem of Mesquite

In the heart of the Mojave, the story of Mesquite's agricultural journey is remarkable. It is a tale not merely of cultivation, but of an tireless spirit, determination, and a community's unwavering commitment to the land. The Mesquite Dam has been rebuilt a remarkable five times symbolizing the enduring spirit of Mesquite's farming community.

The Oasis Dream: Mesquite's Agricultural Inception

Where others saw barren lands, the early settlers of Mesquite envisioned verdant fields and bounteous harvests. This wasn't mere optimism, but a reflection of their profound connection to the land. They knew that beneath the sunbaked surface lay the potential for life and sustenance. However, realizing this dream required more than vision—it demanded tenacity.

The Mesquite Dam: A Testament to Perseverance

The Mesquite Dam played a vital role in Mesquite's agricultural plan to control the Virgin River's waters. But nature, in its unpredictable demeanor, posed challenges. The forces of nature tested, battered, and brought down the dam multiple times. Yet, with each destruction, Mesquite's resolve only strengthened. The community rebuilt the dam five times, each reconstruction symbolizing their undying spirit and their refusal to let their agricultural dreams wither away.

Harvests of Hope: The Fruits of Determination

This unwavering spirit transformed the once arid terrains around Mesquite into patches of green. The waters of the Virgin River nurtured the corps, bearing fruits, vegetables and grains. Every harvest became a celebration, not just of the yield, but of the relentless determination that made it possible.

Agricultural Roots of the Virgin Valley: From Mesquite to Beaver Dam

The Virgin Valley has a rich farming history that's hard to overlook. Mesquite's soil tells stories of success; its pomegranates and Thompson seedless grapes took home first place at the San Francisco World's Fair in 1906. But it wasn't just Mesquite that shined. Nearby Beaver Dam had its own moments in the spotlight. An esteemed horticulturalist successfully grew Indian melons using ancient seeds found in a northern Utah cave.

Beaver Dam is also home to a tight-knit group of DIY and small-batch farmers who produce everything from pistachio trees to melons. Mesquite's agricultural accomplishments, like the dam reconstruction, demonstrate the determination and spirit of the Virgin Valley's farming community. Together, Mesquite and Beaver Dam stand as reminders that, with hard work and community support, dreams can take root and thrive.

Rural Robberies & Crime Chronicles: From A Bank to A Casino

Overton and Mesquite, known for their tranquility and charm, have experienced unsettling moments. At the heart of these tales are heinous crimes that disrupted these close-knit communities. Their stories remain etched in the memories of the residents, reminding them of the vulnerabilities that even the smallest of towns can face. Here, we delve into three such incidents that have become infamous chapters in the history of Overton and Mesquite.

1. August 29, 1967 - Overton's Darkest Hour at Valley Bank

The Crime: In a bank heist at the Valley Bank of Nevada in Overton, the perpetrator escaped with $35,000 after tragically taking the lives of the bank manager and two clerks, stacking the bodies in the bank vault.

Aftermath: The criminal was apprehended near Warm Springs Ranch just hours after the crime. This horrifying event shattered Overton's sense of security. The same bank would later be the site of another robbery. Today, the building has been transformed into a real estate office. Decades later, a poignant moment occurred between the perpetrator's father and a victim's daughter. The perpetrator's death in 1999 from diabetes complications reopened painful memories for both the victims' families and his own.

2. September 7, 1984 - The Helicopter Gang's Return to Valley Bank

The Crime: Landing at Perkins Field in Moapa Valley in a silver-grey and blue Cessna 210, two culprits abducted three individuals, including a father and son, and the airport caretaker.

Heist: Accompanied by their hostages, they targeted the Valley Bank of Nevada in Overton, making off with $126,000.

Twists in Escape: Their escape was impeded by an ink pack and smoke bomb explosion. They were quickly apprehended thanks to crucial evidence, including pill bottles and a left-behind bag, clear camera footage, and an unexpected encounter with law enforcement nearby.

3. August 25, 1994 - The Virgin River Casino Heist in Mesquite

The Crime: An armed robber confronted a security guard and an Assistant Cage Manager during a bank run, making off with $220,000 in unmarked bills from the casino's payroll.

Suspicion: Odd occurrences, such as the absence of regular staff and a different transport van, initially raised suspicions of an inside job, but these were eventually dismissed.

The Investigation: A firearm found in an unrelated domestic dispute led the FBI to a local pizza parlor owner. Despite growing evidence, the suspect vanished.

National Spotlight: This intriguing heist was featured in an episode of "Unsolved Mysteries," broadcast on April 12, 1996. Authorities later apprehended the suspect in Los Angeles and convicted him of money laundering connected to the robbery. However, the total cash was never recovered, and some locals still speculate that others might have been involved.

The landscapes of Overton and Mesquite, with their peaceful small-town atmosphere, have witnessed these significant crimes. These events underscore how a few individuals' actions can deeply affect entire communities.

While these crimes have jolted Overton and Mesquite, other criminal activities have further tarnished the area's image. The busy I-15 corridor, for example, has been a notorious site for smuggling. A notable incident included a police chase, where suspects drove across a local golf course's greens in a high-speed pursuit. The nearby Glendale gas station has seen its share of illegal activities, with numerous incidents over the years. These occurrences are stark reminders that no place, however picturesque, is exempt from challenges.

Takeaways from Mesquite's "Battle for Decency"

In the heart of Mesquite, a significant standoff between community values and the First Amendment took center stage in the 1990s. The dispute centered on the Pure Pleasure Adult Book and Video store, which faced opposition from the community. The town's residents demonstrated their power and the balance between individual rights and community values. The nearly three-year journey stood as a reflection of the lasting impact of community activism on the enduring spirit.

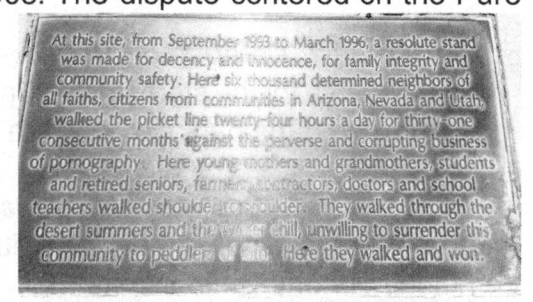

Here are a few takeaways from this chapter in Mesquite's history:

1. Community Mobilization:
The people of Mesquite rallied together, regardless of age, profession, or religious affiliation. Their joint effort shows the power of collective action. When a community unifies in its purpose and works together, its members can achieve significant impact.

2. The Role of HOME (Help Our Moral Environment):
The grassroots organization represented the community's vehement opposition to the store, which was licensed under false pretenses. Only on the day of the store's inaugural opening did city officials and local residents grasp the true nature of the business.

3. A Prolonged Battle:
Led by locals and neighboring residents, the community protests outside the store lasted nearly three years, enduring both the intense heat of the summer and the chill of the winter. This was purportedly the longest continuous picket in US history, showcasing immense resilience and determination.

4. Legal Dimensions:

The store faced multiple legal challenges. In 1996, a U.S. District Judge ruled that Mesquite City Ordinance 103, which was adopted by the City to regulate adult bookstores, was constitutional.

5. Societal Implications:

The community viewed the store as morally offensive, leading to significant opposition. This situation underscored the broader societal debates about morality, free expression, and local autonomy.

6. Support and Unity:

Local businesses and groups, apart from individual citizens, came together to support the cause. This collective stance amplified the opposition against the store.

7. Defense on the Grounds of the First Amendment:

The defense for the store, though in the minority, centered on the First Amendment. This highlighted the balance between freedom of expression and community values.

8. Legacy and Impact:

Today, there is an empty lot with a commemorative plaque symbolizing the community's commitment to its moral fabric and the lengths they will go to uphold their values.

For more information, please contact Dena Hoff, founding member of HOME (Help Our Moral Environment).

The Confluence of Time Zones: The Tri-State Experience

Nestled in the American Southwest, the region surrounding Mesquite offers a unique and diverse landscape. Here, the ticking of the clock isn't just a measure of time, but an embodiment of the rich diversity and interconnectedness of this unique region. The mix of Pacific and Mountain zones gives the region its distinct charm and diverse experiences.

Temporal Tapestries: The Quirks of Time Travel

Mesquite's position in the heart of the Tri-State area allows for easy access to majestic landscapes while also traveling through time. If you travel east to the Arizona Strip, time aligns with Nevada for half the year, and with Utah for the other half because Arizona doesn't observe of daylight saving time.

To the north, Utah, with its majestic landscapes, beckons from the Mountain Time Zone. This proximal shift, though minor, infuses the region with a whimsicality. Imagine dining in one state, then taking a dessert in another, all within an hour yet technically at the same moment.

Daylight Dancing: Making the Most of the Sun

This temporal confluence isn't merely an amusing quirk; it offers tangible benefits. Businesspeople in the tri- state area can take advantage of longer daylight hours for scheduling meetings or deliveries. Nature enthusiasts, too, can chase the sun, maximizing their outdoor adventures by simply journeying east or west.

Stories at the Crossroads: Time Zone Anecdotes

The local lore is rich with tales of these time zone adventures. Some residents enjoy celebrating birthdays twice in a row or having two New Year's Eve countdowns. Such stories, shared with twinkling eyes and hearty laughter, have become a cherished part of the region's oral tradition.

More Than Just Time: A Fusion of Cultures and Experiences

But it isn't just about the hours and minutes. The Tri-State arrangement brings together the vibrancy of three distinct states. There are many experiences to discover; the neon lights of Las Vegas, the rustic appeal of the Arizona Strip, and the scenic vistas of St. George. Each state adds its own hue, its own flavor, and its own rhythm to the collective symphony of the region.

Woven Together: Beyond Boundaries

The confluence of time zones in the Tri-State region, anchored by Mesquite, is more than a geographic phenomenon. It symbolizes the seamless blending of communities, cultures, and histories. It reminds us that while time might delineate our days, shared experiences and stories transcend these boundaries. In this corner of the Southwest, time isn't just a measure; it's an experience, a story, and a testament to the rich tapestry of life at the crossroads of three states.

The Oasis Casino: A Beacon in the Desert

Legends are born form the stories of ambition, vision, and reinvention in the ever-shifting sands of the American Southwest. The Oasis Casino in Mesquite is a shining example in the desert's gaming and entertainment history.

The Humble Beginnings: From Trucks to Jackpots

In the 1960s, what would one day become a landmark in Mesquite's history started humbly as the Western Village Truck Stop. Serving as a respite for weary travelers and truckers, it offered a break from the relentless desert sun and long stretches of road. However, in the hands of a visionary, even a truck stop can transform into a hub of entertainment and excitement. William "Si" Redd, a figure renowned in the gaming world, saw the potential and purchased the truck stop in 1976.

Evolution of an Oasis: The Rise of Peppermill's Western Village

By 1981, the truck stop had been re-imagined and renamed Peppermill's Western Village, signaling a new era. It wasn't just a place to refuel and rest anymore; it was a destination. For nearly a decade, it stood as Mesquite's sole casino, drawing locals and travelers alike to its gaming tables and entertainment venues.

Si Redd's Vision: A Legacy Etched in the Sands

In recognition of the man behind its transformation, they renamed the casino Si Redd's Oasis in 1993. Later, in a nod to simplicity and elegance, they shortened it to the Oasis. Under Redd's leadership, the establishment thrived and became synonymous with luxury, entertainment, and the thrill of gambling.

Changing Hands, Changing Fortunes

The turn of the millennium brought significant changes for the Oasis. In 2001, it underwent a change in ownership, marking a new era under a different management company. However, by December 2008, the Oasis began to struggle, reflecting the broader economic downturn of the Great Recession. The establishment faced closure due to financial difficulties, and by 2010, its casino operations ceased. The hotel remained operational for a while, serving as overflow accommodation for guests visiting other casinos in Mesquite owned by the same company, but its closure was imminent.

In 2011, a major reorganization occurred, leading to the formation of Casablanca LLC, with a new CEO at the helm, which eventually became known as Mesquite Gaming. Today, Mesquite Gaming runs two of the three major casinos in Mesquite. There are speculations about a potential new buyer, reportedly linked to a large global hedge fund. The future remains uncertain, but it seems likely that gaming will continue to be a significant part of Mesquite's economy for the foreseeable future.

Remnants of a Bygone Era

Despite being demolished in 2013, the spirit of the Oasis continues to endure.. Bits of its architecture and essence remain in the town, sparking conversations and fueling rumors, evoking nostalgia for Mesquite's glory days. For many, the Oasis serves as a poignant reminder of the town's rich past—a beacon in the desert that once was.

From its modest truck stop beginnings to its stature as a desert luminary, the Oasis Casino's journey reflects the Southwest's spirit of determination, ambition, and embracing change.

###

Part 3: Booms, Busts, and Resurgence
The Fastest Growing City in the USA: The Rise of Mesquite

Mesquite became more than a blip on the national radar after the Great Recession. As excavation changed the landscape, a tide of tourists, entrepreneurs, and new residents flooded in; transforming this sleepy town into one of the most sought-after destinations in the country. The buzz around Mesquite was palpable as it quickly climbed the ranks to become the fastest-growing city in the USA.

Reshaping the Desert: An Excavation Explosion

The volume of dirt being moved in Mesquite was staggering. Excavators and construction sites were everywhere, symbolizing both physical change and the city's desire for transformation . At this time, there was more earth being excavated here than in almost any other part of the USA, a testament to the scale and pace of the development.

Spotlight on Tourism: From Obscurity to Fame

Mesquite's tourism sector experienced an unprecedented boom. Word was spreading about this desert gem, leading to a surge in visitors keen to experience its offerings. Hotels, casinos, golf courses, and recreational areas became hotspots, pulling in tourists from near and far. Mesquite was no longer just a pitstop; it was becoming the main event.

Del Webb's Vision: Sun City Mesquite

Among those who recognized Mesquite's potential was prominent developer Del Webb. They envisioned Sun City Mesquite as a sprawling oasis for active adults, offering luxury and leisure in the heart of the desert. The project was more than just houses and golf courses; it was a testament to Mesquite's growing appeal and the faith big developers had in its future.

The Media's Darling: Headlines and Accolades

National magazines, newspapers, and television channels couldn't resist the Mesquite story. Many articles praised its rapid rise in development, economic growth, and reputation as a tourist and business hub. For a while, Mesquite was the poster child for American urban success.

Lost Dreams: Projects that Never Saw Daylight

In the heady days of growth, Mesquite buzzed with optimism. Everywhere you turned, signs announced exciting new projects, from grand resorts to elaborate entertainment centers. The promise was palpable, the vision boundless. But as the dark clouds of the Great Recession gathered on the horizon, many of these dreams crumbled under its weight. The vibrancy of those plans dimmed, leaving behind stark relics of grand ambitions interrupted.

The sight of these unfinished projects is eerily reminiscent of the abandoned mines that dot the region. Both bear silent testament to hopes and pursuits cut short. The mines in the region are storied chapters in its history, chronicling tales of those who sought riches in mineral wealth.

Both stories share a narrative of adaptation, strength, and an determination. In both tales, dreams are delayed and adaptability becomes crucial.

Now, wandering past a deserted construction site or discovering an old miner's relic, one can't help but feel the weight of history and draw parallels. These remnants from different times remind us of the region's enduring spirit of resilience and adaptability.

The Evolving Frontier: Arizona Strip in the Modern Era

The Arizona Strip, a sprawling wilderness and desert area nestled between Utah and the Grand Canyon, is a testament to human tenacity and the longing for freedom. Spanning over 8,000 square miles, it exists almost defiantly independent of state and federal governance. The residents of this vast territory embody a fierce independence, yearning for a life less bound by the regulations and constraints of modern society.

Echoing through the years is the sentiment that the Strip's allure isn't just its vastness, but also the spirit it embodies. It represents rural living, spaciousness, and being one's own person amidst nature's grandeur.

In this large territory, where traditional governance is minimal, a unique blend of individuality and community-driven initiatives emerges. This is evident in how Mohave County administers its expansive communities with just a few sheriffs and a single justice of the peace, creating a realm where the extraordinary becomes almost ordinary.

One intriguing aspect of the Arizona Strip was the now-defunct Temple Bar in Littlefield. It was a sanctuary with its own unique laws and governance, embodying the region's penchant for individual governance and autonomy.

The Strip's spirit of resilience, however, faces challenges. The 2023 decision by the federal government to annex additional land has sparked intense debates and concerns over increased government intervention.

The region is grappling with the challenges of rapid development and technological limitations. Its growth often outstrips digital mapping, creating a sense of being "off the map" in a world reliant on online navigation.

In nearby Southern Utah, there's a deep-seated distrust of federal oversight, with concerns ranging from socialism to the risk of totalitarianism, reflecting a desire for more autonomy. This area is known for its rugged individualism, lore, and secretive tales. An old article once mentioned a covert gathering place near Zion National Park, known as the "New Jerusalem," managed by a group inspired by Israeli history, adding intrigue and concern among locals.

A resident of the region once aptly stated, "Trust in the government here is about as scarce as water." This sentiment encapsulates the spirit of the inhabitants who value their autonomy and resist overarching authority.

The Arizona Strip, with its rich history, individualism, and contemporary challenges, stands as a symbol of the American frontier spirit – a vast landscape where the indomitable spirit of its residents continues to shape its evolving narrative.

Mesquite's Underbelly: Murder, Mystery, and History

Mesquite, with its scenic desert landscapes, inviting retirement communities, and tranquil vibes, often attracts those seeking calm and many considered it a haven. Beneath its calm facade, deaths, and unspeakable crimes that have shaken the tight-knit community.

The Political Minefield

The journey begins with a charismatic Mayor, poised for a successful second term. However, his path became tumultuous amidst swirling rumors of an FBI investigation. Doubts about his professional integrity arose, including questions about his use of city resources and involvement in dubious financial dealings. Unfazed, he firmly countered these allegations, hinting at potential political motives behind them. Despite the controversy, his impact on Mesquite's political landscape remained significant.

But Mesquite's political scene faced another startling episode. A respected two-term City Council member was embroiled in a scandal over a seemingly minor, misreported $94 expense. This minor oversight spiraled into a shocking murder-suicide, deeply affecting the town and casting a shadow over its sunny disposition and tight-knit community.

These incidents, years apart, showcased the intense and occasionally volatile political climate of Mesquite. The tragedy involving the Council member garnered significant media attention, revealing the city's complex dynamics and prompting community reflection.

In 2013, the city's narrative was further darkened by another distressing event. Two men, one from nearby Hurricane, Utah, and another from Mesquite, were involved in the gruesome murders of two individuals. The night's terror began with one of the men ominously stating, "It's time for this guy to go to sleep," leading to a chilling series of events: an assault on one victim and the smothering of another with a plastic bag, with their bodies concealed. A third potential victim narrowly escaped, later guiding authorities to the horrific scene.

While one of the assailants confessed, facing a life sentence, the other's trial was complicated by questions of mental stability. The community and local law enforcement were left reeling from these brutal acts, unprecedented in their usually peaceful town.

Lurking Shadows and Haunting Memories

Amid these events, whispers of even darker deeds permeated the local folklore. Rumors spoke of unidentified victims, possibly murdered, their remains burned and cast into desolate mine pits. There were also whispers of unknown leaders trapped in unexplained circumstances, who ended their lives in eerie suicides. These tales, though not always substantiated, added layers of mystery and apprehension to the city's psyche.

Despite its share of challenges, Mesquite's resilience shines through. Although these stories contain dark elements, they emphasize the complexities of a community. Mesquite continues its march forward, aware of its past, yet hopeful for a brighter, safer future.

The Great Recession – Boom or Bust: Weathering the Economic Storm

As the American Southwest sun cast long, shimmering heatwaves over the arid landscapes of Mesquite, a different storm was brewing on the horizon. It was one that would shake the foundations of the nation's economy and test the resilience and adaptability of its people. The Great Recession caused financial instability everywhere, from the city's bustling streets to the tranquil byways of desert towns.

Financial Forecasting: Signs of a Brewing Tempest

By the mid-2000s, the economic skies seemed ever sunny. Real estate was booming, and consumer confidence soared. Beneath the surface, the waters were churning. Subprime mortgages, over-leveraged banks, and complex financial derivatives caused instability.

The First Raindrops: Wall Street's Gloom

In 2008, the storm hit. Major financial institutions faltered, with some collapsing entirely. The stock market plummeted, and a cloud of uncertainty engulfed businesses and households. The financial distress wasn't merely a Wall Street woe—it was a nationwide crisis.

Deserted Dreams: Mesquite's Mirage

In places like Mesquite, which had ridden the wave of economic boom, the sudden downturn was jarring. Property values dropped, and businesses, like the iconic Oasis Casino, faced insurmountable challenges. The echoes of bustling corridors and ringing slot machines grew fainter.

Shifting Sands: Adapting to a New Economic Landscape

Adversity often leads to innovation. Amid soaring unemployment and shrinking GDP, Mesquite started its own journey of reinvention. Entrepreneurs pivoted, new industries gained foothold, and the community rallied together.

Recovery and Resilience: The Sun After the Storm

The Great Recession's effects lingered, but over time, green shoots of recovery emerged. National policies and local initiatives worked hand in hand to restore confidence. Mesquite Gaming's success in the 2010's showcased the city's resilience.

A Desert Lesson: Beyond Boom and Bust

The Great Recession left a lasting mark on Mesquite's history, highlighting economic vulnerabilities. It demonstrated the power of a united community, showing that even in tough economic climates, the desert can thrive.

Mesquite's Trails and Parks: Promoting an Active Lifestyle

Where Desert Meets Vitality

Nestled in the Mojave Desert, Mesquite offers an exciting outdoor lifestyle and a wealth of history and culture. The city's extensive network of trails and parks stands as a testament to its commitment to well-being, recreation, and a communion with nature.

Paths Through Time and Terrain

Winding through Mesquite's varied landscape offers enticing trails that attract both adventurers and contemplative souls. Whether meandering beside the Virgin River or ascending the desert's hills, each path shares stories of ancient civilizations, pioneering spirits, and nature's rhythms. These trails connect destinations and guide travelers through geological and human history.

Mesquite's parks, like precious jewels, are scattered throughout the city. From playgrounds filled with children's laughter to tranquil picnic spots under the shade of the Joshua Trees, these parks are where community bonds are fostered and nature is revered. They are the canvas for festivals, the stage for local musicians, and the sanctuary for those seeking tranquility.

From Passive Relaxation to Energetic Pursuits

Beyond their aesthetic appeal, Mesquite's parks and trails serve as conduits for an active lifestyle. Joggers greet the dawn, cyclists tackle the desert's steep slopes, and families bond over picnics and games. The mindset here is unmistakably clear: a life in motion harmonizing with nature's cadence.

Mesquite's commitment to its trails and parks is more than just recreational; it's ecological. Each trail is designed with careful consideration to minimize its footprint, and parks are maintained with an emphasis on sustainability. Native vegetation thrives, bird songs fill the air, and we respect and preserve the delicate balance of desert ecosystems.

There's another layer to these green and sandy expanses. The parks host cultural events that resonate with Mesquite's rich tapestry of traditions. From local art showcases to community gatherings, these events blend culture with the outdoors for a holistic experience.

The trails and parks of Mesquite are more than mere recreational spaces; they are the city's arteries, pulsating with life, history, and culture. Walking, jogging, or relaxing in these spaces give you a feeling of being connected to a bigger story - a dance between people, history, and the vast Mojave expanse. Mesquite offers endless exploration of nature's wonders and the human spirit's zest.

Mojave Mavericks: Rugged Ingenuity Amidst the Desert Sands

Amidst the sweeping landscapes of the Mojave, Mesquite, has earned a reputation for determination and invention. The desert is a beautiful but unforgiving place, with hidden stories of cowboys and mighty steam engines.

From Cattle Herders to Innovators

The vast plains and arid stretches of the Mojave were both a boon and a challenge for the cowboys of Mesquite. Their lives deeply entwined with the land, marked by the rhythm of galloping hooves and the distant sounds of cattle. Still, the desert's scarcity of water posed a constant challenge. The cowboys, however, were undaunted.

The Dance of Steam and Sand

One fateful day, as legends often start, a group of cowboys stumbled upon an abandoned steam engine near the shimmering water of the Virgin River. While it may have looked like discarded machinery to most, to these men of the desert, it radiated with potential. Through a melding of cowboy practicality and the spirit of innovation, they reimagined this relic of the steam age into a beacon of hope and progress.

With deft hands, worn from reins and ropes, they repurposed the engine, crafting a water pump that would draw life-giving water from the earth's depths. As steam rose and mingled with the desert air, water flowed, quenching the thirst of both man and beast. This event highlighted the Mesquite cowboy's ability to adapt to scarcity.

Legacy in the Sands

Today, as you navigate Mesquite's modern avenues, this spirit echoes in the wind. The story of the steam engine and the cowboys who breathed new life into it transcends time. It reflects Mesquite's essence, where the ruggedness of the cowboy spirit dances with the elegance of innovation.

The Mojave, with its stark beauty and relentless challenges, has always been a backdrop to tales of resilience and imagination. As Mesquite's history unfolds, stories like these remind us of the magic that happens when determination meets opportunity. The cowboys and their steam engine are not just a part of Mesquite's past; they are the embodiment of its enduring spirit.

Long Drive, Rodeo, and All Stars: Mesquite Spectacular Showcase

Mesquite's desert landscape is known for its golden sands, endless sunshine and a rich tapestry of events, personalities, and culture,. Mesquite's reputation is not just based on its charm, but also the exciting events and the famous people it has attracted.

The Power and Precision: World Long Drive Championship

Foremost on this impressive list is the World Long Drive Championship. Golfers from around the world have flocked to Mesquite, swinging their clubs and sending balls soaring. The competition is a combination of sheer power and pinpoint precision, making Mesquite a focal point for sports enthusiasts.

Riding the Dusty Tails: Mesquite's Rodeo Legacy

Nearby rodeos, including the Clark County Rodeo and Fair, are deeply rooted in our local culture. The rumble of hooves, daring riders, and the bond between man and beast capture the essence of the American West. It's more than just a sport in Mesquite; it's a heartfelt celebration of tradition and skill.

But the rodeo isn't the only event that tried to encapsulate this spirit. Inspired by Pamplona, Spain's famous bull runs, Mesquite played host to America's very first Bull Run. The initial event was a hit, drawing in 700 runners and a crowd of 10,000. Despite its initial success, participation decreased the following year, partly because of Mesquite's remote location and the desert's summer heat.

The Bull Run also brought unexpected challenges. The Promoter faced legal hurdles and even a brief jail stint. Despite significant media attention, the event didn't turn a profit and eventually moved elsewhere. Mesquite's tryst with the Bull Run, though short-lived, adds a fascinating layer to its storied past.

Community and Celebration: Mesquite Days and Stalwart Residents

'Mesquite Days' is not merely an event; it's an embodiment of the city's spirit, its history, and its aspirations. The revelry, parades, and cultural showcases are a testament to a community that is deeply interconnected and proud of its legacy. Amplifying the town's allure is the array of leaders from the realms of politics and sports who have chosen Mesquite as their home. Their presence intertwines with Mesquite's identity, adding layers of depth to its cultural fabric.

The Entertainment Capitals: Proximity and Distinction

Located comfortably between the glamour of Las Vegas and the beauty of Utah, Mesquite offers the best of both worlds. While the neon lights of Vegas and the canyons of Utah beckon, Mesquite remains resolute in its unique offerings. It's not just a stopover but a destination, an oasis of events and experiences.

On the Rocks: Golf Resorts & Recreation

Mesquite, with its sun-drenched landscapes and azure skies, is more than just a desert town. It's a golfer's paradise, a shimmering oasis where the sport isn't just played but revered. With seven premier golf courses, Mesquite is a popular destination for golfing enthusiasts worldwide. The challenging and captivating terrain appeals to both experienced and new golfer, eager to swing their clubs against the backdrop of rolling hills and rocky outcrops.

Legends and Legacy: Palmer's Prestigious Designs

Two of Mesquite's golfing marvels have the unique distinction of being designed by none other than golfing legend, Arnold Palmer. These courses are not just stretches of greens and fairways; they are masterpieces that embody Palmer's vision, expertise, and love for the sport. Playing on these courses, one isn't just striking a ball; they're tracing the steps of a legacy.

Gaming Meets Golf: Wolf Creek's Virtual Fame

When a golf course graces a video game, you know there's something special about it. Wolf Creek isn't just another golf course; it's an experience. The appealing greens, the challenging hazards, and stunning views have made it a standout feature in Tiger Woods' PGA Tour Golf video game series. The course, with its real-world challenges and beauty, has captured the imaginations of both virtual gamers and actual golfers alike.

The Fantastic Five: Diverse Terrains for Every Golfer

In addition to Palmer's creations and Wolf Creek, Mesquite has five other golf courses, each with their own unique character and challenges. Whether you're a seasoned pro looking for a challenge or an amateur seeking to learn amidst nature's beauty, there's a course here for you. And for the spectators, the thrill isn't just in the game but in the panoramic vistas that serve as the backdrop.

The Gathering Spot: A Hub for International Golf Lovers

Every year, Mesquite becomes a magnet for a global community bound by their love for golf. The town is alive with golf tournaments, championships, and casual rounds. People exchange stories of great shots and shared admiration for the desert courses. Golf clinics, training camps, and special events pepper the calendar, making Mesquite a year-round hub for golfing activity.

Beyond the Green: Recreation and Respite

Mesquite's golf courses aren't just about the game. They're about the experience. The resorts accompanying these courses ensure that once the game is over; the relaxation begins. Spa treatments, gourmet dining, or just lounging by the pool. The experience is holistic.

In Mesquite, golf isn't just a sport. It's a celebration, a communion with nature, and a testament to the town's commitment to offering nothing but the best. Prepare for an exceptional golfing experience, whether you're playing Palmer's designs, tackling the Wolf Creek, or enjoying the ambiance of the other five courses.

Federal Influence: Protection & Restriction

The ever-evolving narrative of Mesquite has been influenced by federal decisions that have sculpted surrounding land. Presidents tried to protect beautiful landscapes, but there were unintended consequences.

The Grand Canyon-Parashant and Gold Butte national monument declarations by Bill Clinton and Barack Obama aimed to protect nature but are seen by locals as federal overreach. These communities feel the decisions, which restrict activities like mining and ranching, were made without their input. This has sparked a debate about federal control versus local autonomy, highlighting the need for involving local voices in environmental conservation decisions.

The Majesty of Grand Canyon-Parashant

President Clinton designated the Grand Canyon- Parashant a National Monument in 2000, acknowledging its beauty and ecological importance. Covering more than a million acres, this expansive area became a sanctuary for diverse wildlife and, stunning landscapes. The move recognized the significance of the indigenous peoples history and culture while preserving their land.

Yet, with protection came restriction. Locals grappled with limited access and a sense of distance from lands they once freely roamed. Economic activities, especially in agriculture and grazing, were constrained by new boundaries, impacting livelihoods and shaping perceptions of federal control.

Gold Butte's Golden Proclamation

Gold Butte was designated a National Monument by President Obama in 2016, preserving its mosaic of red sandstone, twisting canyons, and ancient rock art. Ensuring it would remain undisturbed for generations. Gold Butte's proclamation celebrated the rich tapestry of flora and fauna, as well as the deep-rooted histories of native cultures.

However, the protective shield also gave rise to concerns. Locals were once again restricted and felt ignored in the conservation efforts. The economic impact was a point of disagreement, especially for ranchers and local businesses depending on visitors.

Weighing the Balance

At the heart of these monumental designations lies a balance of untouched landscapes. These parks and preserves serve as a reminder that nature's wonders are timeless, waiting just beyond the horizon for those eager to explore.

Mesquite in Popular Culture: Echoes of Gold Butte's Whispers

Nestled within the vast landscapes of the Mojave Desert, Mesquite emerges as a city filled with wonders, both natural and historic. In the silence of the desert, Mesquite echoes with captivating stories and legendary celebrity hideaways.

The Mesquite Celebrity Affair

The allure of Mesquite's tranquility hasn't escaped the discerning eyes of many celebrities. John Wayne and Clark Gable, for instance, once sought refuge in the Beaver Dam Lodge, a sanctuary that allowed them to escape the ever-watchful public eye. Many believe that figures like Howard Hughes recognized the region's potential; Hughes, known for acquiring property throughout Las Vegas, including areas like Gold Butte and Echo Bay, was one such individual.

The attraction of Mesquite extends beyond Hollywood fame. Prominent families, particularly from sectors such as the confectionery and seafood industries, often choose Mesquite as their vacation destination. Drawn by its serene ambiance and distinctive landscape, celebrities frequently visit the area. It's also a popular spot for golf enthusiasts, including famous professional players, who are often seen on Mesquite's greens. Furthermore, Mesquite is the hometown of a former NBA player, underlining its appeal to a diverse range of notable individuals. This player not only grew up in Mesquite but also attended the local Virgin Valley High School, adding to the city's rich tapestry of famous connections.

Gold Butte's Legacy

Gold Butte plays a significant role in the history of Mesquite, characterized by stories of its numerous mines, old wagon tracks, and the footprints of Spanish explorers dating back to the 18th century. Although many of the area's historical features have been altered over the years — including the removal of some mining equipment due to factors like theft and federal permits — it continues to symbolize the region's industrious past.

It is also noteworthy that Gold Butte has connections to remarkable individuals. This includes a whistleblower, known for disclosing secrets about the S4 base near Area 51. Rumors suggest that a local resident, knowledgeable about the area's mining history, might have shared stories related to Gold Butte with a friend. These stories included topics like aliens and secret activities at Area 51. This friend, an aviation magnate dubbed as 'probably the most influential source of UFO conspiracy theories', once held a large mining claim in this region.

These conversations have contributed to Gold Butte's mystique. Intriguingly, there was a prediction of a UFO appearance that coincided with a significant sighting during a local parade, a prediction that turned out to be surprisingly accurate.

The Intriguing Characters of Gold Butte

Gold Butte's history is adorned with a colorful array of characters, including the legendary "Crazy Eddie" and the enigmatic duo of Bill Garrett and Art Coleman, famously known as the "Odd Couple." Bill is the subject of persistent rumors claiming he is the nephew of Pat Garrett, renowned for his involvement in the Billy the Kid saga. However, recent historians have cast doubt on this connection, suggesting it may be more folklore than fact.

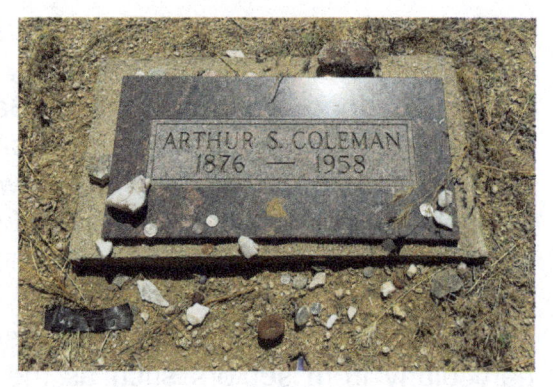

RUMOR HAS IT:

The authenticity of Bill Garrett's relationship to Pat Garrett remains a topic of debate, adding an air of intrigue to the region's history. In addition, Art Coleman, a cherished prospector, reappeared in Gold Butte's narrative after a peculiar grave robbery rattled the community, rekindling memories of a bygone era and contributing yet another bizarre chapter to the region's storied history. Gold Butte transcends mere historical significance; it's a landscape imbued with extraordinary tales and captivating personalities, all of which enrich the area's cultural heritage. While some of these stories may be veiled in uncertainty, they persist in enhancing the mystique of this remote and fascinating land.

Ghostly Adventures in Gold Butte

The renowned TV series "Ghost Adventures" turned its lens to Gold Butte, diving deep into the region's eerie tales. Their research into the chilling legends of Lake Mead and Devil's Cove has made Gold Butte an internationally fascinating destination, blending history with the supernatural. Gold Butte is an amazing blend of history, celebrity tales, captivating landscapes, and mysteries waiting to be unraveled. As travelers wander through its terrains and delve into its stories, they find a city that speaks to adventures, historians, and dreamers alike. And in every nook and cranny, there lies a tale waiting to be told, a secret waiting to be discovered.

Nature's Wonders: State & National Parks Around Mesquite

Mesquite, a jewel of the American Southwest, boasts more than its fair share of entertainment and culture. Yet, it's the natural tapestry that unfolds beyond its borders that truly captures the heart. The state and national parks nearby are like living paintings, showcasing the beauty of nature.

Echoes of the Past: Valley of Fire State Park

Only a short drive from Mesquite, the Valley of Fire unfolds in a burst of radiant reds, oranges, and pinks. The park's name is no exaggeration. As the sun casts its golden rays, the Aztec sandstone formations appear to ignite in flame. With petroglyphs dating back over 2,000 years, it's a portal into the world of the ancient Ancestral Puebloans.

Vistas and Valleys: Zion National Park

Further afield, but worth every mile, Zion National Park is a symphony of stone. Towering cliffs of cream, pink, and red stand as sentinels over verdant valleys. The meandering Virgin River, has carved the park's landscape, resulting in breathtaking views like the Zion Narrows.

Desert Bloom: Snow Canyon State Park

This park, closer to Mesquite than Zion, but smaller than both, is no less enchanting. A medley of lava flows, petrified sand dunes, and red rock vistas, Snow Canyon is a testament to nature's artistry. And in spring, the desert blooms, painting the park in hues of lavender, gold, and coral.

Beyond the Horizon: Grand Canyon-Parashant National Monument

Lying on the Colorado Plateau, this less-traveled section of the Grand Canyon is raw, remote, and utterly mesmerizing. Devoid of the crowds of the main canyon, Parashant offers a tranquil and intimate communion with nature. Starlit skies, rugged landscapes, and deep canyons beckon the intrepid traveler.

The Water's Edge: Lake Mead National Recreation Area

The shimmering blue expanse of Lake Mead stands in stark contrast to the surrounding desert. Created by the Hoover Dam, it's a haven for water sports, fishing, and leisurely cruises. The rugged surroundings of the lake offer a stunning backdrop for a wide range of outdoor adventures. The allure of the desert isn't limited to its urban offerings. It's in the call of the wild, the whisper of the wind through canyon walls, and the serenity of the surroundings.

A Line in the Sand: Bunkerville & the Struggle for Sovereignty

In early April 2014, Bunkerville, a small town in Nevada, unexpectedly gained national attention. In the heart of the American Southwest, Bunkerville became the stage for a decades-long dispute over federal land usage and grazing rights.

Rooted in Foundational Principles

Understanding the events of Bunkerville requires recognizing the character of the American Revolution. The pursuit of independence and the right to determine one's own fate on one's own land are concepts deeply embedded in the American psyche. Cliven Bundy, a cattle rancher, and his kin had grazed their livestock on the public lands of Bunkerville for several generations. Bundy found himself in conflicts over grazing rights and land use because of shifts in federal policies, particularly those focused on conserving habitats for species like the desert tortoise.

Bundy and the Federal Challenge

Over the years, the stalemate between Bundy and the Bureau of Land Management (BLM) intensified. The BLM cited environmental regulations and demanded payment for grazing fees, while Bundy argued for ancestral rights and questioned the need for increased federal jurisdiction. As the fees accumulated and patience waned, the BLM moved to confiscate Bundy's cattle, a decision that would lead to a highly controversial standoff.

When Tensions Boiled Over

Word of the BLM's actions traveled fast, drawing supporters to Bunkerville. Bundy's predicament reminded many of the challenges faced by early American colonists against distant, detached governance. The town was quickly filled with people, some armed, standing in unity with Bundy against what they saw as federal intrusion.

As federal agents and Bundy's supporters squared off, the atmosphere grew thick with anticipation. Hundreds of protesters, including various militia members, gathered in solidarity with the Bundys. Many carried guns and aimed their rifles at federal agents who had positioned snipers pointing at them. Some were on horseback, and some yelled obscenities. Authorities shut Interstate 15 down.

Amidst this tension, the spirit of 1776—a yearning for self-governance and freedom from perceived tyranny—was palpable. Yet, despite the brewing storm, people averted outright conflict. The BLM, weighing the potential outcomes, opted for de-escalation, pulling back their forces and releasing the cattle they had seized.

Echoes of the Past, Lessons for the Future

The Bunkerville events showcased the intricate connection between individual citizens and federal authorities. The standoff reminds us of the values that the United States was built on and raises questions about their relevance today.

Bunkerville's 2014 standoff will not be forgotten. In the annals of its history, this moment underscores the enduring American spirit—a spirit that seeks to assert and preserve its sense of autonomy and freedom.

A Spiritual Oasis: God's Work & the Flourishing Faith of Mesquite

When you think of Mesquite, you often picture its iconic golf courses, bustling casinos, and the allure of the rugged outdoors. While known for its recreational offerings, this lively town also has a rich spiritual heritage. Beyond the rolling greens and neon lights, Mesquite has been a quiet haven for spiritual seekers and believers.

Awakening the Unknown: The Modern-Day Renaissance

Mesquite has experienced a strong spiritual awakening in recent times. Over 10 local churches now offer sanctuaries for worship and community in the town. Each, with its own unique character, contributes to the spiritual tapestry that Mesquite is becoming known for. This isn't just a historical remnant, but a modern-day revival.

Beyond Recreation: A Deeper Connection

In the heart of Mesquite, a profound spiritual resurgence is taking place, particularly within the Protestant community. This revival, deeply rooted in historical faith and flourishing in modern times, is infusing an additional layer of depth into the town's identity. As people are drawn to Mesquite for its physical appeal, an increasing number are finding themselves captivated by its spiritual richness. This reawakening is not just about rediscovering faith but also about acknowledging the Holy Trinity and the divine calling of individuals to serve the community. In a town that may seem to be stagnant in some respects, this dedicated Protestant resurgence is breathing new life, with people feeling called to serve for the betterment of the community and in devotion to the Lord. The intertwining of Mesquite's worldly charm with this profound spiritual movement is creating a unique and compelling narrative, where physical and spiritual sustenance can coexist and thrive.

Focusing on spiritual connections in a place known for leisure and recreation may seem unexpected, yet it is this very contrast that endows Mesquite's community with its unique and profound character. The town provides more than an escape from the mundane; it offers a journey into profundity and a path to new beginnings through Christ.

Exploring Modern Mesquite: Safety, Natural Resources, & Future Prospects

In the heart of the Mojave, where ancient stories intertwine with the whispers of the wind, Mesquite stands poised on the threshold of tomorrow. Today's Mesquite is a synthesis of its resilient past and the promise of a future replete with possibilities. The city is committed to safety and the responsible use of natural resources with a forward-thinking mindset.

Safety First: A Community Commitment

In Mesquite, the well-being of its residents and visitors stands paramount. With its modern infrastructure, and effective law enforcement, and emergency services, the city remains a safe haven in the desert. Community policing initiatives build trust between residents and law enforcement, creating a safe and united environment.

The city's convenient location, away from the noise but still close to major cities, further adds to its reputation as a safe and convenient place to live. It's a place where children can play in the open expanses and families can create memories without the looming shadow of concern.

Nurturing Natural Resources

Mesquite's respect for its environment has not waned with modernization. It has intensified. Embracing a sustainable outlook, the city focuses on conserving water, a resource as precious as gold in this arid landscape. By using innovative agricultural practices, efficient water management systems, and community awareness campaigns we are committed to preserving the Virgin River for future generations. Protecting natural habitats, plants, and animals is a top priority of Mesquite's ecological efforts. The city actively pursues growth and development while minimizing environmental impact, ensuring the thriving of deserts, canyons, and wildlife.

Future Prospects: A Visionary Outlook

As Mesquite steps into the future, it does so with vision and verve. The city is emerging as a hub for sustainable tourism, capitalizing on its rich history, natural beauty, and cultural festivals. Mesquite's location between Las Vegas and the natural wonders of Utah makes it an ideal destination for those seeking both excitement and tranquility.

Economic diversification is also on the horizon. Besides traditional sectors like agriculture that continue to be vital, there is a focus on technology, renewable energy, and service industries. Educational and training initiatives aim to equip the youth with the skills required for tomorrow's challenges, ensuring that Mesquite remains vibrant and relevant in the evolving economic landscape.

Modern Mesquite is more than just a city in the desert; it's a testament to human adaptability, resilience, and foresight. As it cherishes its safety and natural resources, it also casts an eager eye towards the prospects of the future. Mesquite's story unfolds in the dance of shadows and lights on the desert sands, Mesquite's story continues to unfold, promising a journey that respects its roots while embracing new horizons.

The Current State of the Tri States

The region where Southeast Nevada, Southern Utah, and Northwest Arizona come together is a testament to the American spirit of reinvention and resilience. The Tri-State area is a mosaic of Mesquite, the Arizona Strip, southern Utah, and Moapa in Nevada. It represents diverse cultures, shared histories, and new-age aspirations. This junction, in the heart of the American Southwest, is a perfect blend of peaceful landscapes and vibrant city life. Now, more than ever, it's exuding a palpable sense of renewal and ambition, heralding a promising future for its inhabitants.

Southern Utah's Ascension

Southern Utah, renowned for its red-rock beauty and national parks, is not just a traveler's dream anymore. Cities like St. George are flourishing, with rapid growth driving economic vibrancy and cultural dynamism. As communities here expand, they do so with an eye on sustainability and a heart full of local pride.

Arizona Strip: Nature's Undiscovered Gem

The Arizona Strip is a hidden gem with untouched landscapes and close-knit communities. As more people explore it, there's a delicate balance between development and conservation to preserve its beauty for future generations.

Moapa and Beyond: Nevada's Rising Stars

Moapa, along with other outliers in Nevada, is exemplifying the state's can-do spirit. Moapa is blending Nevada's history with its future by improving infrastructure, establishing new businesses and promoting community well-being.

The Mesquite Metamorphosis

Mesquite, previously known for gaming and entertainment avenues, is now becoming a diverse urban center. With a mix of diverse populations, it is growing in culture, economically, and recreationally.

Interconnected Dreams and Shared Futures

Mesquite weaves a story that spans millennia, a tale rich in history, culture, and natural beauty. From caves with ancient secrets to Spanish trails, this land is full of narratives. Pioneer settlements overcame obstacles, showcasing the strength and determination of the human spirit.

Nestled amidst this historical backdrop is a vibrant small- town America, alive with whispers of old tales and contemporary rhythms. While Mesquite has seen its share of rumors and political drama, it stands today as a beacon of enduring values and traditions. The sweltering heat and rugged terrains have turned this town into an adventure paradise. Drawing outdoor enthusiasts to its vast landscapes and natural beauty.

At the crossroads of the past and the present, Mesquite offers a unique blend of heritage and modernity. It's a destination that beckons travelers with its charm, and where residents take immense pride in their shared legacy. Mesquite is a hidden gem in the desert, with a rich history and an exciting future.

The strength of the region is rooted not just in the individual richness of each state, but in their combined synergy. Arizona, with its sprawling deserts and bustling urban centers, brings economic dynamism. Nevada, a mix of entertainment hubs and vast wilderness, adds a touch of allure and adventure. Utah, with its majestic mountains and spiritual sanctuaries, infuses a sense of serenity and depth. Economic collaborations, environmental initiatives, and cultural exchanges demonstrate how these three states seamlessly integrate. Businesses and communities are committed to preserving the regions natural beauty and cultural heritage. The balance between growth and conservation, tradition and innovation, is a testament to the shared vision of its inhabitants.

Each chapter in its history, whether marked by prosperity or beset by challenges, speaks to the region's unwavering resilience. Despite tragedy and disaster, this land and its people have grown stronger through hope and determination.

A unique allure persists here, beckoning a diverse array of individuals. A sense of divine purpose draws many, seeking both sanctuary and a place to make their mark. They join the ranks of those who have come before, honoring the traditions and values that have shaped this region for generations.

As we pay tribute to the rugged history of the Tri-State area, we also cast our gaze forward, envisioning a future that melds the old with the new. While innovation and change beckon, the region remains anchored in the foundational principles that have guided its journey. The path ahead is lit with the promise of opportunity, but the footsteps echo with the reverence of the past.

###

© Copyright Desert Covenant Books, LLC.   All Rights Reserved.

Like what you read?
Join Our Facebook Group!

All Around Mesquite Nevada
History, Trails, & Destinations

www.facebook.com/groups/allaroundmesquite

★ Get the latest updates first! ★
★ Access exclusive insights. ★
★ Connect with a passionate community. ★
★ Never miss out on important info. ★

#StayUpdated #JoinToday #AllAroundMesquite

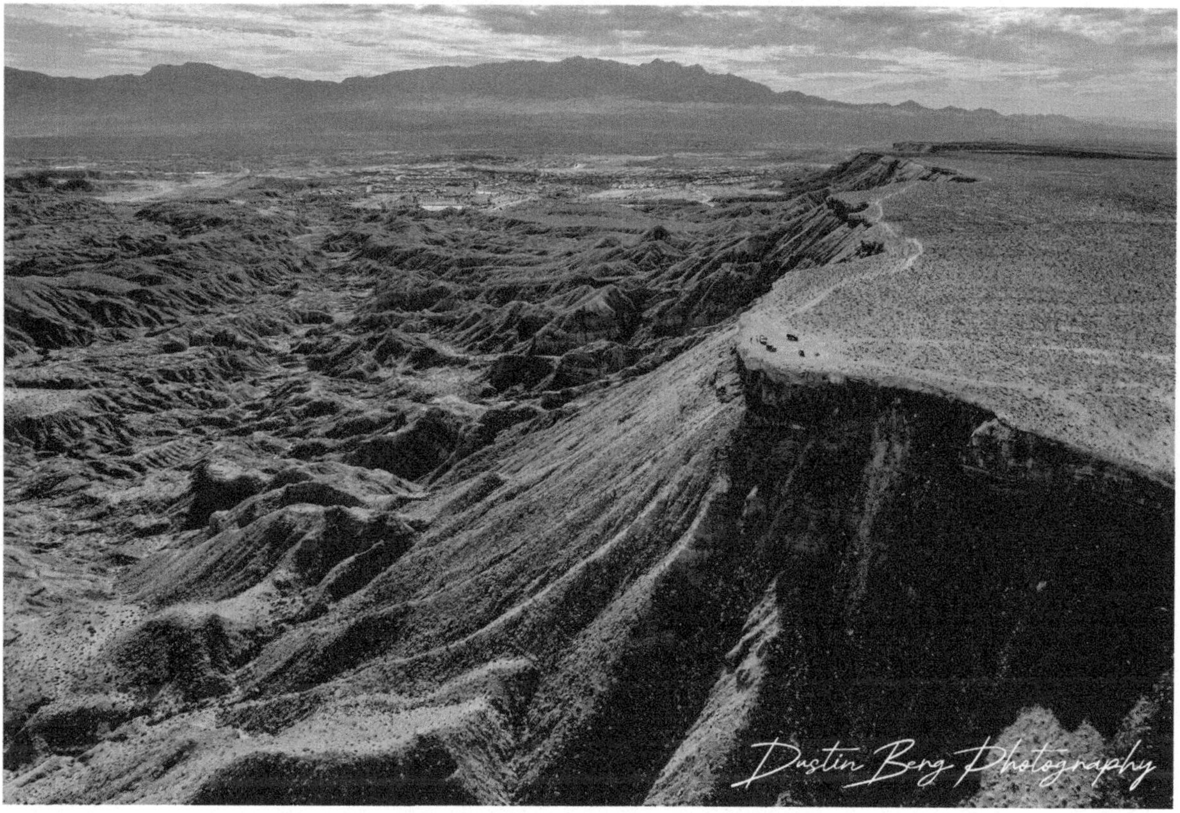
Dustin Berg Photography

Mesquite Rock Carvings along Flat Top Mesa Trailhead by local artist, Pete Karns.

Mesquite Regional Sports and Event Complex- Home of the Long Drive.

Urban Information

Mesquite, with its blend of small-town allure and contemporary comforts, presents an ideal setting for those seeking an active lifestyle. This community is a haven for outdoor enthusiasts and sports lovers, offering a plethora of activities like walking, hiking, biking, and jogging. The well-designed urban spaces and natural landscapes provide the perfect backdrop for a range of sports, including those tailored for the retirement community.

The Senior Games, a highlight in Mesquite, feature an array of tournaments ranging from Cornhole to Pickleball and even pistol shooting, catering to diverse interests and promoting a healthy, competitive spirit.

Beyond its active lifestyle offerings, Mesquite charms with its local boutiques, quaint eateries, buzzing casinos, and serene parks. The town's urban planning emphasizes a strong community vibe while ensuring a variety of attractions are available. This unique mix of a cozy, neighborly atmosphere and the energy of city life makes Mesquite an attractive destination for both residents and visitors. Whether you're seeking a peaceful retirement community with plenty of activities or a vibrant town with modern amenities, Mesquite offers a fulfilling experience blending the best of both worlds.

Chamber of Commerce(s)

We are fortunate to have many great partners in our region that help facilitate events and economic development. If you are interested in learning more about various events in the area, we would encourage you to visit the three main Chamber of Commerce organization websites:

http://www.mesquitenvchamber.com
http://www.moapavalleychamber.com
https://stgeorgechamber.com

PARKS & TRAILS

There is a myriad of options for whatever adventure awaits.
Enjoy the amenities of Mesquite's various parks!

Animal Control Dog Park
795 Hardy Way

Desert Rose Park
640 W Old Mill Rd

Hafen Park
450 W Hafen Ln

Hillside Arboretum
501 Hillside Dr

Hunter Sports Park
500 E Mesquite Blvd

Jensen Trailside Park
770 2nd South St

Library Park
121 W 1st North St

Marilyn Redd Park
251 Marilyn Pkwy

Mesquite Regional Park Trailhead
Lower Flat Top Dr

Mesquite Welcome Center
460 N Sandhill Blvd

Old Mill Park
50 W Old Mill Rd

Old Mill Pickleball Courts
49 W Old Mill Rd

Pioneer Park
501 Hillside Dr

Pulsipher Park
303 2nd South Str

Recreation Center Park
100 W Old Mill Rd

Redd Hills Park
665 Fountain View Ln

Riverside OHV Staging Arena
680 Riverside Rd

Senior Center Picnic Pavilion
102 W Old Mill Rd

Sports & Event Complex
1635 World Champion Way

Veteran's Memorial Park
501 Hillside Dr

Woodbury Park
100 Woodbury Ln

Contact the City at (702) 346-8732 for more information

EVENT CALENDAR

AS OF FALL 2023 - COLOR CODED BY REGION

These are some popular regional holidays and the typical months upon which they fall.
Dates not guaranteed, do your own research.

JAN
Mesquite Motor Mania

Hot Air Balloon Festival

FEB
ELKS Golf Classic

Parade of Homes

MARCH
Mesquite MX

Mesquite Senior Games

APRIL
Clark County Rodeo

MAY
Mesquite Days

Mesquite Amatuer

JUNE
Flag Day

National Arizona Day

JULY
Fourth of July

Pioneer Day

AUG
Chamber Golf

Peach Days

SEPT
Mesquite Gaming Ribfest

Mesquite Gaming Super Run

OCT
MV Car Show

Shriekreeka

Corn Maze

Nevada Day

Hump 'n Bump

NOV
Veteran's Day Parade

Pomegranate Festival

Small Business Saturday

1000 Flags Over Mesquite

St George Downtown Tree Lighting Ceremony

DEC
Parade of Lights

Mingle & Jingle

Legend:

● Mesquite   ● Moapa Valley   ● Arizona Strip   ● Southern Utah

Notable Event Information

1000 Flags over Mesquite:
Visit in November - the "1000 Flags over Mesquite" is a breathtaking display of one thousand American Flags illuminating the west field of the Mesquite Recreation Center around the clock, come rain or shine. Lit up during nighttime and safeguarded by dedicated community volunteers day and night, this awe-inspiring spectacle serves as a vivid testament to patriotism. The Exchange Club of Mesquite takes immense pride in this annual tradition and warmly welcomes everyone to participate in or witness this majestic sea of flags.

Mesquite Days
Celebrating an annual tradition of more than 30 years, Mesquite Days in May features cherished events such as the Mayor's Pancake Breakfast, Family Fun Night, and the iconic Mesquite Days Parade. The spirit of our town is showcased brilliantly during these festivities. For a complete schedule and more details, please visit the News section on the city's official website.

The Entertainment Capital of the World
From our quiet town of Mesquite, the dazzling lights of Las Vegas shimmer in the distance, standing as a testament to its reign as the entertainment capital of the world. The city's ever-evolving spectacle of world-class shows, legendary performers, and extravagant casinos are both awe-inspiring and slightly overwhelming. Yet, while we appreciate the allure and magic Las Vegas offers, there's a shared contentment here in our serene escape, just a stone's throw away from the hustle and bustle.

Clark County Fair & Rodeo
Since 1988, Logandale has proudly hosted one of the top PRCA and WPRA Rodeos in the nation. Over 500 professional athletes take part in the five-day event. It offers a festive, fair atmosphere with food, entertainment, thrilling rides, and top quality livestock. The Clark County Fair & Rodeo seamlessly blends athletic competition and community festivities, making it a must-visit for all ages.

Notable Event Information

Hot Air Balloon Festival
Our annual hot air balloon festival promises breathtaking launches each morning, conditions allowing. Experience the enchanting night glow on Friday and Saturday evenings, coupled with live entertainment in the Skydome Lounge. Don't miss the grand balloon launch finale on Sunday morning.

The Lantern/Lights Fest in Arizona Strip is an annual spectacle that beautifully punctuates the region's event calendar, although the exact timing may vary from year to year. Participants gather to release lanterns against the backdrop of the desert sky, each symbolizing personal sentiments, be it hopes, memories, or dreams. Accompanied by food, music, and camaraderie, the festival's increasing popularity sometimes redirects Las Vegas traffic our way. Due to its growing demand, many prospective attendees often find themselves missing out.

Car Shows
Mesquite is a popular destination for car enthusiasts. They host events like Mesquite Motor Mania, sponsored by Mesquite Gaming, Casa Blanca Resort, and Virgin River Resort, featuring a variety of cars from vintage classics to custom beauties. The Las Vegas Cruisin' Association presents the Super Run Car Show, another thrilling event in Mesquite's car show circuit. Nearby Moapa hosts two beloved car events: the Moapa Valley Car Show, with a 23-year legacy, and the Dan Bailey Memorial Car Show.

Trail Hero (Southern Utah)
The Trail Hero off-roading event emphasizes trail riding and rock crawling across stunning landscapes, set against large mountainscapes. Dedicated to preserving the trails we cherish, this event is chock-full of activities including riding, camping, music, and much more!

Other Events to consider (NOT an exhaustive list):
Beaver Dam Lawnmower Races,
Mesquite Senior Games,
Taste of Southern Utah,
Parade of Homes,
Various 4th of July Events,
Mesquite Gaming Ribfest,
Mesquite & St. George Theatre Performances (and Tuacahn).

Golf Courses
Mesquite, Moapa, Arizona Strip

Beaver Dam Lodge
(928) 347-2222
historicalbeaverdamlodge.com

Conestoga
(702) 346-4292
www.conestogagolf.com

The Oasis Golf Club
(702) 919-6040
www.theoasisgolfclub.com

Coyote Springs
(877) 742-8455
www.coyotesprings.com

CasaBlanca
(702) 346-6764
www.casablancaresort.com

Wolf Creek
(702) 346-1670
www.golfwolfcreek.com

The Palms
(702) 346-4067
www.casablancaresort.com

Coyote Willows
(702) 345-4222
www.coyotewillowsgolf.com

Falcon Ridge
(702) 346-6363
www.golffalcon.com

CasaBlanca & Palms Golf
(877) 438-2999
www.golfingmesquite.com

Mesquite Golf Pass
(866) 720-7111
www.mesquitegolfpass.com

Golf Courses
Southern Utah

Sand Hollow Resort
(435) 656-4653
www.sandhollowresort.com

Copper Rock Golf Course
(435) 215-4845
www.copperrock.com

Sky Mountain Golf Course
(435) 635-7888
www.skymountaingolf.com

Coral Canyon Golf Course
(435) 688-1700
www.coralcanyongolf.com

The Ledges of St George
(435) 634-4640
www.ledges.com

Entrada at Snow Canyon
(435) 986-2200
www.golfentrada.com

Green Spring Golf Course
(435) 673-7888
washingtoncity.org/recreation/golf

Sunbrook Golf Club
(435) 627-4400
www.sunbrookgolf.com

Southgate Golf Course
(435) 627-4440
www.southgategc.com

SunRiver Golf Course
(435) 986-0001
www.sunrivergolf.com

Dixie Red Hills Golf Course
(435) 627-4444
www.redhillsgolf.com

St George Golf Club
(435) 627-4404
www.stgeorgegolfclub.com

MESQUITE & BUNKERVILLE HISTORICAL SITE MAP

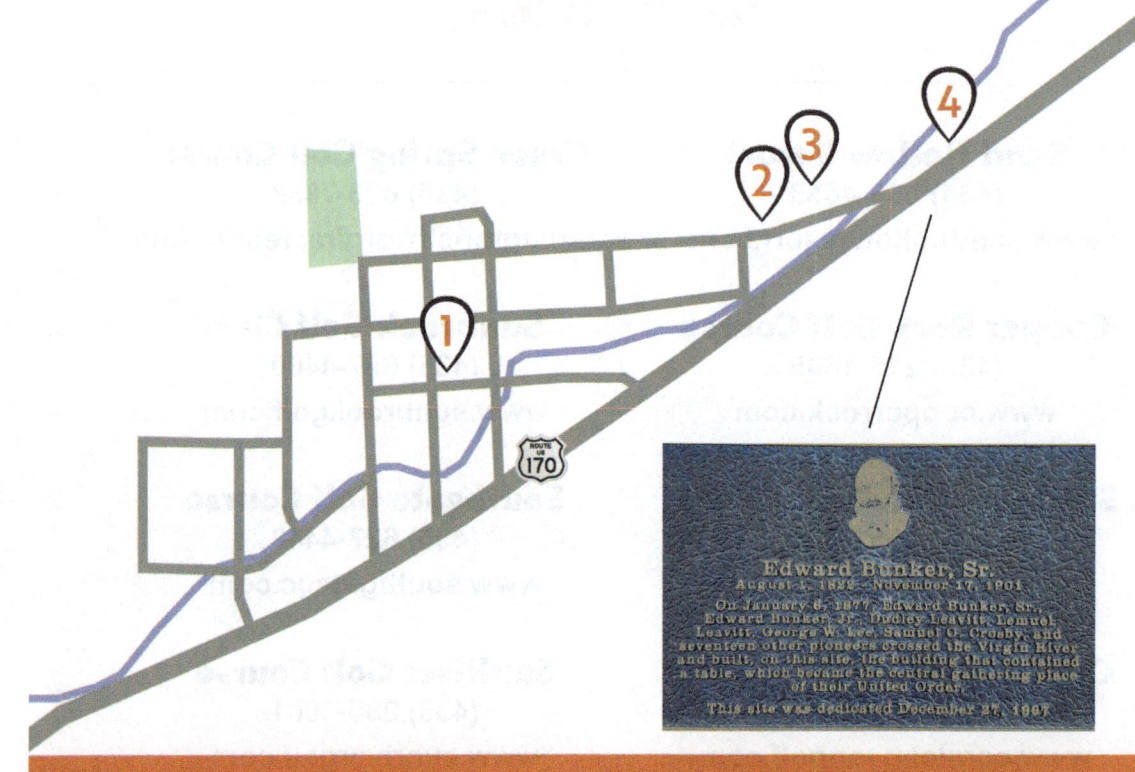

Edward Bunker, Sr.
August 1, 1822 – November 17, 1901

On January 5, 1877, Edward Bunker, Sr., Edward Bunker, Jr., Dudley Leavitt, Lemuel Leavitt, George W. Lee, Samuel O. Crosby, and seventeen other pioneers crossed the Virgin River and built, on this site, the building that contained a table, which became the central gathering place of their United Order.

This site was dedicated December 27, 1997.

LEGEND

BUNKERVILLE

1 - Thomas Leavitt House
2 - Parley Hunt House
3 - Bunkerville Cemetery
4 - Bunkerville Historical Monument

MESQUITE

1 - Egg House/Telephone Building
2 - The Old Spanish Trail
3 - Abbot Way Station
4 - Museum & Fire House
5 - Virgin Valley Heritage Museum
6 - School & Gymnasium Block
7 - Rock House
8 - John David Pulsipher Home
9 - Charles Hardy Home
10 - Open Air Dance Hall
11 - Drug Store/Bakery
12 - Abram Woodbury Home & Gas Station
13 - Charles Arthur Hughes Home
14 - Tithing Lot
15 - History of Mesquite
16 - William Elias Abbott Statue
17 - Mary Jane Leavitt Abbott Statue
18 - William Abbott Home/Abbott Hotel
19 - Ervin "Casey" Jones House
20 - Dairy Barn

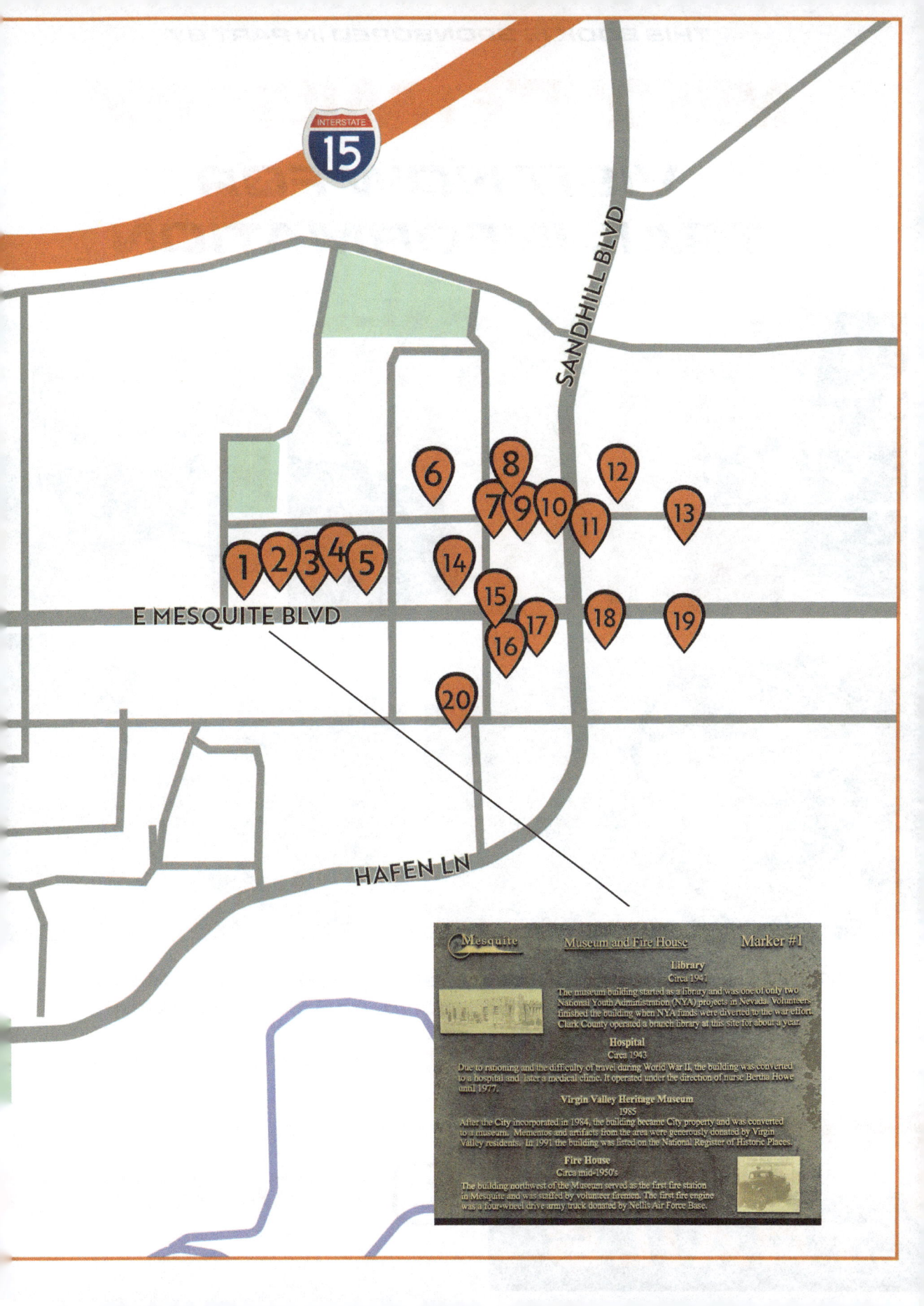

Museum and Fire House — Marker #1

Library
Circa 1941

The museum building started as a library and was one of only two National Youth Administration (NYA) projects in Nevada. Volunteers finished the building when NYA funds were diverted to the war effort. Clark County operated a branch library at this site for about a year.

Hospital
Circa 1943

Due to rationing and the difficulty of travel during World War II, the building was converted to a hospital and later a medical clinic. It operated under the direction of nurse Bertha Howe until 1977.

Virgin Valley Heritage Museum
1985

After the City incorporated in 1984, the building became City property and was converted to a museum. Mementos and artifacts from the area were generously donated by Virgin Valley residents. In 1991 the building was listed on the National Register of Historic Places.

Fire House
Circa mid-1950's

The building northwest of the Museum served as the first fire station in Mesquite and was staffed by volunteer firemen. The first fire engine was a four-wheel drive army truck donated by Nellis Air Force Base.

THIS BOOK IS SPONSORED IN PART BY

MESQUITETRAILS.COM

VISIT NOW FOR TRAIL INFORMATION

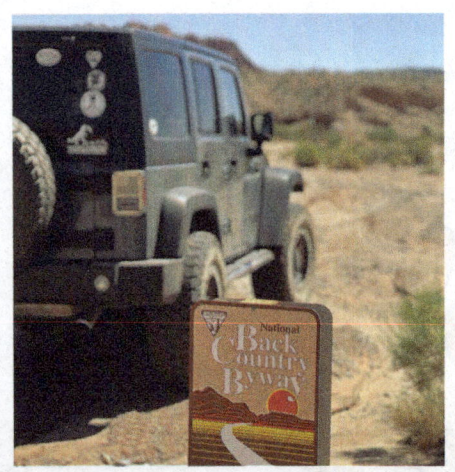

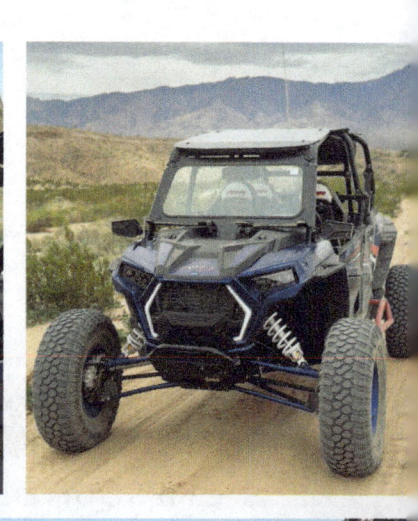

Your place for trails & destinations in & around Mesquite, Logandale, the Arizona Strip, and Southern Utah.

Tag #RideMesquite to be featured!

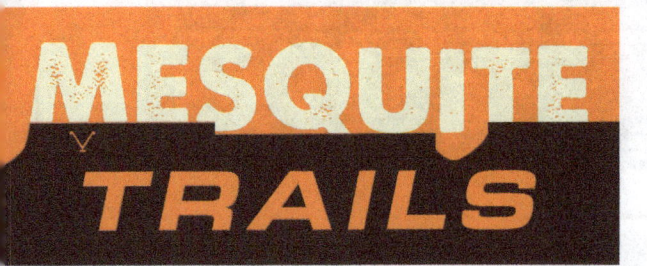

MESQUITE TRAILS

@RIDEMESQUITE

OHV Awareness

CAUTION: RESPECTING NATURE'S PATH

In your thrilling journey through the trails and annals of history, be ever vigilant of the scars left by Mother Nature. Especially after a storm, the paths you tread may bear the marks of her fury. Washed out roads, as depicted in the adjacent image of a deep, treacherous rut, can be not only dangerous but also deceptive.

Ensure your safety, and the safety of those traveling with you, by always proceeding with caution. Preserve the trails for generations to come; understand the history, respect the terrain, and most importantly, know when to reroute. Safe travels, OHVers!

TORTOISE AWARENESS & INVASIVE SPECIES AWARENESS

PLEASE DO NOT TOUCH WILD DESERT TORTOISE. LET THEM BE WILD.

Desert Tortoises are protected under the federal Endangered Species Act as a threatened species. Under the Endangered Species Act, it is illegal to harass, harm, pursue, hunt, shoot, wound, kill, trap, capture, or collect a wild desert tortoise.

TORTOISE AWARENESS BEST PRACTICES FOR OHV USERS:

1. Look underneath your tires for desert tortoises before moving your vehicle.
2. If you see a desert tortoise in the wild, leave it alone, let it be wild.
3. Take pictures of desert tortoises, and enjoy from afar.

Thank you for not handling or disturbing desert tortoises. Their survival depends on it.

NON-NATIVE SPECIES AWARENESS

DON'T GIVE WEEDS A FREE RIDE!

Invasive weeds compete with native plants and animals and result in more frequent and intense fires. Washing off your OHV will help prevent the spread of non-native weeds.

BEST PRACTICES FOR OHV USERS TO MINIMIZE THE SPREAD OF WEEDS:

1. Stay on designated routes and trails.
2. Clean vehicles by washing the undercarriage and brushing all dirt and mud off tires before entering and exiting a recreation site.
3. Clean boots and other gear that can carry dirt and seeds before moving to new areas.

Thank you for staying on designated routes and trails and cleaning your vehicle. For more information, please visit MojaveMax.com

Travel & Exploration Tips

1. Planning & Research:
Maps and Routes: Before you go, check topographical maps and detailed trail guides of your chosen destination before setting out. Many regions, especially remote ones like the Arizona Strip, have limited or no cellular reception.

Local Knowledge: Speak to local rangers, tour guides, or seasoned travelers. They can offer insights and updates on trail conditions, water sources, and potentially hazardous areas.

2. Safety Precautions:
Weather Checks: Desert regions can experience extreme temperature fluctuations. Check local weather forecasts, and be prepared for sudden changes, especially flash floods in canyon areas.

Emergency Kit: Always carry an emergency kit containing a first aid box, a multi-tool, waterproof matches, an emergency blanket, and a whistle.

Communication: Satellite phones and personal locator beacons can save lives in areas without cell service. Part of being in the desert means having limited or no service in many surrounding areas.

3. Gear Essentials:
Water and Hydration: In arid regions, it's recommended to carry at least one gallon of water per person per day. Consider hydration packs for convenience.

Footwear: Invest in sturdy, comfortable hiking boots that offer ankle support and have a grip suitable for rugged terrains.

Navigation: Even if you're using a GPS, always carry a compass and a physical map. Batteries can die, and electronics can fail.

4. Environmental Responsibility:
Leave No Trace: Always pack out everything you bring in, including all trash and food waste.

Camping: If camping, use established sites. Avoid making new fire rings, and always put out campfires completely before leaving.

Travel & Exploration Tips

Wildlife: Keep a safe distance from wildlife. Never feed wild animals as it can be harmful to them and alter their natural behavior.

5. Health & Wellness:

Acclimatize: If traveling from a low-altitude area, give yourself time to acclimatize, before heading to regions with high elevation.

Nutrition: Pack high-energy, lightweight snacks such as trail mix, protein bars, and dried fruits.

Stay Informed: Know the symptoms of heat exhaustion, dehydration, and altitude sickness.

6. Additional Tips:

Photography: Early morning and late afternoon often offer the best light for photographs. Always ask for permission before photographing individuals, especially in indigenous communities.

Local Customs and Regulations: Familiarize yourself with local customs, especially if traveling or camping near indigenous lands.

Group Travel: If possible, travel with a companion or in a group. There's safety in numbers, and shared experiences often enhance the journey.

Embarking on an adventure requires more than just the spirit of exploration; it demands preparation and respect for the environment and its history. These tips aim to ensure that your journey through regions like the Arizona Strip is not only memorable but also responsible and safe. Safe travels and happy exploring!

OHV PREPARATION CHECKLIST

1 - PERFORM GENERAL SERVICE
Ensure all necessary repairs are complete.

2 - CHECK FUEL LEVELS
Top up main tank and spare gas can if required.

3 - INSPECT TIRE PRESSURE
Adjust to your preferred level.

4 - PACK EMERGENCY SUPPLIES
First aid kit, tools, spare tire/repair kit, jack, etc.

5 - TEST RADIO
The ride leader will provide frequency for a radio check

PERSONAL PREPARATION CHECKLIST

1 - BUCKLE YOUR SEAT BELT
This ensures your safety even when you have roll bars.

2 - FILL A SPRAY BOTTLE W/ WATER
Useful for cooling off, cleaning windshield, or treating wounds.

3 - WEAR A HELMET
Mandatory for anyone under 18.

4 - DON A MASK
Necessary to protect lungs from common dust.

5 - APPLY SUNSCREEN
Consider wearing lightweight hats, gloves, long sleeves, & long pants for extra protections.

6 - DRESS APPROPRIATELY
Layer your clothing to adapt to temperature changes.

7 - STAY HYDRATED
Remember to drink water frequently.

8 - PACK MEDICATIONS
Bring any medications you might need.

9 - ADDRESS HEALTH ISSUES
If you have any specific health conditions, inform the leaders.

10 - CARRY WET WIPES
Handy for multiple uses like tissues or rags.

RECOMMENDED SUPPLIES

1 - Properly mounted spare gas container
2 - Tire repair kit, tire pump, lug wrench, & tire gauge
3 - First Aid kit
4 - Prescription Medications
5 - Water, lunch, snacks, energy/food bars, & extra water
6 - Fire Extinguisher
7 - Flashlight/lantern for night rides
8 - Personal protective gear: helmet, goggles, sun glasses, leather gloves, dust mask
9 - Sunscreen, coat/jacket, hat, socks, rain gear
10 - Cell phone, GPS, compass, map of the area, two-way radio
11 - Toilet paper, tissues, paper towels, rags, wet-wipes, goggle lens cleaner
12 - Tool kit (wrenches, screw drivers, sockets/ratchet, pliers, etc)
13 - Spare belt, spark-plugs, fuses, & any parts known to fail
14 - Tow strap, rope (heavy & light), tie-downs, bungee straps
15 - Shovel, knife, axe, hand saw
16 - Tape (electrical/duct), tie-wraps, zip ties, steel wire
17 - Jumper cables or spare battery pack
18 - Cooler (preferably hard sided) to keep food & water cool
19 - Cleanup/lubricate: WD-40, brake cleaner, cleaning brush, nitrile gloves
20 - Come-along, snatch blocks, winch (vehicle mounted or portable)
21 - Engine fluids: engine oil, transmission oil, differential oil, antifreeze
22 - Survival items: lighter/matches/fire-starter, signal device/whistle/mirror, emergency blanket
23 - Silicon/glue/epoxy, hose/tubing clamps, shrink-wrap
24 - Electrical wire, wire connectors, extra bolts/snaps
25 - Orange or yellow tape/tarp/rain suit so you are seen from a distance
26 - ...other items that you deem necessary

MESQUITE
BUNKERVILLE

GOLD BUTTE TRAILHEAD

THE MESQUITE LOOP

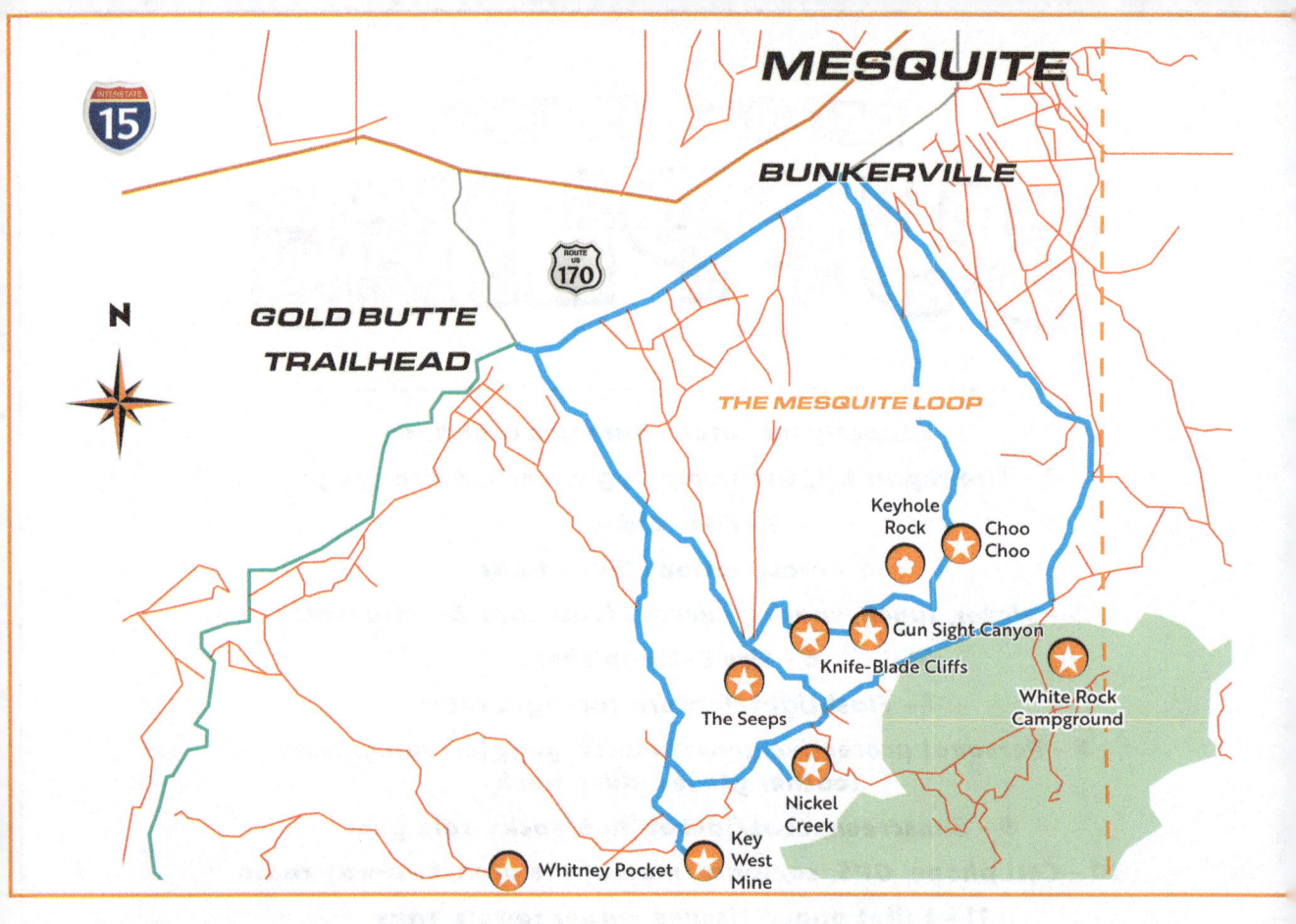

- Keyhole Rock
- Choo Choo
- Gun Sight Canyon
- Knife-Blade Cliffs
- The Seeps
- White Rock Campground
- Nickel Creek
- Whitney Pocket
- Key West Mine

Rocky Mountain Off Road

(208) 691-5554
ROCKYMTNOFFROAD.COM
120 RIVERSIDE RD, MESQUIT

MEET OUR UTV REPAIR SPONSOR..

Trails and Destinations by Region

Mesquite
Introduction and Significance of the Region

**What's it known for? Golf & Casinos.
Best Eats? Thai, Mexican, Greek, Italian.**

Located in the northeastern corner of Clark County, Nevada, the Mesquite Region offers a captivating blend of desert beauty, fascinating history, and modern amenities. Its landscapes—dotted with rugged hills, lush golf courses, and the crucial Virgin River—are a testament to God's artistry and human innovation. Mesquite is a playground for the trail enthusiast with a variety of terrains, from sun-kissed desert flats to mountain pathways. The Mesquite region combines thrilling trails with beautiful views of the Mojave.

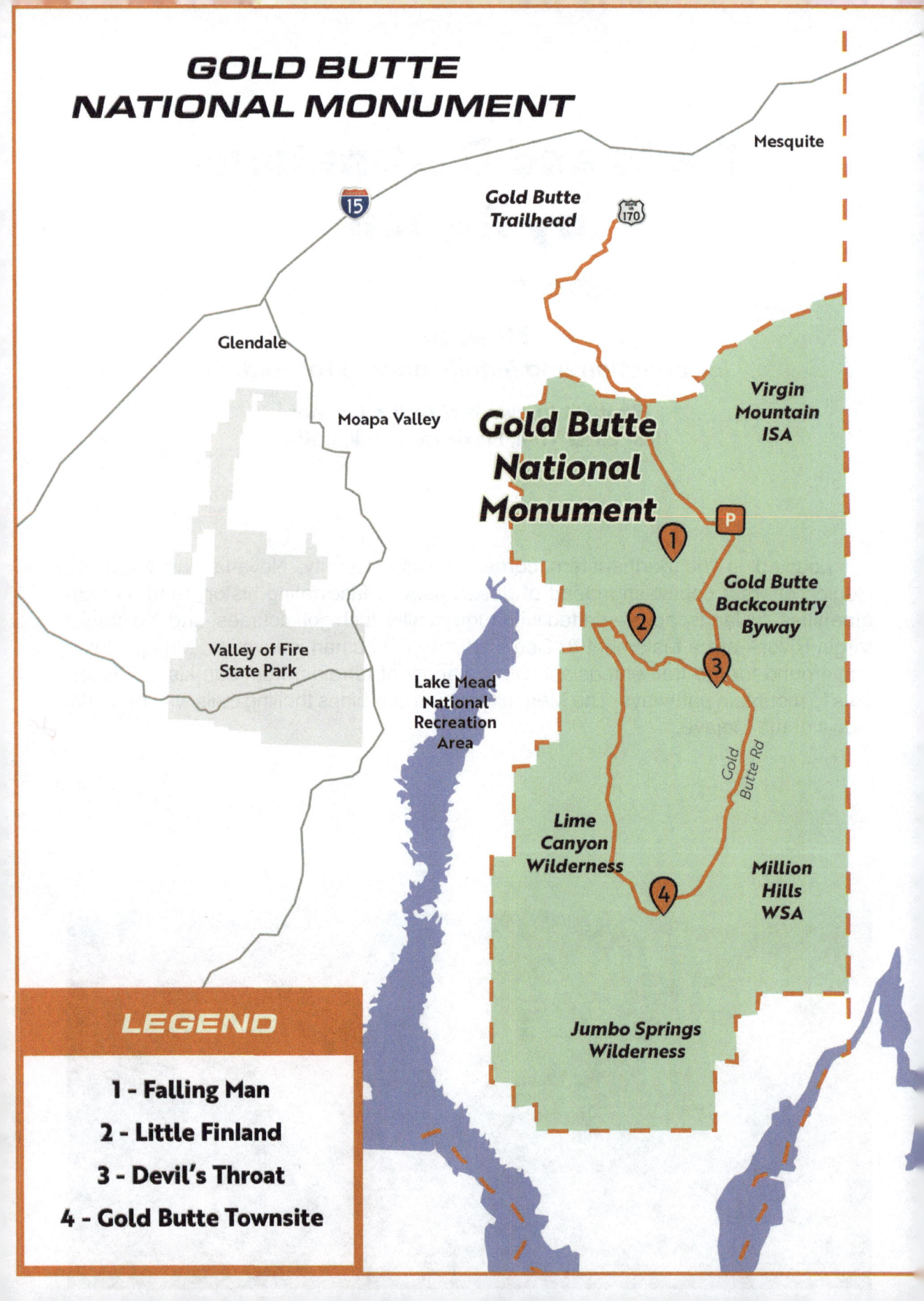

GOLD BUTTE NATIONAL MONUMENT

Mesquite

Gold Butte Trailhead

Glendale

Moapa Valley

Gold Butte National Monument

Virgin Mountain ISA

Gold Butte Backcountry Byway

Valley of Fire State Park

Lake Mead National Recreation Area

Lime Canyon Wilderness

Gold Butte Rd

Million Hills WSA

Jumbo Springs Wilderness

LEGEND

1 - Falling Man
2 - Little Finland
3 - Devil's Throat
4 - Gold Butte Townsite

GOLD BUTTE

Just outside of Mesquite, near Bunkerville Bridge, lies Gold Butte National Monument. Gold Butte spans 300,000 acres in southeastern Nevada, showcasing a captivating mix of red sandstone, canyons, and hints of the Mojave Desert's past. Here, ancient rock art tells tales of bygone civilizations, while remnants of old mining towns give a glimpse into the area's vibrant history. From hiking and exploring ghost towns to spotting wildlife, there's much to see and do. Designated a national monument by President Barack Obama in 2016 after much advocacy, it remains a cherished yet debated landmark. Dive in and discover what Mesquite's backyard offers!

Nearby Camp Sites

- 1 - I-15 Exit 110 Rest Stop
- 2 - Flying J Gas Station
- 3 - Casablanca Casino
- 4 - Virgin River/Littlefield
- 5 - Beaver Dam Wilderness
- 6 - Courtney's Red Rock Canyon
- 7 - Cedar Pocket Campground (Fees Apply)
- 8 - Virgin Mountains
- 9 - Overton Wildlife Management Area
- 10 - Snowbird Mesa
- 11 - Sand Mine Road
- 12 - Dirt Road near Valley of Fire
- 13 - Fire Cove (Permit Required)
- 14 - Stewart's Point (Permit Required)
- 15 - Echo Wash (Permit Required)
- 16 - Whitney Pockets
- 17 - Grand Canyon-Parashant National Monument Pakoon Springs
- 18 - South Cove

MESQUITE

MOAPA VALLEY

GOLD BUTTE NATIONAL MONUMENT

GRAND CANYON-PARASHANT NATIONAL MONUMENT

LAKE MEAD NATIONAL RECREATION AREA

Mesquite & Moapa Valley Trails & Destinations

ROAD & TRAIL INTERSECTIONS

1: Unnamed Trail Intersection
2: Camp Rd - Kern River Pipeline Rd
3: Camp Rd - Sand Hollow Rd
4: Rainbow Pass Rd - Water Haul Rd - S Fork/Camp Rd
5: Rainbow Pass Rd - Horse Hollow Rd
6: Gourd Springs Rd - S Fork/Camp Rd
7: Gourd Springs Rd - Sheep Pens Rd - S Fork Rd
8: Kern River Pipeline Rd - Phone Cable Access Rd
9: Kern River Pipeline Rd - Lower Toquop Rd
10: Kern River Pipeline Rd - Phone Cable Rd
11: Phone Cable Rd - Sand Hollow Wash Rd
12: S Fork Rd - Sheep Pens Rd
13: Kern River Pipeline Rd - S Fork Rd
14: Hackberry Springs Rd - Rainbow Pass Rd
15: Kern River Pipeline Rd - Comm Tower Rd
16: Halfway Washington Rd - Lower Toquop Rd

1: Kern River Pipeline Rd - Camp Elgin Rd - Rainbow Pass Rd
2: Toquop Wash Rd - Lower Toquop Rd
3: BLM 242 - Lime Kiln Cnyn Rd
4: East toward Hole in the Wall
5: Unnamed Trail Intersection
6: Hen Spring Rd - Unnamed Trail
7: Hen Springs Rd
8: Gold Butte Rd - Fishermans Wash Rd
9: Fishermans Wash Rd - Virgin River Access Rd
10: Virgin River Access Rd - Fisherman's Cove Rd
11: Narrow N Rd - Gold Butte Wash Rd
12: Gold Butte Wash Rd - Red Bluff Springs Rd
13: BLM 113 - Gold Butte Rd - St Thomas Gap Rd
14: Red Bluff Spring Rd - Gold Butte Wash Rd
15: Scanlon Ferry Rd - New Gold Butte Rd
16: Gold Butte Wash Rd - Scanlon Ferry Rd
17: Scanlon Ferry Rd - END

TRAILHEADS & PARKING

P1: Gold Butte Road Parking
P2: Witwer Trailhead Parking - Access to Virgin Mesa
P3: Riverside OHV Staging Arena
P4: Logandale Trails System

POINTS OF INTEREST

*1: Stupa Aviation Navigation Site
*2: Aviation Navigation Arrow
*3: Trailhead to Toquop Wash from Virgin Mesa
*4: Overlook - Virgin Mesa American Flag Monument
*5: Riverside Power Station
*6: Camel Safari Las Vegas
*7: Riverside Ghost Town
*8: Toquop Wash Rd - 1-15
*9: Indian Pictograph Park
*10: Peace Garden
*11: Heart of the Mesa
*12: Double Negative
*13: Hole in the Wall
*14: Choo Choo
*15: Budweiser Fence
*16: St Thomas Ghost Town
*17: Whitney Pocket
*18: The Cistern
*19: Aravada Springs
*20: Little Finland
*21: Devil's Nostril
*22: Seven Keyholes Slot Canyon Trailhead
*23: Devil's Throat
*24: Gold Butte Ntnl Monument

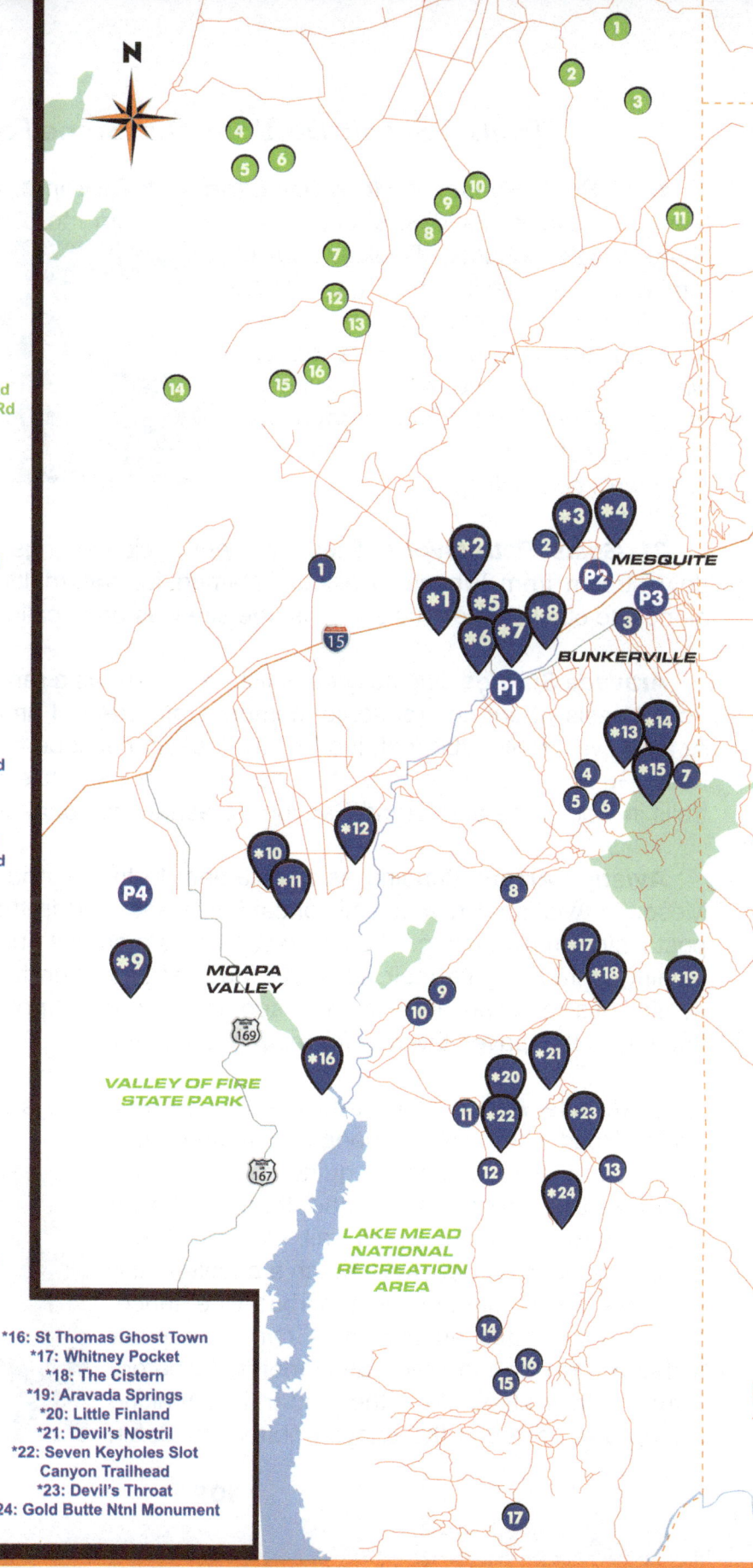

Trails & Scenic Destinations (Some Favorites)

1880 Rock House: A Mesquite Landmark Built in 1880, the Rock House is Mesquite's oldest standing structure. Initially, a home to pioneers from St. George, Utah, it later housed Dudley Leavitt's family. Despite facing harsh conditions and river floods, it saw various residents and modifications over the years. With walls built from native rocks, it witnessed the lives of many until 2003. Today, owned by the City of Mesquite, it is a testament to the town's rich history.

21 Goats Petroglyphs These ancient rock carvings, are found in a wash downstream from Whitney Pockets. Named for the multitude of goat depictions alongside other mysterious symbols, the site was once called "Indian Writings".

Aravada Springs Originally established in 1910 as a ranch, Aravada Springs is a desert oasis where unforgettable memories are created amid stunning landscapes. At an elevation of 4,200 feet, it offers a refreshing escape from the desert's summer heat. Guests can rent cabins, and camp in groups, while enjoying extensive ATV trails in Gold Butte and Grand Canyon Parashant National Monuments.

Aviation Arrow Standing as a testament to the ingenuity of early aviators, the Mesquite Aviation Arrow is a historical landmark used in the early 20th century for postal system navigation. The arrow served as a crucial guidepost for airmail pilots, helping them navigate their way over the vast and often featureless landscapes. A symbol of aviation history, this arrow serves as a reminder of the pioneering spirit and innovation that paved the way for modern air travel.

Budweiser Fence A local treasure, Budweiser Fence is a popular spot along Hen Spring Road where visitors hang aluminum cans on an old cattle fence, creating a quirky tradition. Start your hike on Cabin Canyon Road, then head west onto Hen Spring Road, a jeep trail. After a 1.3-mile climb of about 500 feet, you'll reach a saddle at the canyon's head, marked by a barbed-wire fence. Visitors often hang an aluminum can (remember to bring wire) on the fence as a memento before retracing their steps along the jeep trail or making a loop down through the canyon bottom to Cabin

Canyon Road. The trailhead is a short distance up the road to the right.

Cabin Canyon Road: An Exciting 4WD Route Experience a thrilling 4WD adventure on Cabin Canyon Road from Mesquite, to Grand Canyon- Parashant National Monument. Although initially appearing well-graded, keep in mind that weather can alter its condition. The road traverses challenging bedrock sections, making more than just a grader necessary for upkeep. The toughest parts are in higher elevations, with lower sections usually accessible to 2WD vehicles with moderate clearance. This route can be part of a scenic loop around Virgin Peak or a journey into the Great Backcountry further south.

Cabin Spring Rock Cabin In the heart of Gold Butte National Monument lies the Rock Cabin, a mortarless stone structure hinting at past prospectors' dreams. Perched in Cabin Spring Canyon with a dried-up spring inconveniently below, it's surrounded by discarded cans that whisper of its era. A visit evokes wonder about its hardy inhabitants and offers sweeping canyon vistas.

Choo Choo In Southeast Nevada's Virgin Mountains, locals repurposed an old steam train car into a lifeline for farming and ranching, by using its tank to channel water from a mountain spring to a makeshift trough. The project promoted agriculture and a vibrant ecosystem, with a variety of wildlife from bighorn sheep to quails. The initiative stands as a beacon of resourcefulness, and a unique destination.

Devil's Cove Nestled in the remote desert landscape near Mesquite, Devil's Cove offers a journey to the extreme edges of solitude and nature's grandeur. Once connected to Lake Mead and the Colorado River, this area now stands as a testament to the ever-changing forces of nature. Visitors can witness breathtaking scenery and wildlife in this desolate yet captivating location. Devil's Cove has an intriguing history involving natural wonders and mysterious past events. In 2023, Ghost Adventures investigated the area and uncovered an unusual connection to unexplained incidents.

Devil's Throat A striking sinkhole, Devil's Throat stands as a reminder of the unpredictable forces of nature. In the arid landscapes, its vast, gaping maw beckons explorers and geology enthusiasts. Its ominous name and impressive depth (100+ feet deep on average) make it a notable landmark in the region. People refer to a smaller sinkhole nearby as Devil's Nostril.

Falling Man Petroglyph The Falling Man Petroglyph, an ancient and fascinating rock art depiction located in the Gold Butte National Monument, continues to intrigue and captivate those who visit. This enigmatic petroglyph, etched into the desert varnish of the rocks, provides a window into the artistic and communicative expressions of earlier times. While there is speculation about its meaning, it is likely a warning to the adventurous, especially considering the nearby tall and potentially slick rocks that pose a danger to climbers. As you observe this historic artwork, it invites cultural reflection and wonder about the narratives and significance it has carried through the ages. Be sure to also check out the nearby **Newspaper Rock**, a boulder featuring many differently sized petroglyphs.

Firebrand Cave A hidden gem in Southern Nevada, this cave is proof of the region's rich indigenous history. The secluded site holds great cultural and historical significance, particularly to the Paiute people. Experts and historians believe that Firebrand Cave served as a focal point for ceremonial rituals and gatherings in ancient times.

UNLV's meticulous archaeological dig at the site unveiled remarkable artifacts that shed light on the cave's past. The discoveries of ceremonial attire, evidence of maize cultivation, and weapons help decode the practices, diets, and defense tactics of the indigenous people in the area.

To protect the site and to respect the wishes of the Paiute people and local tribes, the Bureau of Land Management has placed restrictions on sharing the exact location. For those genuinely interested in Firebrand Cave and its intriguing discoveries, a specialized research paper from UNLV is exclusively available at the Library of Congress. Similar cultural caves have been reported in the Moapa Valley. Be warned, it is a dangerous trek and the cave itself is very unstable after a recent collapse.

Fisherman's Cove Tucked away in the vast expanse of Gold Butte National Monument, Fisherman's Cove is a blend of natural serenity and historical significance. In the early 20th century, it was a key section of the Arrowhead Highway, linking Las Vegas with Salt Lake City. When Lake Mead expanded in 1938, transportation improved and they moved the primary route to the current location of Interstate 15. This left Fisherman's Cove a secluded remnant of days gone by. Today, visitors to the cove are treated to the tranquil waters of the Virgin River, which is a welcome sight after navigating the rugged dirt roads leading to the cove. While it's advisable to make the journey during the cooler months to avoid the desert's intense heat, the experience is worth it. Whether you're drawn by the call of history or the allure of a peaceful riverside haven, Fisherman's Cove is a destination that offers both.

Flat Top Mesa stands as a majestic geological formation, its flat summit etching a distinct silhouette against the vast desert sky. This monumental mesa, characterized by its plateaued peak, serves not only as a natural landmark but also as a testament to the region's rich geological history. For both residents and visitors alike, Flat Top Mesa is not just a geological wonder, but also a symbol of the enduring spirit of the desert landscapes of the American Southwest & Mesquite.

Gold Butte Cistern Built by the Civilian Conservation Corps (CCC) during the Great Depression, showcases water preservation in Nevada's desert. Positioned within the rugged terrain of Gold Butte, this structure has provided vital water storage for the region. Today, it stands as a symbol of the CCC's enduring impact and their commitment to environmental stewardship.

Gold Butte Townsite Once a bustling mining town, the Gold Butte Townsite now stands as a reminder of the vibrant history of the American Southwest. Nestled in the heart of the desert, it was once home to nearly 2,000 people who sought their fortunes in the nearby mines. Today, visitors can explore the remains of this once-thriving community, including old mine shafts and decaying structures. They can also learn about the challenges and successes of the people who lived here. It's a place where history comes alive, telling the story of a bygone era. Be sure to look for the **Cradle of Humanity**, a notable hole in a large boulder that lends itself well for a photo-op with people. While there, pay your respects to the **Gravesite** of longtime Gold Butte residents, Bill Garrett and Art Coleman.

Great Eastern Mine Located in the Virgin Mountains in the Bunkerville mining district, the Great Eastern Mine is famous for its copper and nickel deposits. This site, in Section 14, 23 of T15S R70E, boasts a geological structure characterized by the Key West Thrust and many faults. The peridotite found here has changed into hornblende and biotite through alteration processes, making it a interesting place for mineral exploration.

Little Finland, Gold Butte Little Finland, nestled in the Gold Butte region, is a captivating natural wonder for explorers and nature lovers. This remarkable site showcases intricate rock formations shaped by the patient hands of time. Prepare to be amazed as you explore this magical place, where geological forces have shaped nature's stunning artwork for countless decades.

Key West Mine in Nevada serves as a reminder of the state's vibrant mining history. Located amidst rugged terrains, it offers a glimpse into the challenges and aspirations of past miners. The remains of this site attract both history enthusiasts and adventurers, transporting them into a gritty bygone era.

Keyhole Rock Also called the Portal or Hole in Rock, is a captivating natural wonder and can be found near the "Knife Blade Cliffs." It beckons adventurers to explore its beauty, accessible via a quick scramble off the main trail. While enjoying the picturesque surroundings, you might hear a local legend that claims this rock is an ancient portal, responsible for bringing various elements to the desert. This charming narrative adds an extra layer of fascination to the site's allure.

Knife-Blade Cliffs Close to the trail leading to Keyhole Rock, a unique geological marvel unfolds. The northern hills look like someone has meticulously turned them on edge, resulting in sharp, pointed peaks. These formations, aptly named "knife-blade cliffs," stand as a testament to nature's sculpting prowess, offering a dramatic backdrop to those venturing towards Keyhole Rock.

Lower Toquop Road This road, connects Camp Road and the Northwestern exit from Flat Top Mesa to the Toquop Wash, serving as an important trail that unites northern and southern Mesquite. Although it offers stunning desert views and a unique off-road experience, caution is advised, especially following storms. The northwest road descending from Flat Top Mesa is prone to washing out. The power district regularly maintains the road to keep it passable, grading it back to navigable conditions. This route showcases the beauty of Mesquite's rugged landscape and its sturdy infrastructure.

Mesquite Healing Garden/Labyrinth This tranquil spot in downtown Mesquite is perfect for anyone seeking a moment of meditation or a peaceful walk. The garden's labyrinth offers a unique journey, with every twist and turn designed to help visitors reflect and find inner peace. As you navigate its path, you might encounter trinkets and treasures, that add to its charm. While it's now a popular destination for many, the Mesquite Healing Garden holds a special backstory. Mary Louise Shurtleff, a local author and spiritual coach, lovingly created it. Today, it stands as both a tranquil oasis and a beautiful tribute to Mary's vision and spirit.

Mesquite Medicine Wheel / Labyrinth Resembling a traditional Native American Medicine Wheel, this sacred site in the desert serves as a tribute to the profound spiritual and cultural importance of these symbols. Although it's not an authentic Native American ceremonial site, it provides a space for contemplation and meditation, celebrating Native traditions. The nearby Mesquite Regional Sports and Event Complex also features a unique labyrinth. Designed in the classic 7-circuit pattern, this labyrinth invites mindful meditation, set against the backdrop of Mesquite's breathtaking landscape, and is open to all, free of charge.

Lot's Wife Near Bunkerville Ridge, lies a distinctive landmark affectionately known as Lot's Wife. This natural rock formation resembles a woman made of salt, reminding us of the biblical account from the book of Genesis, where Lot's wife was turned into a pillar of salt. It portrays a visual narrative that intertwines the grandeur of nature with ancient stories, evoking a sense of awe and reverence in those who view it.

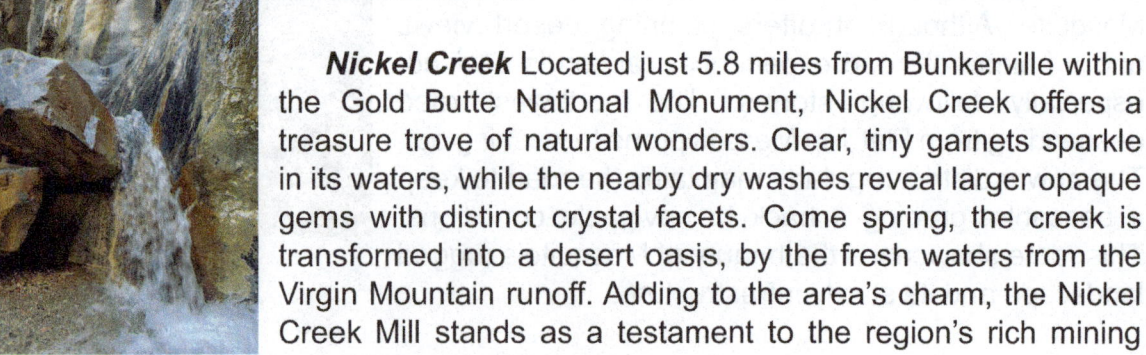

Nickel Creek Located just 5.8 miles from Bunkerville within the Gold Butte National Monument, Nickel Creek offers a treasure trove of natural wonders. Clear, tiny garnets sparkle in its waters, while the nearby dry washes reveal larger opaque gems with distinct crystal facets. Come spring, the creek is transformed into a desert oasis, by the fresh waters from the Virgin Mountain runoff. Adding to the area's charm, the Nickel Creek Mill stands as a testament to the region's rich mining heritage. Adventure seekers take note: for the best experience at Nickle Creek, a high-clearance or 4X4 vehicle is recommended.

Radio Tower In the rugged terrains of the Virgin Mountains, a Radio Tower stands as a modern sentinel, facilitating vital communications in the region. The tower fits perfectly with the natural backdrop, combining technology and nature. Those that venture to the top of the hill will be rewarded by an unobstructed view of the Virgin Mountains and Virgin Peak itself.

Red Bluff Spring In the captivating Mud Wash below Little Finland road, Red Bluff Spring is a natural oasis unlike any other in the vicinity. This spring has a distinct slot canyon below it, with towering walls that resemble cobblestones and stand upright in the desert. The journey to this geological wonder begins with a brief walk from the Lake Mead border sign, marking the entrance to a world of natural wonders. It's important to note they strictly prohibit vehicle access beyond the border sign to preserve the pristine beauty of this remarkable desert terrain.

Riverside Ghost Town Located 10 miles southwest of Bunkerville on Riverside Rd., Riverside Ghost Town is a hidden gem for nature enthusiasts. This once popular location features abandoned buildings and a special grove of large pine trees, perfect for photography. Visitors can also access the nearby river, but note that the dirt road leading here can be challenging. Riverside has become a hotspot for underage partying, resulting in litter and graffiti. Please be aware that it's now private property.

Seven Keyholes The Seven Keyholes in Gold Butte are fascinating natural rock formations that tell a captivating story. These fascinating geological wonders have drawn adventurers and nature enthusiasts for ages. As you stroll through this enchanting landscape, you'll be amazed by the stunning beauty of nature and the powerful forces that have shaped this remarkable place over many years.

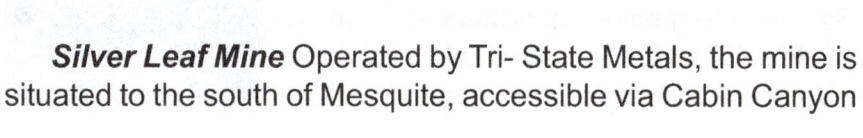

Silver Leaf Mine Operated by Tri-State Metals, the mine is situated to the south of Mesquite, accessible via Cabin Canyon road. Geologically, the mine boasts higher tungsten values primarily found within quartz veins. The mine features hornblendite dikes, though these contain limited amounts of expansible hydrobiotite. Positioned along the south-central stretch of a mineral belt that extends from the Arizona border, 1.5 miles northeast of Virgin Peak. The trail up is a very steep incline and is mostly inaccessible, even for a UTV. In the spring, it becomes a creek, making it even more difficult to access.

The Submarine Legend speaks of the "Mesquite Submarine," a vessel shrouded in mystery and tales of old. Born at the dawn of WW2, she was a prototype, a beacon of hope and innovation. Yet, she never tasted salty ocean waters or saw battle. Scrapped in the desert, she stands as a silent tribute to a brave crew hailing from the arid landscapes of Southern Utah and Nevada. Some say she's just a mirage, a nickname given to a ghost that never truly existed. But those who believe search the sands, hoping to glimpse this elusive testament to history.

RUMOR HAS IT:

The Old Spanish Trail Near Mesquite is a historical route that encapsulates centuries of exploration and trade. Cutting through the breathtaking Mojave Desert, it once connected Santa Fe and Los Angeles during the 19th century. Today, it offers a glimpse into a rich and vibrant past, beckoning modern-day explorers to trace the steps of early pioneers.

The Pyramid A sign near the Gold Butte entrance documents the historic residence of Clyde, Pakoon Jim, Dora, and Pyramid Bob at Juanita Springs. Clyde built a pyramid across from Gold Butte Road, for Pyramid Bob's extraterrestrial communications. However, legend has it that Pyramid Bob's interactions eventually deterred the aliens.

The Seeps Critical to local ranchers, the Seeps is a secluded area in a hidden canyon where water often trickles and forms pools because of the natural drainage. Historically known as Seeps Canyon, it is the last canyon on the western side of the Bunkerville Mountain Range; channeling its waters northward into the Virgin River Valley. The Seeps, also called Hidden Canyon, is where nature's aqueous artistry reveals itself.

An unusual Berm on Toquop Wash

Toquop Wash Named after a Paiute word for a native tobacco-like plant, Toquop Wash winds through the Nevada wilderness, creating a stunning tapestry. The wash gracefully merges with the Virgin River, combining sandy desert vistas with lush riparian beauty. Explore this captivating landscape, where history, indigenous heritage, and the power of nature come together. Toquop Wash is the main road connecting various destinations, like Rock Houses, Mormon Mountains, Davidson Gravesite, Navigation Arrow and more. It is also the area most recognizable from the Bundy Standoff where the FBI setup snipers on the I-15 bridge, overlooking the wash.

White Rock Campground Offering a rustic and secluded camping experience, in a cool, elevated location. With minimal amenities and a rugged access road, White Rock Campground is best suited for campers with high-clearance vehicles who can bring their own supplies. The campground has stone tables, a concrete pad, plenty of room to spread out, and breathtaking views of the surrounding desert landscape. Locals call this place the Alien Temple because of the abandoned settlement's concrete pad and unusual rock features.

Whitney Corral Resting near the foot of Virgin Peak, Whitney Corral stands as a poignant symbol of a bygone era of ranching. The spring used to quench cattle's thirst is now dry, but the Cowboy Campsite nearby has a rich history to explore. Old truck tires, rusty chairs and skeletal remains of an old farm truck, tell stories of ranchers surviving in this rugged landscape.

Whitney Pocket At the north end of Gold Butte National Monument, Whitney Pocket offers a captivating spot to explore. Its white, red, and orange sandstone formations provide a striking contrast to the rugged grey peaks surrounding it. Popular among campers, ATV enthusiasts, and off-road adventurers, this remote destination is accessible by a bumpy road, with high clearance and 4x4 strongly recommended for further exploration. Whitney Pocket boasts an intriguing history, with petroglyph panels reflecting its ancient past and a short-lived gold rush in the early 1900s.

Virgin Mountains At 8,074 feet, Virgin Peak stands as the tallest point in the Virgin Mountain range, nestled northeast of Lake Mead in Clark County, Nevada. This natural wonder in the Gold Butte National Monument, has rugged terrain and stunning red rock formations for adventurous hikers. The South Ridge route is the best choice for hikers to enjoy the area's unique geology and towering Yellow Pine trees.

V Day on the Mesa The giant white V overlooking I-15 in Mesquite is a longstanding emblem of the local community. Like ancient petroglyphs, it reminds us of our impact on the landscape and needs regular maintenance to keep its fresh appearance. The tradition of updating the V, has lasted for over a century, connecting past and present generations of the Virgin Valley High School community.

Moapa Valley

Introduction and Significance of the Region

**What's it known for? Valley of Fire & Logandale Trails.
Best Eats? Pizza, Ice Cream, Food Trucks, Coffee.**

Situated just north of the frenetic energy of Las Vegas, Moapa Valley offers a serene oasis amidst the vastness of Nevada. This verdant expanse is a stark contrast to the typical barren stretches of the Mojave Desert. The Muddy River supports a diverse ecosystem and has a rich cultural heritage. Explore the stories of Moapa Valley, from ancient Native American sites to tales of frontier resilience. The trails are gateways to a captivating mix of history and natural beauty, perfect for adventurous explorers.

MOAPA VALLEY HISTORICAL SITE MAP

1 - Glendale and "Glendale Nick" Nicolaides
2 - Early Settlements in the Moapa Valley
3 - Fay Perkins, Sr.
4 - Lost City Museum
5 - Pueblo Grande de Nevada
6 - Moapa Valley Pioneers
7 - Pioneers
8 - Valley of Fire Behind the Camera
9 - Silica Dome
10 - Atlatl Rock
11 - Beehives
12 - Valley of Fire
13 - Nevada's First State Park
14 - The Cabins
15 - In Memory of Sergeant John J Clark
16 - Arrowhead Trail
17 - Powell of the Colorado
18 - A Town at the Bottom

Trails & Scenic Destinations

Black Mountain Black Mountain boasts ancient petroglyphs, providing a fascinating window into the past. These time-worn carvings on the mountain's rocky canvas hint at the rich history and beliefs of its early inhabitants. A visit here is like stepping back in time, offering a tangible connection to the region's ancestral cultures.

Double Negative In Moapa, Nevada, the earthwork sculpture "Double Negative" is a fusion of art and the desert landscape. Michael Heizer crafted this grand trench in 1969, and its allure has been drawing worldwide attention ever since. Art dealer Virginia Dwan initially funded the purchase of the 60-acre site, and in 1969, Heizer transferred the property deeds to her. Later, in 1971, Heizer halted Dwan Gallery from selling the artwork, leading to its donation to the Museum of Contemporary Art, Los Angeles (MoCA) in 1984. Heizer initially believed in letting nature take its course, opposing conservation efforts from MoCA, but recent remarks suggest he now wants the piece restored.

Lakeside Mine Perched at the far reaches of Gold Butte National Monument, offers a panoramic view of Lake Mead and a glimpse into mining history. Operating sporadically from 1937 to 1956, the site features remnants of a miner's camp, several adits, and a mine- shaft adorned with wooden headgear. Because of its remote location, the mine serves as an intriguing pit stop for adventurers heading toward the lake's edge.

Logandale Trails System A Showcase of Nevada's Natural Splendor. The Logandale Trails System in Southern Nevada has 200 miles of trails highlighting the region's desert views and unique geological formations. Designed for off-roading enthusiasts, trekkers, and nature lovers, this network showcases the state's dedication to outdoor pursuits and environmental conservation.

13 Mile Loop The popular 13 Mile Loop is perfect for beginners and who want a serene experience with sand dunes and native petroglyphs. On this trail, visitors can indulge in breathtaking views and possibly even catch sight of local wildlife, such as the Big Horn Sheep. The loop also serves as a gateway to numerous other trails of varying intensities.

Shedder Trail Beyond the 13 Mile Loop, the trail system has a lot more to offer. A standout among them is the Shedder Trail, alternately known as the Shredder or Sh*tter Trail. It promises a heart-pounding experience for those with modified rigs. With challenging obstacles, from the mild Shedder Bowl start to the adrenaline-pumping V-notch descents and waterfall climbs, ending with a challenging finale. Famous for its unofficial night runs, the Shedder Trail is a rock crawler's dream, best suited for rigs with at least 33" tires, a lift, and ideally, a locker.

Hump "N" Bump The Hump'N'Bump event, hosted at the Clark County Fairgrounds in Logandale, is a must for off-roading enthusiasts. This internationally recognized, low-speed, three-day event offers guided trail rides over various terrains. Participants can engage with vendor booths, training seminars, and spectator events. The culmination is a communal dinner followed by raffles, featuring generous prizes from the event's sponsors. Nearby attractions like The Lost City Museum enrich the experience with a glimpse into the area's intriguing human history.

Lost City Located in Overton, Nevada, showcases remnants of ancient Ancestral Puebloan structures, providing a window into a civilization that thrived centuries ago. The ancient ruins, with their fascinating architectural designs, provide evidence of the once sophisticated communities in the region. Today, the site serves as a poignant reminder of the area's rich cultural heritage.

Moapa Valley National Wildlife Refuge Situated in southern Nevada, this Refuge is a sanctuary for the endangered Moapa dace. The warm spring waters provide an ideal habitat for this rare fish, while the refuge itself offers visitors a serene natural escape. Birdwatchers, conservationists, and nature enthusiasts frequent the area, appreciating its unique ecosystem and tranquil beauty.

Moapa Valley Branch of the Bank of Las Vegas / Custom Fit In the small rural town of Overton, the Bank of Las Vegas has witnessed some alarming incidents over the years. A devastating bank robbery in 1967 led to the shooting and killing of three bank employees, deeply affecting the community. The perpetrator was apprehended by authorities within hours, leaving residents to recall the panic and disbelief that enveloped their tight-knit community.

Prior to the robbery, the assailant had a history of criminal activity and was on parole at the time of committing the murders. He showed little remorse and served his sentence until his death. Notably, the victims' families harbored no resentment towards the criminal's family, acknowledging the shared suffering.

History echoed itself in 1984 when the bank was targeted again, this time by a notorious criminal gang known for using a helicopter in their heists. The robbers made several errors during this incident, escaping with tainted money and leaving crucial evidence behind. This led to the FBI quickly tracking them down, initiating the gang's eventual collapse.

Now, the location of the old Bank of Las Vegas houses a contemporary office for a real estate and construction firm. The memories of its turbulent past continue to be an intriguing part of Moapa Valley's history.

The Mormon Mesa In Moapa, Nevada The Mormon Mesa is a significant elevated landform, with a historical connection to early Mormon settlers. It is marked by a prominent "M" symbolizing their heritage. This vast desert landscape showcases unique geological formations and remnants from ancient inhabitants. With its rugged terrain and sweeping vistas, it stands as a tribute to the area's rich pioneer history and natural beauty.

Heart of the Mesa New Land art installations have gained popularity atop the Mormon Mesa near Moapa Valley. The Shambaugh family and Children from the Save Our Mesa organization created "The Heart of the Mesa," a rock formation that has quickly gained popularity among tourists. A second installation, "The Peace Garden," encourages visitors to add their art. Both installations have drawn media attention, emphasizing the beauty of the mesa and concerns over a previously proposed solar plant.

Moapa Navigation Arrow The Moapa Navigation Arrow, located 14.5 miles south of Mormon Mesa Arrow #32, can be accessed by following a gravel road off I-15 leading to what is referred to as Beacon Hill. This 'step-arrow' remains in good condition and measures approximately 44 feet. Pilots used to approach it from a heading of 48° (NE) and depart at 68° (E-NE). While all measurements are approximate, this piece of aviation history has garnered attention on several TV shows. These abandoned navigational aids have become not only great local landmarks but also popular destinations for explorers.

Muddy Mountains Wilderness The Muddy Mountains Wilderness, just an hour's drive from Las Vegas, is a hidden gem along the north shore of Lake Mead. The National Park Service and the Bureau of Land Management oversee this 3,521-acre wilderness. It has unique slot canyons, stunning geological formations, and sweeping views of Lake Mead. Enjoy the solitude and serenity of this place, with abundant Mojave Desert plants like creosote bush, yucca, Joshua trees, and desert willow. Keep an eye out for wildlife like bighorn sheep, the distinctive banded Gila monster, and the iconic desert tortoise. Lake Mead National Recreation Area is the first of its kind in the US and offers a wealth of recreational opportunities. This year-round playground has 1.5 million acres of rugged mountains, canyons, valleys, and two expansive lakes where people can swim, boat, hike, cycle, camp, and fish. Lake Mead NRA has it all - breathtaking landscapes, Hoover Dam and nine designated wilderness areas.

Red Rocks Although not directly in the Moapa Valley, Red Rocks is a must see destination in Clark County. Red Rock Canyon National Conservation Area near Las Vegas, boasts stunning landscapes featuring red sandstone formations. A favorite spot for hiking, climbing, and sightseeing. It highlights the unique ecosystem and geological wonders of the Mojave Desert. This natural haven provides a serene escape from the bustling entertainment of the nearby city.

Rogers Spring Rogers Spring in Moapa is a natural oasis, offering a stark contrast to the surrounding arid desert. Rich in biodiversity, this spring-fed pool provides a sanctuary for various aquatic species. Visitors are drawn to its refreshing waters and the tranquility it offers amidst the desert expanse.

St. Thomas Memorial Cemetery The St. Thomas Memorial Cemetery in Overton, Nevada is historically important because of its connection to early Mormon settlements, specifically St. Thomas, Nevada. Recognized for its heritage, it was added to the National Register of Historic Places on February 1, 2005. In anticipation of the formation of Lake Mead because of the Hoover Dam's construction, they moved the cemetery to its current spot in 1935. Initially dubbed "Mead Lake Cemetery", it eventually adopted its present name. The responsibility of the cemetery's care and upkeep lies with the local community.

Valley of Fire In the heart of Nevada, Valley of Fire is the state's oldest state park, captivating visitors with a mesmerizing tapestry of vivid red sandstone formations. These formations, were sculpted by the elements and serve as a reminder of the passage of time and the transformation of nature. The stark contrast of the crimson rocks against the deep blue skies makes the desert landscape appear as though it is on fire. This breathtaking scenery is not only a feast for the eyes, but also a rich repository of history. Ancient petroglyphs in the canyons and valleys give a glimpse into the lives of the early inhabitants. When people venture into the Valley of Fire, they are treated to its geological splendor and transported to a time where the narratives of ancient civilizations come alive, leaving many in profound reflection and awe of the intertwining tapestry of nature and history.

Warm Springs Natural Area In Moapa, Nevada The Warm Springs Natural Area, with its extensive 1,250 acres, has a history as colorful as its natural beauty. During the ownership of Howard Hughes in the 1970s, the area was more than a site for ranching and farming; it became a secluded retreat. The springs attracted Las Vegas showgirls, who basked in the sun and relaxed in palm-thatched cabanas, adding a touch of glamour to the serene landscape.

This period, however, was just a brief chapter in the area's long narrative. The modern efforts of the Southern Nevada Water Authority (SNWA) have shifted the focus significantly towards conservation. The primary aim is the preservation of this unique ecosystem, especially the endangered Moapa dace. These small, resilient fish are pivotal to the area's biodiversity, found only in the thermal springs linked to the Muddy River system.

SNWA's conservation strategies involve habitat restoration and protection measures, ensuring that the area remains a haven not just for the Moapa dace but for over 28 sensitive species and more than 200 bird species. By balancing the needs of wildlife with public access, the Warm Springs Natural Area today serves as a testament to the possibilities of successful environmental stewardship, turning a once-private luxury retreat into a public treasure dedicated to preserving nature's delicate balance.

Weiser Bowl In the northern Muddy Mountains there is a remarkable geological formation known as Weiser Bowl or "The Bowl." It stands out due to its peculiar bowl-shaped terrain, and can be found near Moapa and Glendale. This natural wonder is formed from unique geological processes, where limestone layers folded and upended during thrust faulting in the area. To reach most sections, high-clearance vehicles are necessary and it's recommended to have 4WD in certain areas for added safety. Additionally, there are a few spots on the west rim that offer shorter walks to scenic overlooks.

LINCOLN COUNTY HISTORICAL SITE MAP

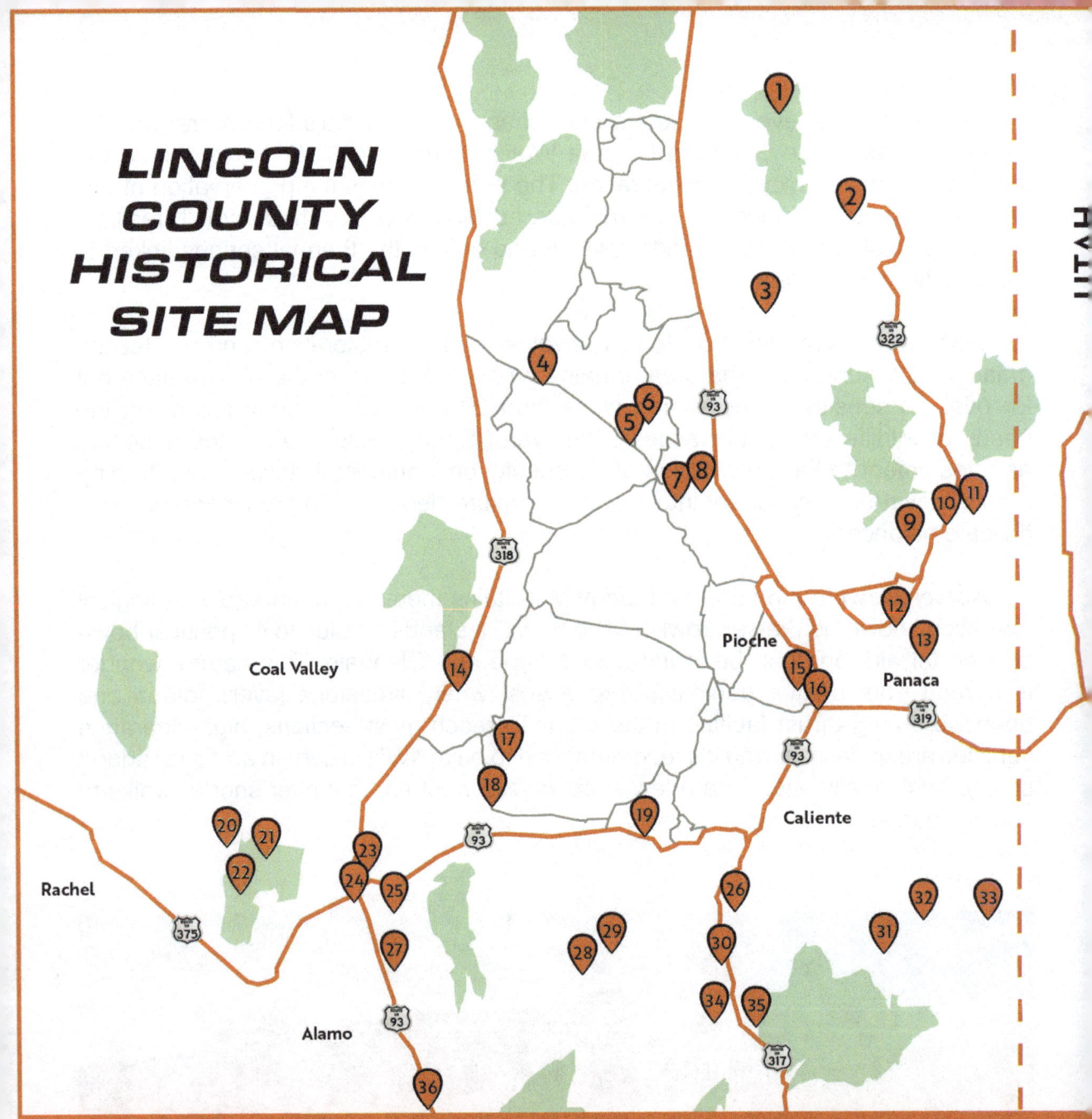

LEGEND

1 - Cotton Wood Canyon Trail
2 - Atlanta Peak
3 - Kalamazoo
4 - Griswold Cabins
5 - Silver Horn Mine
6 - Bailey Spring
7 - Bristol Wells Ghost Town
8 - Jackrabbit Mines
9 - Meadow Valley
10 - Spring Valley State Park
11 - Rice Family Cemetary
12 - Echo Canyon State Park
13 - Panaca Kilns
14 - White River Narrows Archeological Site
15 - Cathedral Gorge State Park
16 - Bullionville Cemetary
17 - Little Boulder Springs Trail
18 - Mecca
19 - Oak Springs Trilobite Site
20 - Crescent Mill
21 - Logan Ghost Town
22 - Mt Irish Petroglyph Site
23 - Nesbitt Lake
24 - Key Pitman Wildlife M.A.
25 - Crystal Wash Petroglyphs
26 - Kershaw-Ryan State Park
27 - Ash Springs Petroglyphs
28 - Delamar Cemetary
29 - Delamar Ghost Town
30 - Rainbow Canyon Scenic Drive
31 - Pine Canyon Reservoir
32 - Matthews Canyon Dam
33 - Beaver Dam State Park
34 - Rainbow Canyon
35 - Elgin Schoolhouse
36 - Pahranagat NWR

Lincoln County

Introduction and Significance of the Region

**What's it known for? The Extraterrestrial Highway.
Best Eats? American and Food Trucks.**

Lincoln County, Nevada An emblematic fusion of the Wild West's rugged history and the diverse, untouched landscapes of the Great Basin. Mesquite was originally a part of Lincoln County and continues to expand into neighboring territories. Sprawling valleys, forested mountain ranges, and remnants of the past make this region a treasure trove for adventure seekers and those interested in history. For trail aficionados, Lincoln County offers more than just paths to traverse; it's a narrative of resilience, where ghost towns whisper stories of yesteryears and the terrain challenges one's limits. Experience the thrills of technical trails and breathtaking panoramas in Lincoln County.

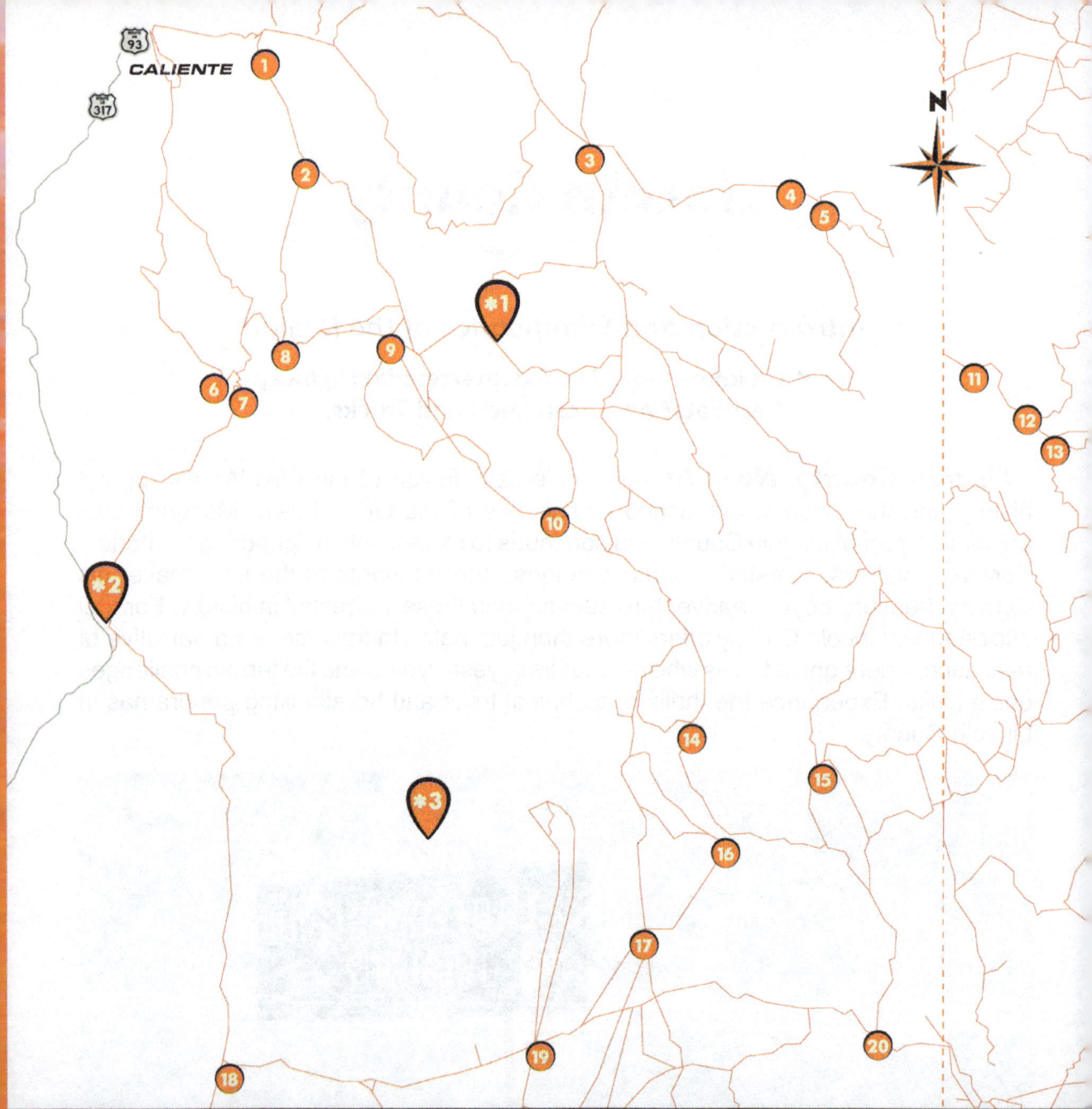

Lincoln County Trails and Destinations

ROAD & TRAIL INTERSECTIONS

1: Clover Creek Rd - Barnes Canyon Rd
2: Barnes Cnyn Rd - Barnes-Ellie Cutoff Rd
3: Beaver Dam Rd - Oak Wells Rd
4: Beaver Dam Rd - Enterprise Rd
5: Beaver Dam Rd - Pine Mtn Rd
6: Ella Mtn Rd - Spring Heights
7: Ella Mtn Rd - Pennsylvania Cnyn Rd
8: Ella Mtn Rd - Fife Rd - Barnes-Ellie Cutoff Rd
9: Fife Rd - Barnes Cnyn Rd
10: Sam's Camp Rd / E Pass Rd - Pine Washington Rd
11: Beaver Dam Rd - Mathews Ranch Rd
12: Mathews Ranch Rd - Cougar Pass Rd
13: Cougar Pass Rd - Slaughter Creek Rd
14: E Pass Rd - Sam's Camp Rd
15: Bull Valley Rd - Bunker Pass Rd
16: Lime Mtn Rd - E Pass Rd
17: Lime Mtn Rd - Sam's Camp Rd
18: Rainbow Pass Rd - 4230
19: Tule Pipeline Rd - Snow Springs Rd - Intersection - Garden Springs Rd
20: Snow Springs - Bull Valley Rd

POINTS OF INTEREST

*1: Pine Canyon Dam
*2: Elgin Schoolhouse
*3: Walter Ray Memorial

Trails & Scenic Destinations (from Mesquite)

Airplane Ridge/Bunker Pass Rd Between Mesquite and Caliente, close to the Utah border, lies a site known as Airplane Ridge, where remnants of a mysterious plane are scattered. Experts believe this debris is from an early US fighter jet, but its origins are mostly unknown. It is located near Motoqua, Utah and north of Lime Mountain, Nevada. Although locals know about this crash site and it likely occurred decades ago, it is important to remember that tampering with aircraft wreckage, including removing or taking parts is a federal crime.

Ash Springs, Nevada This unincorporated community in Lincoln County's Pahranagat Valley is known for ranching and desert ash trees. The area boasts natural hot springs on BLM land, with waters that emerge at about 97°F and cool slightly in a sizable soaking pool. However, caution is advised due to the presence of the harmful brain-eating amoeba, Naegleria fowleri, which tragically claimed a young boy's life in 2023.

Beaver Dam Wilderness A pristine expanse of rugged landscapes and rare plants and animals can be found along the Arizona-Nevada-Utah borders. Its serene canyons and peaks are a haven for hikers seeking solitude. The untouched beauty of this area serves as a testament to the wild wonders of the American Southwest. In 1986, the US Congress designated it as a wilderness area, administered by the Bureau of Land Management.

Davidson Memorial The Davidson Memorial honors the immigrant settlers who tragically died traveling to Utah in 1869. This landmark stands as a quiet reflection of their journey and the unforgiving nature of the desert.

Delamar, Nevada Delamar is a ghost town in eastern Nevada that flourished during the late 1800s because of its rich gold deposits. At its height, it had over 3,000 residents and various amenities. However, a devastating fire, followed by decreased mining activity, led to its decline. A unique aspect of Delamar's history is its link to silicosis, a lung disease from inhaling mine dust, earning it the nickname "The Widowmaker." Presently, stone ruins and old mine remnants mark the town, with wild horses roaming the area. Nearby, a dry lake resembling the shape of Texas serves as a notable landmark.

Elgin Schoolhouse State Historic Site In the ghost town of Elgin, Nevada, this historic one-room schoolhouse served local students for decades before closing its doors in 1967. After a careful restoration, they designated it a state historic site in 2005. Today, visitors can take guided tours to see preserved furnishings and artifacts from its operational years.

Lone Mesa Near the Three Corners Monument in Lincoln County and northeast of Mesquite, Lone Mesa is a standout feature amidst the desert expanse. Its elevated vantage point offers hikers sweeping views at the convergence of Nevada, Arizona, and Utah.

Lower & Upper Lime Mountain Well Perched along the contours of Lime Mountain, these wells stand as a site of refreshment in the scorching Nevada terrain. Their strategic location on Bunker Pass and Bull Valley Roads has been vital for the region's agricultural activities. At 6,936 feet, this is a beautiful wilderness area. Lime Mountain owes its name to the abundant lime deposits peppered throughout the vicinity.

Mormon Mountains Nestled between Moapa and Mesquite in Nevada, the Mormon Mountains rise as rugged formations against the vast desert landscape. These mountains are famous for their unique geology and rich history. You can visit a radio tower with panoramic views, refreshing springs, and caves believed to hold treasures from the Old Spanish Trail. For both outdoor enthusiasts and history buffs, the area holds a blend of adventure and mystery.

Mt. Ella Rising to an elevation of 7,479 feet, Mt. Ella is a prominent feature in the Clover Mountains, south of Caliente and near the Utah border. Besides its natural beauty, people know the mountain for its historic fire lookout, one of the few remaining in Nevada. Just a short distance away, visitors can explore intriguing caves near the Barclay settlement. With its scenic vistas, historical significance, and adventurous opportunities, Mt. Ella is a captivating destination for nature enthusiasts and explorers.

Pine Canyon Dam Situated northeast of Elgin, the Army Corps of Engineers manages this flood control dam to protect the railroad. They upgraded the area with shade structures, picnic tables, grills, fire pits, and vault toilets, making it a great place for outdoor gatherings.

Rainbow Canyon Nestled south of Caliente, Rainbow Canyon is one of Nevada's best-kept secrets. Often overshadowed by famous destinations like Red Rock or Valley of Fire, this southeastern Nevada jewel provides an unspoiled glimpse of the Mojave Desert's beauty, away from bustling tourist areas. The canyon has a variety of colors, from the iron-rich red rock formations to rugged limestone crags. Natural caves, ancient petroglyphs and groves of cottonwood trees line the Meadow Valley Wash. The 21-mile Rainbow Canyon Scenic Drive follows Nevada State Highway 317, highlighting the natural beauty of the area. The occasional sight of Union Pacific locomotives adds a layer of intrigue to the journey, reminding visitors of the area's rich history. Nearby, Kershaw-Ryan State Park has modern restrooms, a spring-fed pool, and volleyball courts, all surrounded by breathtaking canyon views. Rainbow Canyon is not merely a destination, but a vibrant mosaic of nature, history, and adventure waiting to be explored.

Rock Houses Constructed by the CCC near the Mormon Mountain range, these manmade structures are surrounded by rumors. One legend speculates that Governor Steuben of Pioche hosted his mistresses here. No one knows for sure, in fact we were unable to find ANY Nevada politicians with this name - however a more recent report suggested it was actually a former Las Vegas Mayor. BLM archaeologists identified these rock homes as part of a mining camp for Scheelite ore in the 1940s, based on information from the Lost City Museum. The structures might predate this period, but knowledge is limited. You can find water nearby in the Gourd Springs and rumors also swirl of a strange set of petroglyphs near to this site.

RUMOR HAS IT:

The Little A'Le'Inn A quirky motel and restaurant near Area 51 in Rachel, Nevada, drawing enthusiasts of UFOs and extraterrestrial lore. It offers a unique desert experience with themed rooms and memorabilia. This iconic spot is both a rest stop for travelers exploring the Nevada desert and a meeting place for those fascinated by the mysteries of the cosmos.

The Three Corners Monument Marking the unique tri-point where Utah, Arizona, and Nevada converge. Visitors can literally stand in three states simultaneously, making it a popular spot for photos. This geographical point showcases the fascinating borders that carve up America's vast landscape. There are actually two monuments here. An earlier monument built in the early 1900s is located off the boundary about a mile northeast on a nearby mesa.

Walter Ray Memorial The Walter Ray Memorial in Lincoln County honors CIA pilot Walter L. Ray, who died while flying the secret Lockheed A-12 from Groom Lake. Evidence from Ray's crash and another unknown crash remain, revealing the area's complex history. Thanks to Jeremy Krans' dedicated efforts, the site was rediscovered and marked in the 1990s, ensuring that Ray's dedication and sacrifice would not be forgotten.

Arizona Strip

Introduction and Significance of the Region

What's it known for? Grand Canyon North Rim.
Best Eats? Fusion, Cafe, Steakburgers.

Lying to the north of the mighty Colorado River and isolated from the rest of Arizona by its vast expanse, the Arizona Strip stands as a testament to the raw beauty of untamed wilderness. This region, known for its sprawling mesas, canyons, and rugged terrain, offers more than just a challenging landscape; it's a journey into an area rich with American history. The Strip beckons adventurers with its rich history of ancient Native American civilizations, pioneer trails, and iconic landmarks. Explorers on these trails will find spectacular views and ancient stories for a one-of-a-kind adventure.

Dustin Berg Photography

Trails & Scenic Destinations

Bar 10 Ranch A hidden gem beyond the Grand Canyon's edge. Situated deep within the Arizona Strip, the Bar 10 Ranch isn't just a geographic marker: it's a serene journey into a vast wilderness. With the majesty of the Grand Canyon as its backdrop, Bar 10 offers visitors an intimate experience away from the typical hustle and bustle. This isn't your ordinary Grand Canyon visit; this is the Grand Canyon without the crowds. While still operating as a genuine cattle ranch, Bar 10 has grown into the area's top recreational hub. It's not only the ideal start and end point for many adventures, but also a place where visitors can experience the raw beauty of nature. Bar 10 Ranch promises an epic trip to the Grand Canyon's less-traveled paths.

Beaver Dam Lodge Nestled within the northern Arizona Strip, Beaver Dam Lodge stands as a timeless testament to a bygone era. This historic oasis, established in 1929, was a popular stop for Hollywood stars like Clark Gable, Jane Russell, and John Wayne. Whispers of secret passages for discreet celebrity access and ghostly sightings haunt its storied past. Now a popular lottery, golf and lodging destination, Beaver Dam has kept its legendary aura through gold rushes, the Roaring Twenties, and the whispers of mafia figures.

BLM Pakoon Basin Airstrip Located in the secluded Pakoon Basin of Mohave County, Arizona, the Bureau of Land Management (BLM) oversees this gravel airstrip. Situated in a barren, arid landscape, it serves as a crucial base for fire watch teams in the Grand Canyon Parashant National Monument. The well-kept access roads are designed for ATVs and high-clearance vehicles, facilitating swift wildfire responses and regular patrols. The BLM is committed to protecting this unique airstrip in the Mojave Desert.

Arizona Trails & Destinations

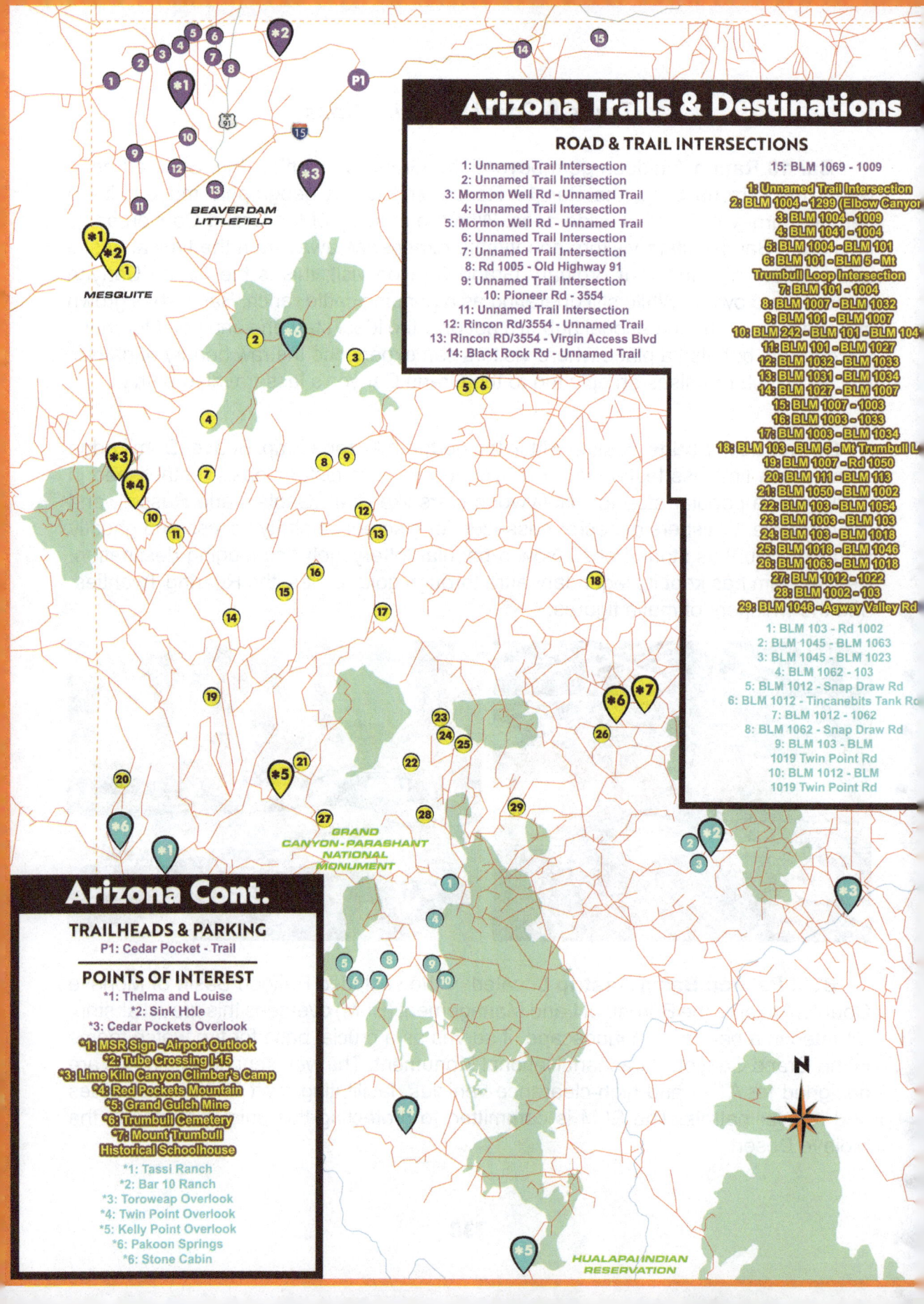

ROAD & TRAIL INTERSECTIONS

1: Unnamed Trail Intersection
2: Unnamed Trail Intersection
3: Mormon Well Rd - Unnamed Trail
4: Unnamed Trail Intersection
5: Mormon Well Rd - Unnamed Trail
6: Unnamed Trail Intersection
7: Unnamed Trail Intersection
8: Rd 1005 - Old Highway 91
9: Unnamed Trail Intersection
10: Pioneer Rd - 3554
11: Unnamed Trail Intersection
12: Rincon Rd/3554 - Unnamed Trail
13: Rincon RD/3554 - Virgin Access Blvd
14: Black Rock Rd - Unnamed Trail
15: BLM 1069 - 1009

1: Unnamed Trail Intersection
2: BLM 1004 - 1299 (Elbow Canyon
3: BLM 1004 - 1009
4: BLM 1041 - 1004
5: BLM 1004 - BLM 101
6: BLM 101 - BLM 5 - Mt Trumbull Loop Intersection
7: BLM 101 - 1004
8: BLM 1007 - BLM 1032
9: BLM 101 - BLM 1007
10: BLM 242 - BLM 101 - BLM 104
11: BLM 101 - BLM 1027
12: BLM 1032 - BLM 1033
13: BLM 1031 - BLM 1034
14: BLM 1027 - BLM 1007
15: BLM 1007 - 1003
16: BLM 1003 - 1033
17: BLM 1003 - BLM 1034
18: BLM 103 - BLM 5 - Mt Trumbull L
19: BLM 1007 - Rd 1050
20: BLM 111 - BLM 113
21: BLM 1050 - BLM 1002
22: BLM 103 - BLM 1054
23: BLM 1003 - BLM 103
24: BLM 103 - BLM 1018
25: BLM 1018 - BLM 1046
26: BLM 1063 - BLM 1018
27: BLM 1012 - 1022
28: BLM 1002 - 103
29: BLM 1046 - Agway Valley Rd

1: BLM 103 - Rd 1002
2: BLM 1045 - BLM 1063
3: BLM 1045 - BLM 1023
4: BLM 1062 - 103
5: BLM 1012 - Snap Draw Rd
6: BLM 1012 - Tincanebits Tank Rd
7: BLM 1012 - 1062
8: BLM 1062 - Snap Draw Rd
9: BLM 103 - BLM 1019 Twin Point Rd
10: BLM 1012 - BLM 1019 Twin Point Rd

Arizona Cont.

TRAILHEADS & PARKING
P1: Cedar Pocket - Trail

POINTS OF INTEREST
*1: Thelma and Louise
*2: Sink Hole
*3: Cedar Pockets Overlook

*1: MSR Sign - Airport Outlook
*2: Tube Crossing I-15
*3: Lime Kiln Canyon Climber's Camp
*4: Red Pockets Mountain
*5: Grand Gulch Mine
*6: Trumbull Cemetery
*7: Mount Trumbull Historical Schoolhouse

*1: Tassi Ranch
*2: Bar 10 Ranch
*3: Toroweap Overlook
*4: Twin Point Overlook
*5: Kelly Point Overlook
*6: Pakoon Springs
*6: Stone Cabin

St. George
Kanab
Mesquite
Fredonia

① Spanish Trail Marker
② Sand Hollow Wash Bridge
③ Pipe Spring National Monument

Grand Canyon North Rim

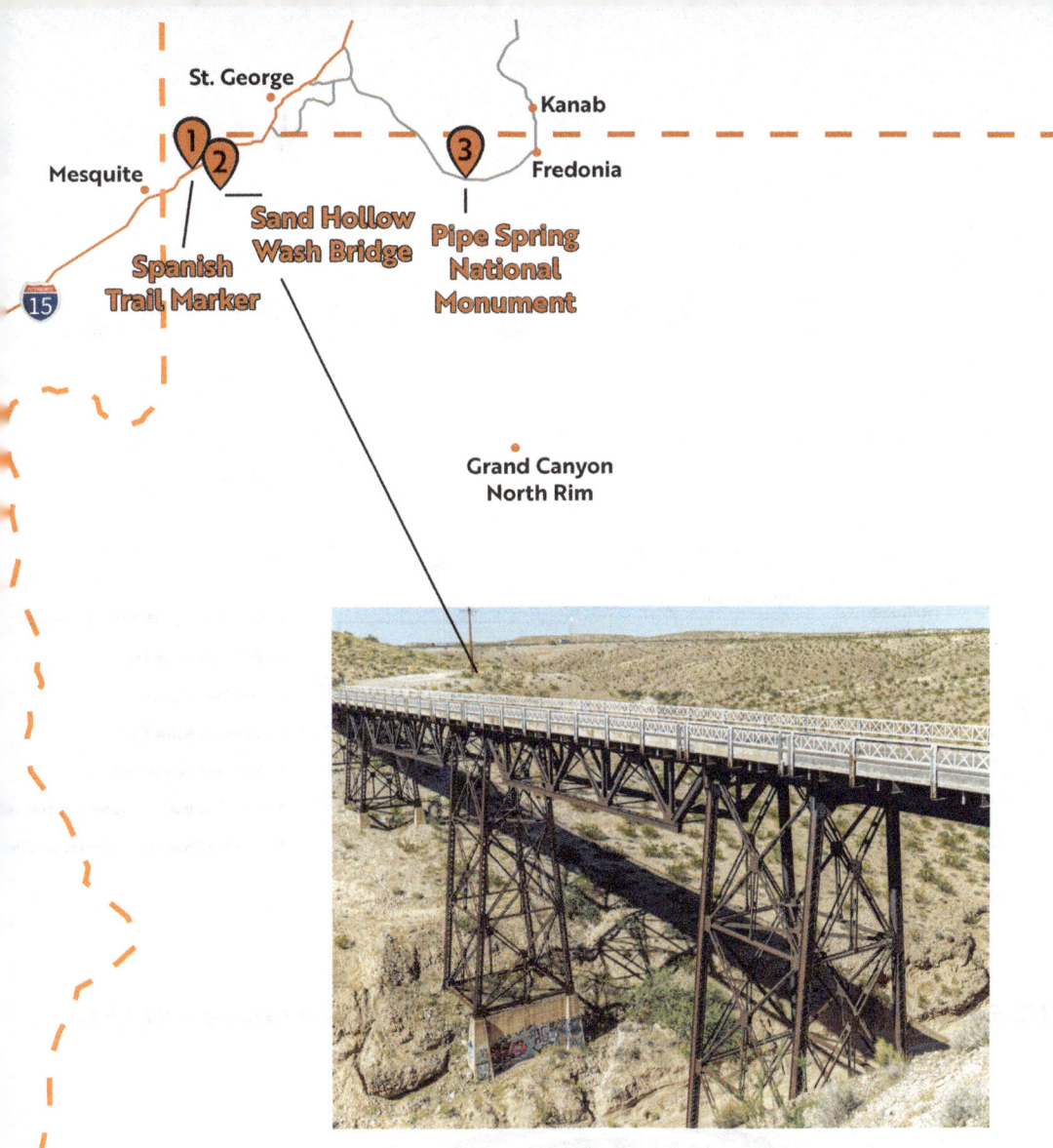

ARIZONA STRIP HISTORICAL SITES

GRAND CANYON NORTH LEGEND

1 - Vermillion Cliffs/White Pocket
2 - Point Sublime Trail
3 - Fire Point Loop
4 - Jumpup Point Trail
5 - Toroweap Overlook
6 - Mt. Trumbull to Grand Gulch Mine
7 - Hidden Canyon/Virgin Mountains

Map labels: St. George, AZ Strip to Mesquite, BLM 1069, Fredonia, Jacob Lake, Mt. Trumbull Schoolhouse, Mt. Trumbull, Tuweep, Bar 10 Ranch, Toroweap, Grand Canyon North Rim

---

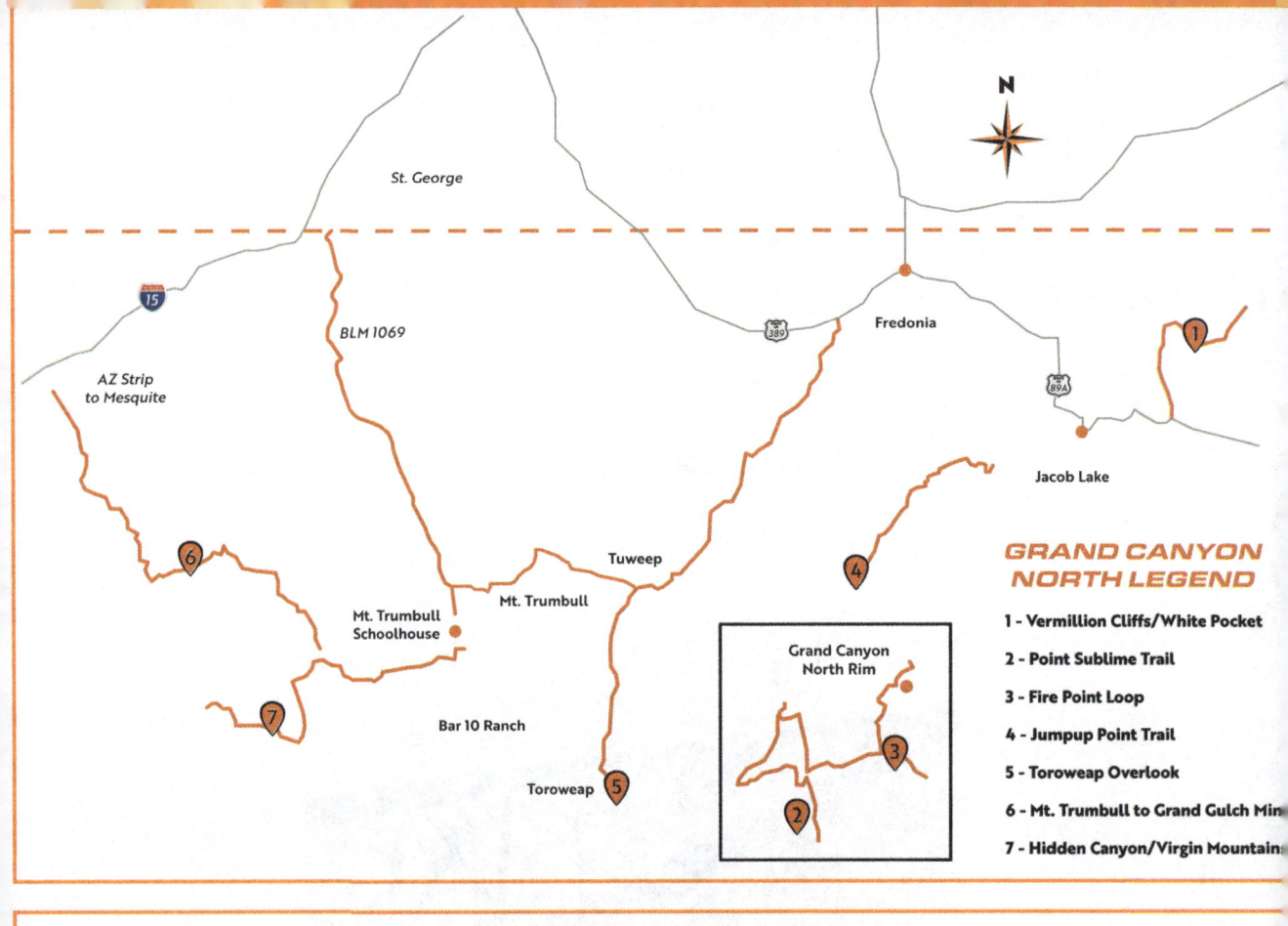

GRAPHICS & MAPS DESIGNED IN COLLABORATION WITH...

MESQUITE BRANDING & DESIGN CO.

(725) 225-5806   MESQUITEBRANDING.COM

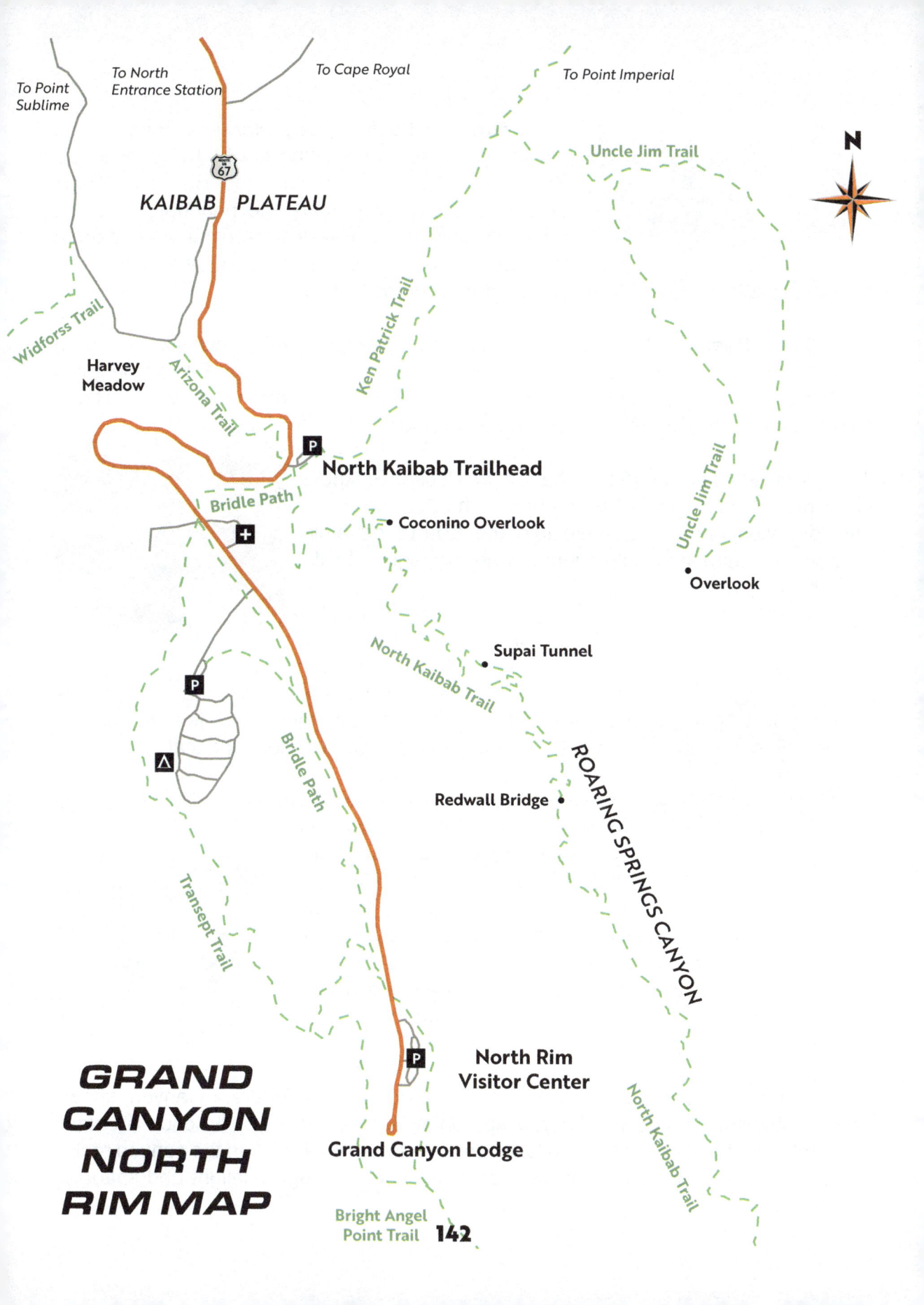

GRAND CANYON NORTH RIM MAP

142

Boundary Peak Survey Markers Perched just outside Mesquite, on a hill north of I-15 opposite the Palms Golf Course, you can find Boundary Peak Survey Markers. They mark the boundary between Arizona and Nevada. These discreet landmarks are a testament to the precision of early surveyors, and can be found all over the region.

Cedar Basin Just over the mountains south of Gold Butte Townsite, this area offers a scenic escape into nature and history. Accessible via Cedar Basin Road, this valley is home to the historic Cedar Basin Corral and other attractions like the Radio Crystal Mine site and the trailhead to Jumbo Peak.

Cedar Pocket Sinkhole The Cedar Pocket Sinkhole is a remarkable geological feature in the Arizona Strip. Its formation offers a glimpse into the Earth's dynamic processes, attracting both tourists and geologists to its depths.

Dinosaur Rock Found near Gibson Jones Ranch in the secluded Arizona Strip, got its name because it resembles a dinosaur's head. This intriguing geological feature adds an element of whimsy to the rugged desert landscape.

Drain Tubes The Off-Roader's Underpass Near Mesquite, where the Sand Hollow Wash and I-15 meet, are the Arizona Drain Tubes — two large culvert tubes that are important for off-road enthusiasts. These tubes are conveniently located under the interstate, making them a popular crossing spot for UTVers, traveling between the north and south sides of town. They symbolize the connection between urban planning and adventure, allowing off- roading to continue despite the town's growth.

Figure Four Canyon Nestled near the Narrows is the Figure 4 Canyon, known for its stunning formations. As you approach Beaver Dam, you'll notice a unique natural formation that looks like a lazily drawn number 4, etched on the canyon rocks. This formation is notable for its lack of vegetation, although sunlight and shadows can sometimes make it harder to see. While it stands as a prominent sight, the true origins of the '4' are entirely natural, debunking many speculations. Rumors exist of naturally formed numbers along the canyon ridge, spanning from 1 to 5, but these sightings have not been confirmed. Various travelers and enthusiasts also claim to identify other formations, such as a Christmas tree.

Mountain Man Of special note is the "Mountain Man", a formation that becomes distinctly visible on neighboring Mt Bangs from Mesquite, particularly when the peaks are dusted with snow.

Photo Courtesy of Virgin Valley Heritage Museum

Frehner Haven Ranch (Cold Springs Ranch) Nestled in the Elbow Canyon Trail, the Frehner Haven Ranch, also known as Cold Springs Ranch, was once a cherished family property. Its rumored fruit trees served as a vital resource for travelers and became a symbol of respite and unity. A dispute over a land lease led to the destruction of most of the structures, leaving only the foundations behind. Despite this loss, it remains a special spot for travelers, preserving the memory of its historical significance. Visitors can still find solace amidst the foundation's remains and appreciate the site's natural beauty.

Garden of Eden AKA Red Rocks (Outcropping) Not to be confused with the Garden of Eden Slot Canyon, this place is simply called Red Rocks or The Garden of Eden by the locals. It's surrounded by a dirt road about a mile and a half ride off the beaten path called Disneyland because of the fun ups and downs. Enjoy a scenic jaunt through cedar trees and red rock wonders on a very sandy road. Recommended as a SxS trip worth exploring!

Garden of Eden Slot Canyon Also referred to as The Grotto by some local ATVers, should not be confused with Kirk's Grotto in Gold Butte National Monument, which lies further to the west and on the Nevada side. The Grotto has a sloping floor that is quite steep. It is a short walk from the parking area to the opening and is a cool place to hang in the heat, with great scenery and shade.

Gibson Jones Ranch Once a private homestead, the Gibson Jones Ranch is a remote outpost nestled within the Arizona Strip, part of the Grand Canyon-Parashant National Monument. Referred to as "the pool" by some local UTVers and "Slats Jacobs" by the local ranchers, this historic ranch offers a rare look into the region's frontier history while offering a peaceful escape in the rugged wilderness of the Arizona Strip area.

Grand Gulch Mine Once buzzing with mining operations, Grand Gulch now stands as a vivid reminder of the area's extensive history of mineral extraction. Nestled in rough landscapes, its remains tell stories of the dreams and resolve of past prospectors. Today, it doubles as a significant historical site, offering a glimpse into a past epoch.

Halloween Point Located near Mesquite and accessible by Taglo Mine Road through Cabin Canyon Road. It provides, a breathtaking view of Middle Canyon. From this vantage point, one can admire expansive sky views and the distant glimmer of Mesquite's city lights.

Ice Cave Despite not being a typical cave, this unique partial slot canyon was named for its refreshing coolness, attracting early settlers and their 4th of July picnics. Keep an eye on the summit, where you might spot a resident owl that frequents the area.

Jacob's Well This historic ranch reveals the Arizona Strip's past with the remains of a dwelling, distinguished by a window and chimney. Near a pond stands a vintage windmill and an old-style water pump, hinting at bygone water systems. Modern stone pathways lead to structures, perhaps added for convenience in muddy conditions. Antique machinery and remnants of an elaborate canal system decorate the area, though some reservoirs are now empty.

Limekiln Canyon In Arizona, Limekiln Canyon offers a picturesque blend of rugged beauty and serene landscapes. Carved over time by natural forces, its intricate rock formations tell tales of geological marvels. Today, it's a sought-after spot for nature enthusiasts and sport climbers seeking a slice of the Southwest's untouched charm.

Little Grand Canyon A desert gem about 40 miles south of Mesquite on the Arizona Strip, lies west of Grand Gulch and Negrohead. This scenic destination is near landmarks such as Willow Spring and Mud Mountain, easily reached via the Pakoon route. Its raw beauty is reminiscent of the vastness of its namesake in miniature form, and with a unique charm of its own.

Little Jamaica Little Jamaica, also known as Littlefield Springs and located in Littlefield, Arizona, was once a scenic oasis by the Virgin River. This charming spot featured small waterfalls and a man-made pool fed by a mountain spring. Conveniently situated near the interstate, it provided a refreshing break amidst the desert. However, due to overpopulation and ongoing I-15 construction expansions, Little Jamaica has been removed. Despite this, a group of local people are hoping to restore this once-popular destination.

Middle Canyon Middle Canyon is a trail in the Arizona Strip near Mesquite, connecting Limekiln Canyon and Cabin Canyon Road. This pathway serves as a link between these two prominent canyons in the region.

MSR Point Just north of the I-15 by the Nevada border is the MSR Sign. It's a super short and fun ride up the bluff to a scenic area where you can get a clear view of the desert, Highway 91, Mesquite Airport, and Wolf Creek golf course. It's especially nice at sunset. The "MSR" in the name stands for Mesquite Sippers and Rippers, a local UTV club. A beautiful spot just outside of town to watch a stunning sunset over the Mormon Mountain range.

Mud Mountain Within the northern section of the Pakoon Basin, between Lime Kiln Pass and Black Rock, stands Mud Mountain. With an impressive elevation of 5,787 feet, this peak is more than just a geographical wonder. Whispered tales of feral hogs roaming its terrains have piqued the curiosity of many hunters. While there's no designated license to hunt these elusive hogs in Arizona, would-be adventurers should note that a general hunting license is required, and there are specific regulations dictating when and where hunting is allowed.

Pakoon Spring Nestled in the Arizona wilderness, is a serene oasis drawing life amidst the arid desert landscape. Its waters sustain a diverse ecosystem, making it a haven for local wildlife. Visitors find its tranquil setting enchanting and a testament to nature's resilience and beauty.

Red Pocket Mountain Located south of Limekiln Canyon, Red Pocket Mountain is a stunning natural landmark in the Grand Canyon-Parashant National Monument. The vivid red colors and unique geological formations make it an attractive spot for adventurers and enthusiasts exploring the remote wilderness.

Shivwits Arch A ceremonial arch, is a prominent and visually striking natural feature visible from Interstate 15 in the Arizona Strip. This remarkable geological formation carries cultural significance in the region.

Tassi Ranch Located in the Mojave Desert is Tassi Ranch, a sprawling 200-acre property north of the Grand Canyon, within the Grand Canyon-Parashant National Monument. The land is adorned with creosote bushes, standing as a testament to human resilience with the towering Grand Wash Cliffs as its backdrop. A stone ranch house from 1938, shaded by cottonwood trees, and remnants of a 20th-century ranch reveal the ranch's rich history. Native Americans and Mormon traders frequently stopped at Tassi Springs, where settlers built a stone house and a well by 1912.

Ed Yates, occupying the ranch from 1929, significantly shaped its destiny. By improving the infrastructure, he turned the ranch into a hub for stock-raising and agriculture, centered around the valuable Tassi Springs. The ranch house made of rocks and the barn built with railroad ties are a departure from typical log construction in the area, representing local ingenuity. The strategic clustering of ranch structures around the spring and their unique design adaptations provide a vivid glimpse into how early settlers thrived in the harsh desert conditions of northern Arizona.

Thelma & Louise This scenic stop represents one of the more popular vistas overlooking Beaver Dam Wash near the Arizona Strip. Local lore suggests that this is where Thelma and Louise made their cinematic cliff dive. Adding a whimsical touch, visitors have started the quirky tradition of hanging bras on the adjacent fences, as a light-hearted tribute. Its secluded position enhances its pristine allure, providing explorers with a distinctive experience.

Toroweap Offering one of the most breathtaking overlooks of the Grand Canyon's North Rim. Perched high above the Colorado River, visitors are treated to unparalleled vertical views, making it a favored spot for photographers and adventurers. Its remote location adds to its untouched beauty, giving travelers a unique Grand Canyon experience.

Virgin River Canyon Recreation Area
The Virgin River Canyon Recreation Area is a natural oasis for outdoor enthusiasts, located on Interstate 15, between St. George Utah and Mesquite. You can have fun and relax with trails, wildlife viewing, and river activities. The area features two designated wilderness areas, making it a haven for nature lovers. Whether you enjoy hiking, observing wildlife, or river exploration, this recreation area has something to offer.

The Virgin Gorge Outlook
Providing breathtaking views of the canyon carved by the Virgin River below. In the Arizona Strip, this vantage point captures the raw beauty and grandeur of the Southwest's rugged landscapes. Visitors often find themselves captivated by the play of light and shadow on the canyon walls, making it a must-visit spot in the region.

White Pocket
Tucked away near Kanab lies the mesmerizing landscape of White Pocket. A surreal tapestry of swirling reds, whites, and pinks, this geologic wonder in the Vermilion Cliffs National Monument appears as if painted by nature's brush. Its intricate patterns and formations, beckon adventurers and photographers alike, offering an otherworldly desert experience. Don't miss **House Rock Valley,** offering stunning views of Buckskin Gulch and the Paria River.

Wolf Hole Valley Nestled within the Arizona Strip in Mohave County, Wolf Hole is a ghostly reminder of times gone by. Once a humble ranching and farming community, all that remains now are a few foundations, and an abandoned house. Its intriguing name, attributed to a mistranslation by Major John Wesley Powell, was originally "Coyote Spring" in Pah-Ute. From 1918 to 1927, there was a post office, but now people come to enjoy the serene history and explore the sprawling Wolf Hole Mountain plateau, about 30 miles south of St. George, Utah. Accessible year-round, this ghost town offers a well-graded route around the mountain, once home to the town and author Edward Abbey.

Don't see your favorite
LOCAL TRAIL DESTINATION?

Let us know. We want to hear from YOU!

Reach out to us at:
INFO@MESQUITETRAILS.COM

and share your insights on the history, trails, and destinations unique to Mesquite. Let's celebrate the beauty All Around Mesquite together!

Connect with our community of trail lovers on social media:
@RideMesquite & @AllAroundMesquite

SOUTHERN UTAH HISTORICAL SITE MAP

LEGEND

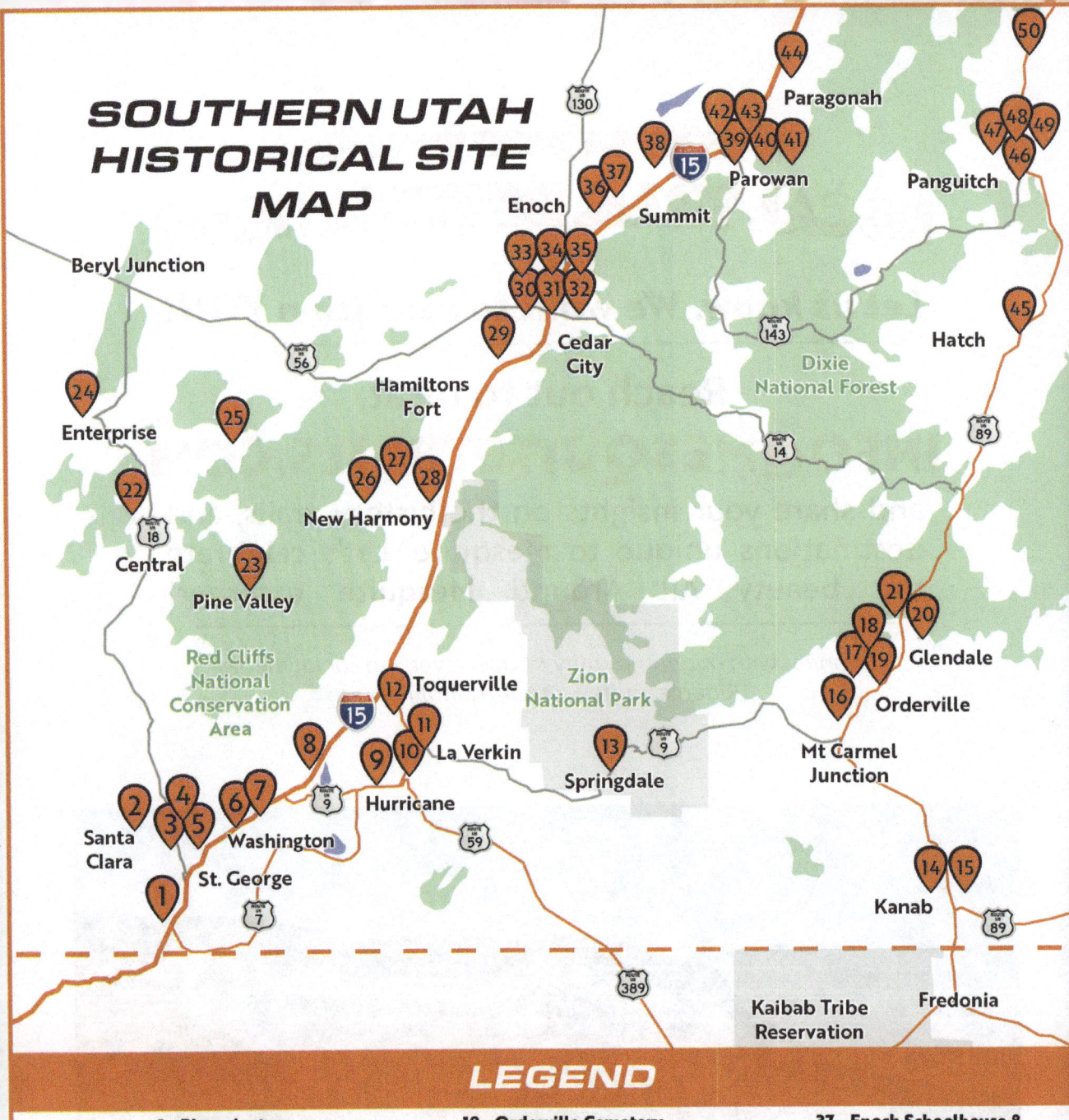

1 - Bloomington
2 - Swiss Colony
3 - St George Tabernacle
4 - Winter Home of Brigham Young
5 - Stone Quarries
6 - Washington Cotton Factory
7 - Covington Mansion
8 - Harrisburg
9 - Hurricane Pioneers
10 - La Verkin
11 - La Verkin Canal
12 - Toquerville
13 - Discovery of Zion Canyon
14 - Jacob Hamblin
15 - Powell Survey
16 - Settlement of Long Valley
17 - United Order Industries
18 - Orderville Bell
19 - Orderville Cemetery
20 - Glendale
21 - United Order Woolen Factory
22 - Mountain Meadow Massacre
23 - Pine Valley
24 - Enterprise
25 - Pinto Settlement
26 - New Harmony
27 - Military Training Campsite
28 - Fort Harmony
29 - Hamilton Fort
30 - Fort Cedar
31 - Cedar City Tabernacle
32 - Chaffin Grist Mill
33 - The Social Hall
34 - Pioneer Cabin
35 - First Cedar Encampment
36 - Johnson's Fort
37 - Enoch Schoolhouse & Tithing Office
38 - Sylvanus Cyrus Hulet
39 - Old Comedy Hall
40 - D.U.P. Relic Hall
41 - Pioneer Rock Church
42 - First School House & Council House
43 - Public Works
44 - Tithing Lot & Relief Society Hall
45 - Hatch Ward Building & Bell
46 - Social Hall
47 - Panguitch Stake Tabernacle
48 - Panguitch Tithing Lot
49 - Panguitch Quilt Walk
50 - Historic Fort Sanford

Southern Utah

Introduction and Significance of the Region

What's it known for? Zion National Park
Best Eats? Lots - Try Indian/Asian and Formal Dining

Southern Utah displays nature's artistry, sculpting a remarkable landscape of towering sandstone cliffs, winding canyons, and expansive plateaus that seemingly touch the horizon. This region has stunning natural features and a fascinating indigenous history, offering an enticing mix of adventure and reflection. For trail enthusiasts, Southern Utah is more than just a hiking destination; it's an experience. Where footsteps echo against ancient petroglyphs and majestic arches carved by erosion. The trails combine technical challenges and beautiful views, providing an experience that lasts long after the trek is done.

MOTOQUA

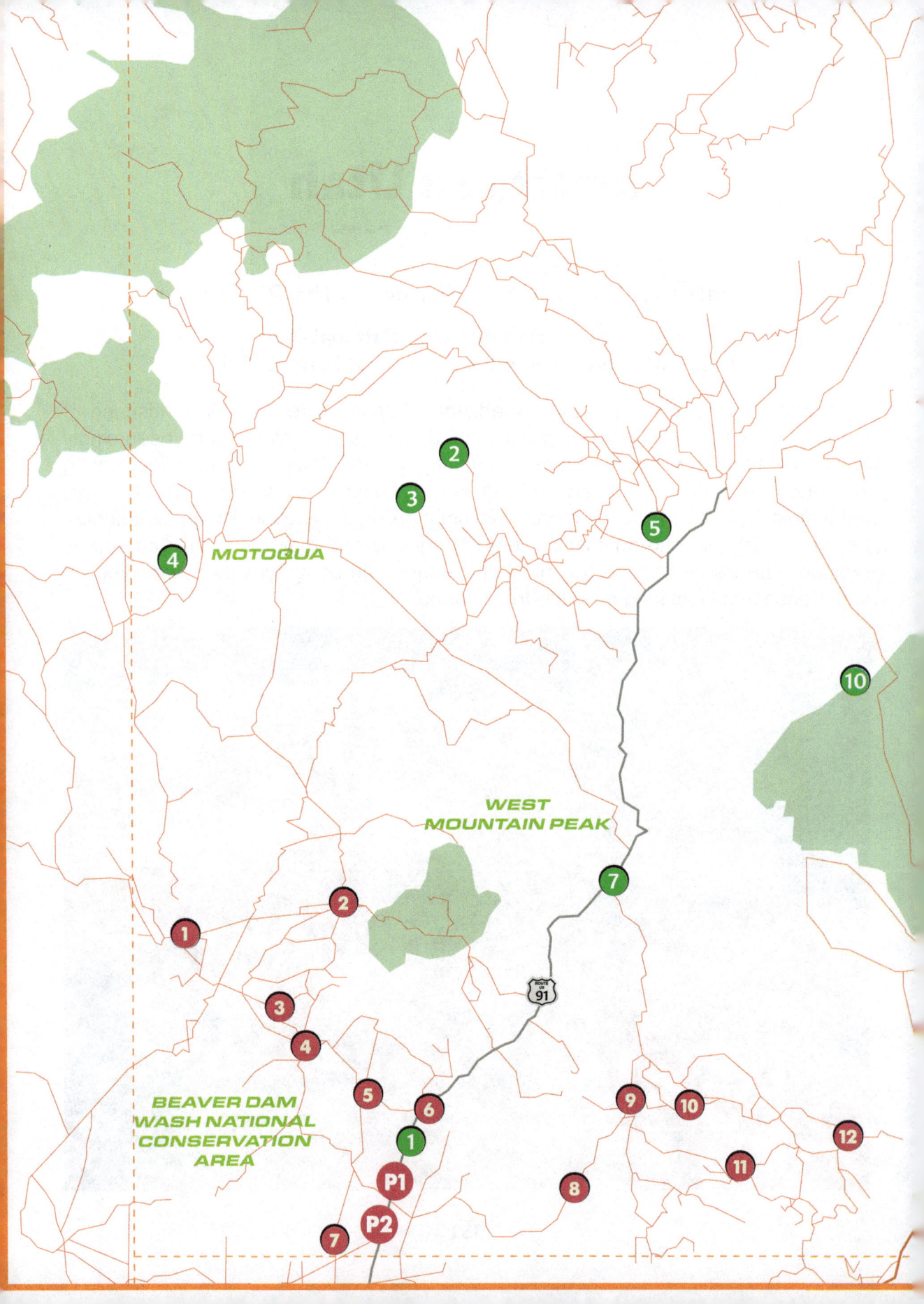

WEST
MOUNTAIN PEAK

BEAVER DAM
WASH NATIONAL
CONSERVATION
AREA

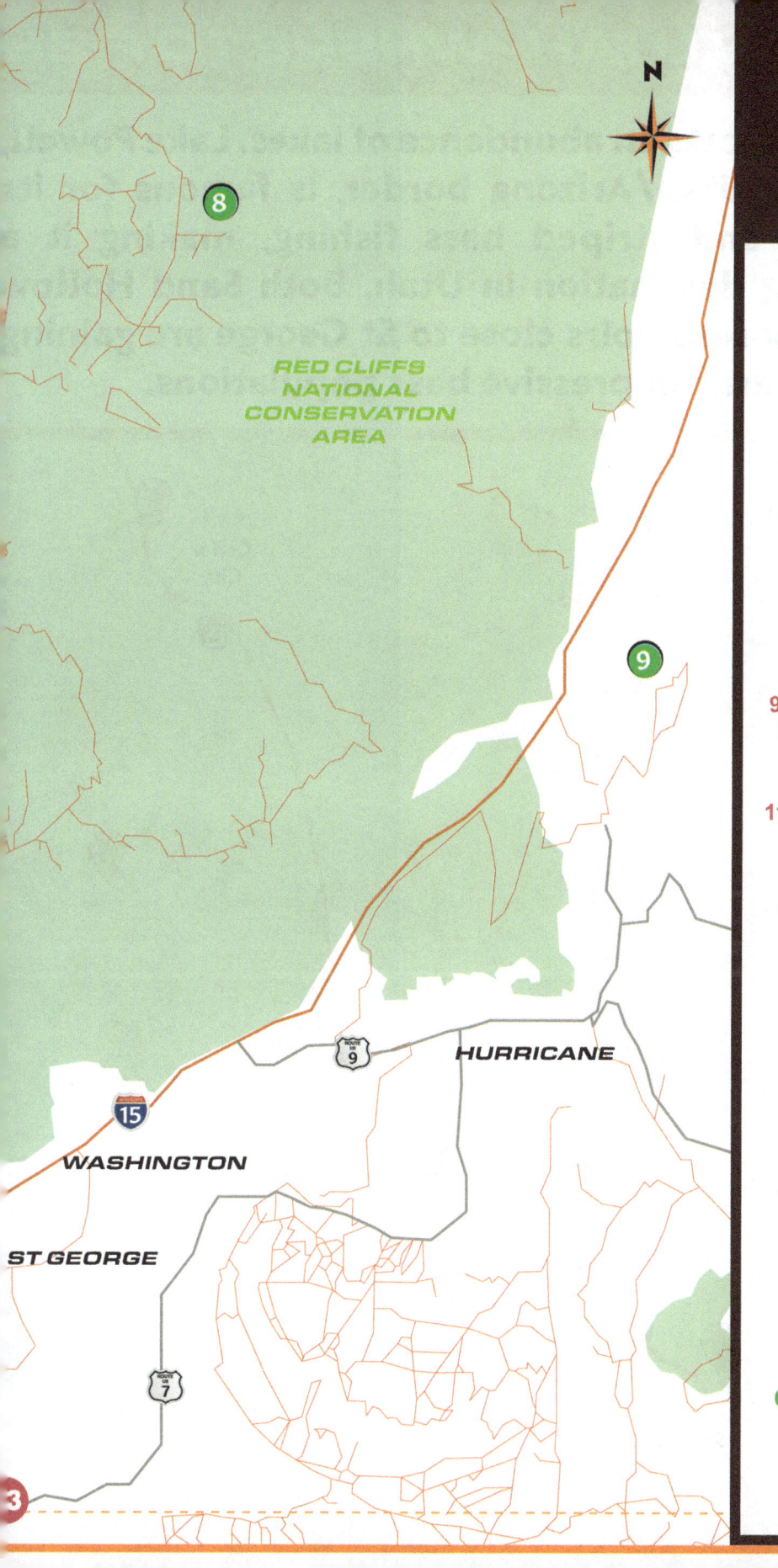

Southern Utah Trails & Destinations

1: Lytle Little Ranch Rd - Eardley Rd - 0029
2: Indian Springs Trail - UT 0074 - 0076
3: UT 0081 - 0082
4: Lytle Ranch Rd - Indian Springs Trail - 0081
5: Lytle Ranch Rd / Eardley Rd - Welcome Springs Rd
5: Lytle Ranch Rd / Eardley Rd - Welcome Springs Rd
6: Lytle Rand Rd / Eardle Rd - Old Highway 91
7: Mormon Well Rd - 0095
8: Bulldog Pass/Ape Rd @ Bulldog Pass
9: Mojave Desert Joshue Tree Rd - Hollow Washington Rd
10: Hollow Washington Rd - Bloomington Cave Rd
11: Unnamed Trail Intersection
12: Hollow Washington Rd - Navajo Dr

TRAILHEADS & PARKING

P1: Mojave Desert Joshua Tree Rd /Bulldog Pass - Apex Rd - Old Highway 91
P2: Mormon Well Rd - Old Highway 91
P3: BLM 1069 - St. George

DESTINATIONS

1: Castle Cliffs
2: B52 Crashsite
3: Pine Arch
4: WW2 Memorial
5: Old Post Corral
6: Bloomington Petroglyphs
7: Shivwits
8: Pine Valley
9: Toquerville Falls
10: Snow Canyon Park

SOUTHERN UTAH - WHERE TO FISH

Southern Utah boasts an abundance of lakes. Lake Powell, located on the Utah/Arizona border, is famous for its excellent bass and striped bass fishing, making it a popular boating destination in Utah. Both Sand Hollow and Quail Creek reservoirs close to St George are gaining recognition for their impressive bass populations.

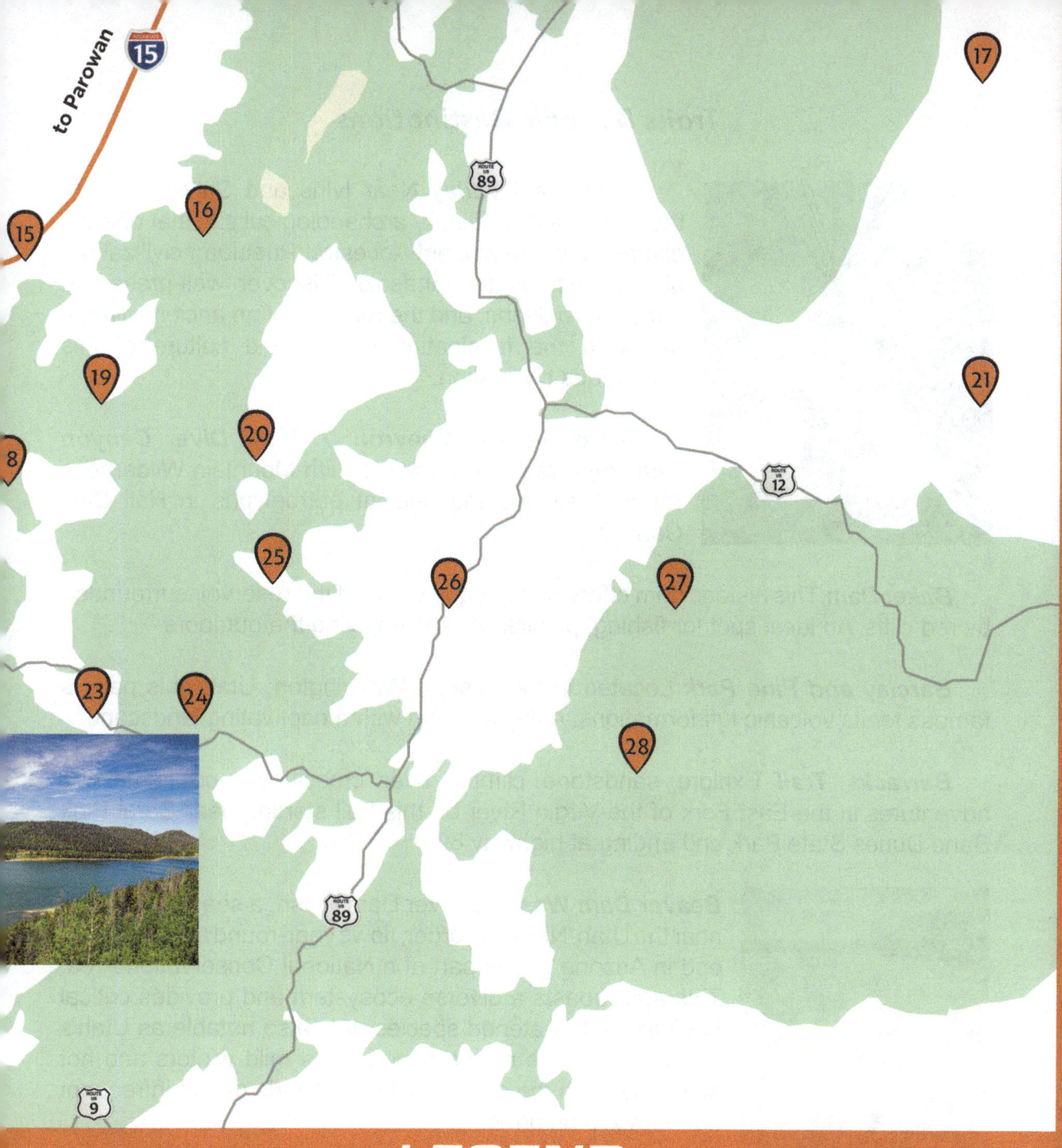

LEGEND

- 1 – Enterprise Reservoir
- 2 – Newcastle Reservoir
- 3 – Lake at the Hills
- 4 – Baker Reservoir
- 5 – Pine Valley Reservoir
- 6 – Kolob Reservoir
- 7 – Gunlock Reservoir
- 8 – Tawa Ponds
- 9 – Skyline Pond
- 10 – Sullivan Virgin River Park Pond
- 11 – Razor Ridge Pond
- 12 – Quail Creek Reservoir
- 13 – Stratton Pond
- 14 – Sand Hollow Reservoir
- 15 – Parowan Pond
- 16 – Paragonah Reservoir
- 17 – East Fork Sevier River, Black Canyon
- 18 – Bristlecone (Brian Head) Pond
- 19 – Yankee Meadow Reservoir
- 20 – Panguitch Lake
- 21 – Pine Lake
- 22 – Woods Ranch Pond
- 23 – Navajo Lake
- 24 – Duck Creek Pond
- 25 – Mammoth Creek
- 26 – Asay Creek
- 27 – Tropic Reservoir
- 28 – East Fork Sevier River, Upper

Trails & Scenic Destinations

Anasazi Valley Near Ivins and Shivwits, Utah, there is an extraordinary archaeological site that offers a glimpse into the ancient Ancestral Puebloan civilization, also known as the Anasazi. Discover well-preserved ruins, petroglyphs, and the remains of an ancient village, revealing the fascinating history and culture of this mysterious civilization.

Apple Valley Chevron / Hell Dive Canyon Petroglyphs Explore the Moquith Mountain Wilderness Study Area and the ancient petroglyphs in Hell Dive Canyon.

Baker Dam This historic dam offers picturesque views of the reservoir surrounded by red cliffs. An ideal spot for fishing, picnicking, and enjoying the outdoors.

Barclay and Pine Park Located in far western Washington, Utah, this park is famous for its volcanic tuff formations. A tiny creation with a captivating landscape.

Barracks Trail Explore sandstone climbs, river crossings, and immersive adventures in the East Fork of the Virgin River on this trail starting near Coral Pink Sand Dunes State Park and ending at highway 89.

Beaver Dam Wash Beaver Dam Wash, a seasonal stream near the Utah-Nevada border, flows year-round at its southern end in Arizona and is part of a National Conservation Area. This area boasts a diverse ecosystem and provides critical habitats for threatened species. It is also notable as Utah's lowest point. The region experiences mild winters and hot summers, with the occasional flash floods due to infrequent but heavy rainstorms.

Black Mountain Features ancient petroglyphs that provide a compelling look at history. These time-worn carvings on the mountain's rocky canvas hint at the rich history and beliefs of its early inhabitants. A visit here is like stepping back in time, offering a tangible connection to the region's ancestral cultures.

Birthing / Conception Cave The Birthing and Naming Caves, a series of petroglyph-rich sites near Gunlock, Utah, offer a unique window into ancient times. Accessible by walking paths near Gunlock Reservoir. This cave, situated on the west side of a large sandstone outcrop, features a rock slab covered in petroglyphs and is more of a shallow alcove than a deep cave. Other caves in the area, such as the Conception Cave, are more remote and may require an off-road trail suitable for jeeps or UTVs, adding an adventurous element to their exploration.

Bloomington Cave Nestled on the east side of the limestone-rich Beaver Dam Mountains, just 15 miles west of St. George, lies the Bloomington Cave. Recognized as the most extensive cave within the St. George Field Office area, it boasts six unique levels and intricate passageways. With a total surveyed length of 1.43 miles, it proudly ranks as Utah's fifth-longest cave. The cavern's layout is complex, characterized by tight squeezes, steep floors, and slippery trails, posing challenges even for experienced explorers. Less experienced visitors may find it more difficult than expected. Though entry requires a permit, getting one is a straightforward process via the St. George Field Office. Venture inside, and you'll traverse one of the five marked routes, each presenting its own set of challenges.

Bloomington Petroglyph Park A Suburban Historical Gem Situated in the center of a Bloomington suburb, the Petroglyph Park is a remarkable attraction that seamlessly blends history and art. Here, ancient petroglyphs provide a rare glimpse into the stories and traditions of cultures long past. For those looking to delve deeper into the area's history, a short drive of just over a mile will lead to the historic Airmail Arrows. There's a small parking pullout near a dirt road that ascends to a water tank, where the prominent arrow is easily spotted. With its mix of suburban living and historical treasures, Bloomington is an intriguing destination for all ages.

Brian Head, Utah A picturesque mountain town at an elevation of 9,800 feet (3,000 m) above sea level, making it the highest town in Utah. Known for its ski resort, vibrant fall colors, and diverse outdoor recreational activities, this charming community serves as a gateway to scenic wonders and adventures throughout the year.

Bullfrog Basin Situated off highway SR-24, this basin provides an immersive experience into the rugged terrains and breathtaking vistas. It's a stone's throw from the iconic Capitol Reef.

Photo Courtesy of Virgin Valley Heritage Museum

Castle Cliff Station In Southern Utah, Castle Cliff Station was once a vital stopover for travelers during the stagecoach era, and serves as a reminder of the region's vibrant history. Nestled amidst the backdrop of the impressive Castle Cliffs, this historic site offers a glimpse into Utah's frontier history. Its preserved remnants continue to attract history enthusiasts and explorers alike.

Cedar Breaks Dive deep into the beauty of Cedar, from its scenic vistas and rock formations to historic sites. Be sure to visit the bristlecone pine trees at Cedar Breaks which are over 1,650 years old. These old-timers have adapted to living on barren slopes and cliff edges.

Cedar Area - Mammoth Cave, Navajo Lake Traverse the depths of Mammoth Cave and the serene waters of Navajo Lake.

Coral Pink Sand Dunes State Park The Coral Pink Sand Dunes State Park near Kanab, is a breathtaking expanse of brilliant pink and red sands sculpted by the wind. This natural wonder, shaped over ages, offers a dynamic dunescape that seems to glow under the sun. An ever-changing outdoor canvas, it's a paradise for off-roaders, photographers, and those seeking to witness nature's artistry in a serene desert backdrop.

Desert Mound Mine A testament to the region's mining history, this abandoned mine narrates tales of old. Explore the remains and machinery from bygone days.

Deer Creek ATV A 2,053 ft moderately popular singletrack trail near Brian Head Utah. The Deer Creek ATV trail allows users to travel in both directions and features a moderate overall physical rating with a 140 ft green climb. On average, it takes 5 minutes to complete this trail.

D.I. Ranch Originally acquired by mobster Moe Dalitz in 1954. Dalitz named the ranch after the Desert Inn in Las Vegas, which Dalitz also owned. Throughout its history, the ranch has been a destination for Dalitz and his family, as well as Las Vegas showgirls, high-rolling customers, and assorted characters. Despite its unsavory past, some Utah polygamists believe the D.I. Ranch has religious significance, while others see it as a potential wilderness retreat for troubled teens. Today, it is owned by a partnership of prominent Washington County individuals and managed by Lemuel "Lem" Leavitt, who oversees cattle operations on this 831-acre property.

Dixie Sugarloaf Standing proudly in St. George, Utah, the Dixie Sugarloaf tells the story of the area's geological history. This distinctive red rock formation, reminiscent of a sugarloaf, has become an iconic symbol of the city. In addition to its geological significance, the Sugarloaf has played a role in local culture and history, with "Dixie" emblazoned on its side as a nod to the area's early settlers. This natural monument reminds both residents and visitors of St. George's unique blend of natural beauty and pioneering spirit. Whether you're capturing its beauty at sunset or admiring it from afar, the Dixie Sugarloaf is lasting symbol of the city's rich heritage.

Enterprise Sinclair Station A point of historical significance and a waypoint on many a journey.

Elephant Arch Elephant Arch is located in the Red Cliffs National Desert Reserve in northern Washington, Utah, and is a stunning natural wonder. This modest sandstone formation, reminiscent of an elephant's trunk and eye, perches partway up a hill, marking the terminus of a rustic hiking path. Its unique shape attracts both adventurers and nature enthusiasts.

Flag Point / Indian Cliff Dwelling & Pit Houses Travel back in time with ancient Indian cliff dwellings and pit houses.

Casto Canyon Renowned for its distinct red rock formations, this trail provides both hiking and off-road adventures. Nearby areas such as Freemont Trail, Hancock Peak, Highway 12, Red Canyon, and Peterson Point add to the experience with their unique landscapes.

Cedar Area Trip Beginning in Parowan and stretching to Brian Head and Panguitch Lake, this journey takes you through terrains like Birch Springs. It's a refreshing high-country trip ideal for warm weather.

Cliffs of Insanity, Warner Valley Nestled in Warner Valley, the Cliffs of Insanity feature the striking Mexican skirt formation. The sheer magnitude and beauty of these cliffs make them a must-visit spot.

Cottonwood Canyon, Bear Valley to Panguitch Lake Traverse from the dense forests of Cottonwood Canyon to the serene shores of Panguitch Lake. The journey offers both mountainous terrains and lush valleys, making it a visual treat.

Crazy Jug Point Bill Hall Lookout Experience the vastness of the Grand Canyon from the vantage of Crazy Jug Point. Nearby, Bill Hall Lookout intensifies the panorama, with layers of geologic history unfolding before your eyes.

Diamond Valley to LEEDS Travel from Diamond Valley through Cottonwood Canyon and culminate your journey in LEEDS. The route showcases old cabins, charcoal kilns, a museum, and remnants of a silver mine.

Fredonia Fire Point Feel the warmth of history and the cool breeze of altitude at Fredonia Fire Point. This lookout stands as a silent guardian, watching over the ever-changing landscape below.

Glitter Mine Situated near the Arizona border and a quick 25-minute drive from St. George, Glitter Mine, or "Glitter Mountain," is a unique geological site. This location has a mound covered in shimmering gypsum pieces and a noticeable pit exposing the gypsum beneath the surface. Visitors are encouraged to enjoy the spectacle from outside the pit. There are gypsum fragments on the ground to take home as souvenirs, making it a fun excursion, especially for kids.

Gold Strike, Utah Dive into the tales of gold mining in Utah, exploring every facet from patios and solution mining to the rich legacy of the Beaver Dam wash.

Gooseberry Mesa Discover the spectacular scenery of Gooseberry Mesa and Hurricane Cliffs in southern Utah's red rock country. These trails, celebrated for both biking and UTV riding, offer world-class experiences with breathtaking mesa rim views.

Grafton Revel in the history of Grafton, a pioneering town located just south of Zion National Park. Known as the most photographed ghost town in the West, Grafton has been featured in several films, including the classic 'Butch Cassidy and the Sundance Kid.

Gunlock Reservoir Enjoy boating, fishing, and swimming in the tranquil waters for year-round recreation and natural beauty, away from the city's hustle and bustle. The reservoir's warm summer waters and the area's mild winter climate make it a perfect destination for any season. Occasionally, the nearby red rocks transform into vibrant waterfalls, offering a breathtaking natural spectacle that enhances the beauty of this picturesque spot.

Gunsight Point A sentinel of the North Rim, Gunsight Point unveils the expansive beauty of the canyon. A vista like no other, it promises views that leave even the most seasoned travelers in awe.

Hell Dive Canyon Pictographs The Moquith Mountain Wilderness is home to the historic Hell Dive Canyon Pictographs. Discover unique depictions protected beneath alcoves, making for an enlightening hike filled with wonder.

Hell Hole Pass Venture along the captivating Hell Hole Pass trail, weaving through Indian Springs and reaching the pinnacle at Utah Mountain. Navigate past intriguing TV towers and bask in panoramic views that span across the expansive region.

Hurricane Cliffs Ascend the historic Honeymoon Trail to reach the summit of Hurricane Cliffs, offering vistas that stretch for miles. Explore historic trails, rock formations, and discover the history of ancient marital journeys to the St. George Temple.

Hurricane Mesa Test Facility Initially an Air Force base, the Hurricane Mesa Test Facility showcases a 12,000-foot test track and played a significant role in aviation testing. Today, it stands as a testament to the advancements in aerospace and a slice of history.

Indian Walkway/Barracks Overlook Dive deep into history at the Indian Walkway, a ceremonial pathway adorned with boundary stones. Situated amidst the Coral Pink Sand Dunes region, the Barracks Overlook offers views of the enchanting Poverty Flats.

Ivins Reservoir Also known as Fire Lake Park, this serene and picturesque body of water in Ivins, Utah, is nestled amidst the stunning desert landscape. The reservoir is a peaceful place for locals and visitors to enjoy fishing, boating, and the beauty of the region.

Jackson Spring Petroglyphs Start at Motoqua Road and unravel a path leading to the intriguing Jackson Spring Petroglyphs and Pictographs. The challenging ascent leads to a mountaintop with ancient rock inscriptions and a secluded pictograph cave.

Kanab A high-desert town in southern Utah, is known for its striking red rock landscapes and status as a gateway to the Grand Canyon, blending its role as a commercial center with a rich history in filmmaking.

Kolob Terrace to Cedar Canyon This scenic trail takes you through beautiful landscapes from Kolob Reservoir to Cedar Canyon. Bask in the coolness of the aspens and pines, while enjoying the stunning views overlooking Cedar City.

Kolob to Kanarraville Navigate through scenic terrains, respecting the gates and the herds they protect. Amid the dense forest cover and scattered cabins, experience the untouched beauty of this journey.

Last Chance Canyon / Hidden Canyon The trail boasts magnificent views from Last Chance Knoll, with blooming cacti and the drive down Rattlesnake canyon. You can also view the remains of a way station used by Grand Gulch miners.

La Verkin Canal Overlook, Hurricane Canal Overlook This trail ride follows along the base of Smith Mesa and Gooseberry Mesa, offering scenic views. There are stops at both the LaVerkin canal and Hurricane canal overlooks.

Lion's Mouth Cave & Petroglyphs A natural cavern known for its entrance resembling a lion's mouth. Close by are some impressive pictographs nestled in an alcove at Lion's Mouth rock formation.

Little Creek Mesa A grand mesa offering breathtaking views, a fishing lake, Anasazi ruins, pottery fragments, and unique petroglyphs.

Lone Pine Arch / Conception Cave Embark on the Sand Cove Trail out of Dameron Valley, leading to Manganese road and Motoqua road. Petroglyphs, the beautiful Lone Pine Arch, and the hidden Conception Cave with its petroglyphs await discovery.

Jackson Spring Petroglyphs A unique combination of natural beauty and ancient artistry.

Long Valley Foothills A picturesque trail that starts at Washington Dam Rd. The terrain varies, offering both challenges and scenic views to the travelers.

Lost Springs Mesa Panoramic overlooks, a view of the Hurricane Cliffs and the Arizona Strip, and the challenge of a washed-out bridge beckons off-roaders.

Lytle Ranch In southern Utah, Lytle Ranch is a unique oasis amidst the desert landscapes, renowned for its rich biodiversity. This lavish paradise attracts researchers and naturalists, who want to study its rich biodiversity. Its serene environment and lush greenery stand in stark contrast to the surrounding arid region, making it a captivating spot for visitors.

Mineral Mountain Experience the scenic trail through General Steam canyon leading to the White Pinnacles and the vastness of Mineral Mountain.

Modina, State Line Mine, Deer Lodge, Jenny Mine Journey through history, from the old railroad town of Modina to the relics of the State Line Mine, Deer Lodge, and the silver mines of Nevada.

Moqui Cave A sandstone erosion cave in southern Utah, sits about 5 miles north of Kanab along U.S. Route 89 and was historically used by Anasazi people. Now, it serves as a natural history museum, featuring an extensive collection of Native American artifacts and dinosaur tracks.

Moquith Mountain Discover the beauty near Coral Pink Sand Dunes State Park, from vast dunes and slickrock plateaus to the hidden South Fork Indian Pictographs. Prep for a demanding hike and be sure to carry water.

Nephi Twist Start at Nephi's Twist in La Verkin and experience the rocky bed of La Verkin Creek, complete with creek crossings and a challenging canyon climb.

North of Beaver Elevated terrains, a picturesque waterfall, and a historical miners' camp await exploration.

Old Irontown A historical site echoing tales of Utah's iron mining legacy. Here, remains of a once-thriving town offer glimpses into the past.

Old Tobin Wash Trail A route that takes you through iconic juniper trees, leading to the serene Pine Valley Mountain. Along the way, you'll encounter landmarks like the Little Red Canyon and the Lone Pine Petroglyphs.

Orderville Gulch to Strawberry Point Start in Orderville, a quaint historical town originally founded with no property rights under the United Order, and journey through Zion Ponderosa and North Fork to Strawberry Point. This location is locally renowned for its panoramic views. The popular trail concludes east of Duck Creek.

Parowan Parowan Gap in southwestern Utah is a natural wonder, carved through red sandstone hills. It's famous for its colorful geology and dinosaur footprints. What makes it special are the hundreds of ancient petroglyphs along the narrowest section. It's a great spot to explore and see these carvings and dino tracks up close, offering a unique blend of outdoor fun and a peek into the past.

Peekabo Slot Canyon to Johnston Canyon Traverse a deep narrow canyon with soft sandy paths and towering sandstone walls.

Pinnacles Trail Near Kanab, Utah, Pinnacles Trail extends 9.2 miles and boasts a moderate rating. A year-round destination, it's a haven for off-road enthusiasts and their canine companions.

Poverty Flats This trail east of Zion, winds through Pinion Pines and Junipers, with scenic views similar to the Barracks trail, but with no river crossings.

Quail Hill Pass Another off-roading haven known for its challenging terrains and vistas. It offers elevated views of Twin Point, a seldom-visited viewpoint overlooking the north rim of the Grand Canyon, nestled amidst dense Ponderosa pines.

Sand Hollow Utah Is home to the stunning Sand Hollow reservoir that attracts both water enthusiasts and anglers. Surrounded by red sand dunes, it offers thrilling off-roading adventures for ATV and dirt bike riders. The area is a popular outdoor destination, combining aquatic recreation with desert exploration.

Sand Mountain Recreation Area ATV riders and dune buggy enthusiasts love this vast area for its adrenaline-pumping rides on sandy terrains. The nearby Sand Hollow Tunnel is an added attraction, offering a unique travel experience.

SAND MOUNTAIN SPOTS INCLUDE:
Top of the World This trail takes riders to elevated viewpoints, with breathtaking panoramas of the surrounding landscape.
Flintstone House Named for its unique rock formations reminiscent of the popular cartoon, this area is a must-visit for geology enthusiasts and those looking for a quirky off-road destination.
The Chute A challenging stretch for off-roaders, The Chute promises thrills with its steep inclines and rough terrains.
Sand Dunes An off-roader's paradise, this area is all about dune bashing and conquering sandy terrains. Expect an adrenaline rush as you navigate through the shifting sands.
Resurrection Trail This trail promises a blend of natural beauty and challenging terrains, making it a favorite among seasoned off-roaders.
Parade Ground Memorial Known for its tranquility and historical significance, this destination honors important events and figures from the past. Surrounded by natural beauty, it's a great spot for both reflection and off-road adventure.

<u>Other Sand Hollow Attractions:</u>
- **Sand Hollow Tunnel**
- **Edge of the World**
- **Papa Smurf**
- **Water Tanks, Staging Area, and Green Gate**

- *Milt's Mile*
- *Fault Line, Lower West Rim*
- *Razzle Dazzle*
- *Wayne's World*
- *Fallen*
- *Double Sammy*
- *Front Range*
- *East Rim & West Rim*
- *Triple Seven*
- *Hot Tub*
- *Washington Dam Underpass / The Tanks*
- *PLAN B*
- *Ledges*
- *Sliplock Gulch*
- *Maze*
- *Soup Bowl*
- *Landslide Trail (AZ Strip Overlook)*

Second Left Hand Canyon to Duck Creek
This scenic drive elevates travelers to over 10,000 ft, revealing the aftermath of the Brian Head fires. Side trails lead to the picturesque Yankee Meadow, with the main trail meandering through a dense forest dotted with summer mud holes.

Seegmiller Mountain / Hole in the Wall
Begin your journey into the Arizona strip on the south River Road, ascending Seegmiller Mountain and then descending to Hole in the Rock Canyon. The Sunshine trail brings you back, but not before offering incredible views and thrilling terrains.

Shinob Kibe Trail Experience the hidden charm of Shinob Kibe Trail, starting in the midst of a bustling community but offering a tranquil refuge. Named after a Paiute deity, this mesa served as a refuge from neighboring tribes and features an ancient medicine wheel near the summit. As a bonus, it houses one of the old aviation navigation arrows used for mail routes from Los Angeles to Salt Lake City. Although the elevation gain is challenging, you'll find the panoramic views and a guest book waiting for you to explore at the summit.

Shivwits Brickhouse In 1986, a historical site lost both its chapel and schoolhouse because of a devastating fire. The location played a significant role in educating Native American children until the early 1940s, highlighting its importance in the Shivwits Paiute community. The establishment of the reservation dates back to 1903, as mentioned in a 1994 article in the Daily Spectrum.

Short Creek Mesa South of Little Creek Mesa, you can enjoy panoramic views of the Honeymoon trail, Mt. Trumbull, Colorado City, Red Cliffs, and the peaks of Zion. The Cookie Cutter Petroglyphs, named for their unique depth, are a short hike away.

Smith Mesa Loop Starting in Virgin and veering onto the Kolob Terrace Road, this trail provides non-stop views of landmarks like Red Butte, Burnt Mountain, and Timbertop. When descending from Smith Mesa to Hurricane Mesa, travelers can catch a glimpse of the rocket sled track and view pictographs, concluding the journey in Virgin.

Snow Canyon State Park Located in Utah's Red Cliffs Desert Reserve, Snow Canyon offers a stunning display of red and white Navajo sandstone formations, ancient lava flows, lava tube caves, and sand dunes, all set against the backdrop of the extinct Santa Clara Volcano. A true desert jewel, it's a perfect spot for picturesque hikes and nature exploration.

Temple Trail / Sunshine Trail A historic path that pioneers used for lumber transport to build the Temple. The trail winds through Warner Valley, reaching highway 7. Also know as the historic Honeymoon Trail, once taken by pioneers on their marital journeys to the St. George Temple. Witness sections of hand-stacked rocks, original trail remnants, and unparalleled cliff-top vistas. **The St. George, Utah Temple is** the longest operating temple of the LDS Church, and the first temple built in Utah.

Tom's Canyon Feel the thrill of navigating Tom's Canyon's challenging terrain, featuring slick rock and sandy ascents. In addition to the off-road adventure, you will be treated to expansive canyon and hilltop views.

Tusher Mountain Offering off-roaders stunning mountain views and diverse terrains.

Tweed Point This is a popular destination offering panoramic views of the Pakoon Basin and Grand Wash Cliffs. A high clearance 4x4 with a short wheelbase is recommended for the journey.

White Dome Nature Preserve Discover a hidden gem of natural beauty, where you can explore unique sandstone formations. Nestled in a pristine setting, it features an abundance of desert plants and animals. The preserve is a testament to conservation efforts, protecting the landscape for future generations.

Vernal Rock Valley Known for its unique rock formations and scenic beauty.

Veyo Nestled in a volcanic landscape, Veyo is renowned for its scenic pool and delectable pies. The region boasts unique geological formations that provide a picturesque backdrop for off- roading.

Zion National Park Among the towering cliffs and breathtaking canyons of Zion National Park, you'll find iconic sandstone formations like Angel's Landing. Initially called Mukuntuweap National Monument, it was later changed to Zion National Monument in 1918 to increase its popularity among visitors. In 1919, it was redesignated as Zion National Park by Congress, with President Woodrow Wilson's approval. In 1937, they declared the Kolob section as a distinct national monument, but merged it into the park in 1956. Congress declared 85% of Zion a wilderness area in 2009. The park's famous red and tan sandstone formations, including Angel's Landing, attract millions of visitors annually.

Enjoyed the journey through Mesquite?

We're thrilled to offer you an exclusive opportunity to enhance your reading experience. Upgrade to the interactive eBook now and dive into a more engaging and immersive way of exploring this story.

Grab the eBook

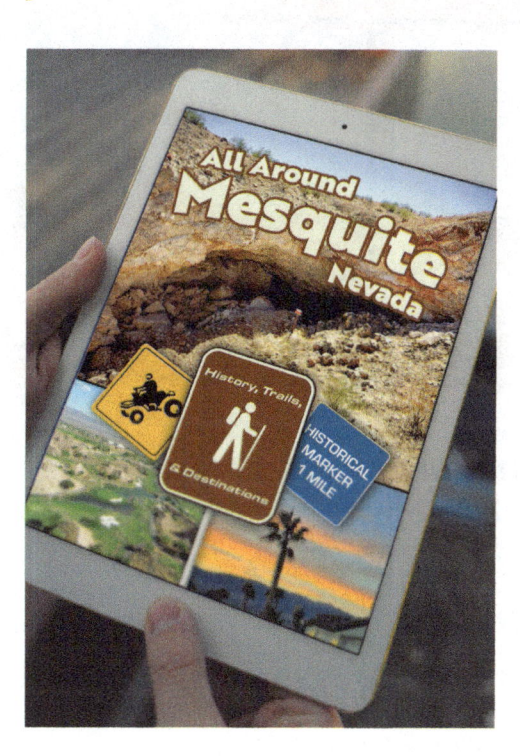

- **Always Updated**
  Get the latest discoveries directly on your Kindle or tablet

- **Digital Maps**
  Navigate routes with interactive digital trail mapping, regularly updated.

- **Mobile History**
  Carry Mesquite's tales and images on any smart device.

- **Quick References**
  Tap into our sources and links directly from your screen.

LEARN MORE BY VISITING...
www.MesquiteBook.com

Other Resources:

Discover what Mesquite, NV and the surrounding region have to offer through these great organizations:

Virgin Valley Heritage Museum
https://www.mesquitenv.gov/departments/museum

The Kokopelli ATV Club - http://kokopelliatvclub.com

Moapa Valley Progress Newspaper - https://mvprogress.com

The Lost City Museum - https://lostcitymuseum.org

OLSHACS - https://olshacs.org

MVRP - https://www.moapavalleyrevitalization.org

EPILOGUE

As the final pages of this guide come to a close, so too does our journey through the enchanting city of Mesquite, Nevada. But remember, every ending is but a new beginning. The trails, histories, and destinations we've explored in this book are only a fraction of the experiences that Mesquite offers. The city is full of untold stories, unexplored paths and hidden landmarks. Mesquite's history, spanning from the days of the Paiute tribe to its modern dynamism, is a testament to the city's resilience and evolution. These trails are just a sample of the many opportunities available, and the listed destinations invite you to explore further.

The true essence of Mesquite lies not just in its history or landscapes, but in its people. The warmth of its residents, the richness of their stories, and the vibrancy of the culture make Mesquite a city like no other. As you explore, converse with locals, and embrace its heritage, you'll find untold stories waiting to be shared with the world. For those who have been with Mesquite from the start, this guide may have rekindled memories and renewed pride in your hometown. May this book ignite curiosity and a desire to explore for newcomers and visitors.

The purpose of this guide is to provide a holistic overview of Mesquite. Like all great cities, Mesquite is constantly changing, with endless opportunities to learn, explore, and appreciate.

So, as you put down this book, consider it not the end but an intermission. Mesquite awaits your next visit, your next adventure, your next story. Embrace the spirit of discovery and adventure in Mesquite, where the journey is as exciting as the destination.

Thank you for joining us on this captivating adventure. Whether you're a resident or a traveler, let the spirit of Mesquite forever inspire you.

Until our paths cross again, safe travels and happy discoveries.

AFTERWORD

Within these pages lies an account of survival, faith, and discovery that I am grateful to be recounting. The grace of a higher power surely intervened during the research of this book.

For the past three years, I've been immersing myself in the history and landscape of the Mesquite, Nevada region, where Jessica and I live. I've been compiling information about the historic sites, trails, and unique aspects of this area for an e-book, this book specifically. But the Firebrand Cave had eluded me. An ancient ceremonial site, it remains unknown to many locals.

In early 2023, I heard whispers of this elusive cave. Firebrand Cave isn't just any landmark; it holds significant historical and cultural importance for the natives of Southern Nevada. Articles disclosing its location have mysteriously vanished or been redacted. My most promising lead? A UNLV study book that is out of print and only available from the Library of Congress. Luckily, I could gather some details from the cover. Archaeologists have unearthed treasures like native pottery, spirit sticks, firebrands, and ceremonial weapons. Yet, much about it remains a mystery. According to legend, Shamanic leaders used to meditate here, seeking spiritual visions.

With insights from Gold Butte locals and exhaustive research, I was confident that I had pinpointed its location. Unfortunately, when we arrived at our intended starting point, unexpected obstacles blocked our way: posts obstructed the trail, and a barbed wire fence further up the hill prevented easy access to the mountain.

The intense summer heat had foiled my initial two expeditions. But this year's Labor Day weekend, with the temperature expected to peak at a more manageable 91 degrees, I felt a renewed resolve. I've driven thousands of miles on the local trail systems and had yet to face anything like what was about to unfold...

Accompanied by my friend Richard, we made the trek to Gold Butte on a lesser-known route. The path led us through areas that had been slippery and wet because of recent flash flooding. We crawled over rocks and blazed new trails to get to what used to be a common area. Finally, we reached the post markers. Armed with essentials like light backpacks, sustenance, flashlights, first aid kits, and a half dozen water bottles, we set off on foot. Our determination wavered momentarily when we realized we had strayed from our path and gone over a mile in the wrong direction. However, our shared tenacity propelled us forward, refusing to let our hard work be for nothing.

After a grueling journey traversing washes, navigating cow paths, and scaling uphill trails, we stood before our destination: the ancient ceremonial cave. Although we wanted to explore more of its history and traverse the cave, the warning signs told us to proceed with caution. We had lunch and felt a sense of accomplishment reflecting on the journey and marveled at finding the historical site. With a mixture of fulfillment and longing, we turned back before too long, opting for what seemed to be the most direct route home.

The return journey proved even more challenging than expected. Dehydration and fatigue posed significant threats, as we quickly weakened under the blazing desert sun. I didn't want to become another statistic — someone who ran out of water and died in the Mojave Desert.

We were facing exhaustion and dehydration, and had to choose between summoning a rescue helicopter via emergency satellite call, or forging ahead on our own.

We were still seemingly miles away from our base camp. The trek, originally planned to be under 3 miles, had already extended over 5 miles so far, with unexpected elevation changes, hotter than expected temperatures, and rugged terrain adding to our challenge. We became painfully aware that we were too drained to continue, exhausted to the core.

I took it upon myself to move ahead, a barrage of prayers on my lips as I envisioned reaching our vehicle and the lifesaving supplies within. Every step felt heavier than the last, my body threatening to give up on me at any moment. The sight of the fence gave me a glimmer of hope, pushing me to venture downhill to the RZR where I could hardly stand.

With newfound energy gained from urgent hydration, I mustered the strength to steer the vehicle closer to Richard by navigating through the fence. We were both at our limits, but together we escaped the danger we found ourselves in. We expressed heartfelt prayers of gratitude and acknowledgment of the divine intervention that guided us.

However, our journey was not yet at an end. Misjudgment induced by fatigue resulted in a hasty retreat. Still in shock from the desert heat, I hit a mound from a bad line, and it sent us toppling into a gully. Luckily, the rig landed tightly across the fall and was stuck in place. Had it rolled over further, it might have sent us down a good-sized drop-off, becoming our demise in our weakened condition. I crawled out and walked sluggishly up the hill, finding a weak cell signal to call for help from a new acquaintance.

Using the upturned vehicle as shelter from the blazing sun, we waited. Our backup supplies were slowly being drained and we were too exhausted to go any where. We were far from any help and waited nearly 2 hours under the small veil of shade provided by my wrecked UTV. It was quiet, and it felt like an eternity before we heard an engine in the wash. Our friend arrived. Alone, with just his dog and a 2-seat XP 1000, I thought our only option would be for him to drive us back to civilization one at a time. I said another prayer, "Lord, you saved us twice so far, but I would love it if we could somehow drive out of here in one piece."

Tipped over UTV provided Shade.

My prayer was answered. With a combination of perseverance and cowboy ingenuity, and the help of a person of distinction (who had ties to a famous off-road recovery show and was a great gentleman I had met just a week prior), we pulled from every angle until the vehicle was high-centered. Finally, we managed to drag it out of the gully and back onto its wheels. Despite minimal damage, we could limp the vehicle down the hill and allow the fluids to settle.

It ran fine! Our friend told us of a quicker route back through Cliven's Landing, saving us precious time. We arrived in Mesquite, immediately sought water and drove home just in time for sunset. What a day!

There are still facets of this adventure I cannot share, for reasons best kept under wraps for now. I can say with complete certainty that we experienced miracles that day, and the Lord was watching over us. I'm grateful to be here, sharing this journey with you.

Desert Covenant Books

In the lead-up to my remarkable experience in the cave, a sequence of events unfolded in Mesquite, each guiding me towards a deeper understanding and faith, including some undeniable divine interventions. These experiences, culminating in the recent adventure that pushed me to my limits, have filled me with profound gratitude. The miraculous nature of my journey, where I escaped with my life not just once but twice, and the ability to drive my vehicle home after the accident, are testaments to a greater promise fulfilled. It's now my duty to honor these experiences by giving glory to God and sharing these stories with the world.

Motivated by this, I founded Desert Covenant Books. Our aim is to narrate not only the fascinating tales of this land but also to illuminate stories of faith, resilience, and divine providence. If you've had a Christian-based experience of your own and are looking for a way to share your testimony, I invite you to join me. Let's work together to bring your story to the forefront.

Desert Covenant Books

desertcovenant.com

ACKNOWLEDGMENTS

Organizations that have helped support this book - directly & indirectly...

The Virgin Valley Heritage Museum, City of Mesquite, Mesquite Fire & Rescue, Mesquite PD, Mesquite Branding, RMOR (Rocky Mountain Off Road), The Rugged Outdoorsmen, Juniper Outpost Boutique Store, Adventure Rentals, Bundy Exhaust Brake, Desert Rats, Sun American Mortgage (The Utleys), The Kokopelli ATV Club, Polaris World CANAM, Mohave County Sheriff's Office Search and Rescue, Moapa Valley Revitalization Project, Slurp Smoothies, Mesquite Technologies, Moapa Valley Chamber of Commerce, BirdandHike.com, Friends of Gold Butte, Mesquite Trails RV Park, Mesquite Chamber of Commerce, Virgin Valley 4x4 Club, St. George Jeepers, First Baptist Church Mesquite, The Historical Beaver Dam Lodge, The Virgin River Coalition and The Lost City Museum.

Thank you sincerely to everyone who has helped along the way. I apologize if I've inadvertently left anyone out, but please know that your support has been greatly appreciated.

Thanks for sharing this Mesquite experience with us.
To God Be the Glory!

-Dustin Berg

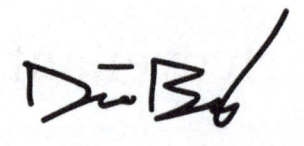

ACKNOWLEDGMENTS

By the grace of God, I had planned for a long time to write a book, but it wasn't until we moved to Mesquite, Nevada that I found the passion & drive to do so. Here's to the first of many.

Special thanks to my wife, who empowered me to believe in myself and demonstrated that I can follow through. Thank you, Jessica Berg, for being my number one supporter.

Thank you to my entire family - biological, extended and adopted! Thank you to my Mom, Dad, Step Dad, Grandparents, Daughters, Aunts, Uncles and everyone in between!

This book wouldn't be possible without the trail contributions, stories, or general inspiration from these individuals: Geoffrey Slater, Richard Cook, Krissy and Val Woods, Elspeth Kuta, John Belanger (The Rugged Outdoorsmen), Wayne Rasmussen, Dan Schwartzman, Lori Johnson, Justin Teerlink, Colton Teerlink, Arden Bundy, Ryan Bundy, Carol Kolson, David Neufeld, Julie Pershing, Debra Yergen, Annie Black, Vernon Robison, Kasen Kolhoss, Sonny Graham, Lyle Palmer, Larry Conner, Shane Butehorn, John Getchel, Andrew Bird, and likely many others.

Special thanks to Trenton Robison for his help in putting this together and managing a rolling deadline with countless revisions. I appreciate your help and patience.

REFERENCES

A River and a Road:
In Honor of Mesquite, Nevada's Centennial 1994
Frehner Thurston, Dorothy Dawn. Thurston 1994

Mesquite and the Virgin Valley
White Zarate, Geraldine. Arcadia Publishing 2010

Lords of St. Thomas
Ellis, Jackson. Green Writers Press 2018

Muddy: Where Faith and Polygamy Collide
Hughes, Dean. Deseret Book, 2019

The Desert Between Us
Barber, Phyllis. University of Nevada Press 2020

The Settlements on the Muddy 1865 to 1871:
"A God Forsaken Place"
Fleming, L.A. Utah Historical Society 1967

Crazy Ed's Sagas and Secrets of Desert Gold
Bounsall, Eddie. Bounsall 1992

Crazy Ed's Sagas and Secrets of Desert Gold 2
Bounsall, Eddie. Bounsall 1993

The Prehistory of Gold Butte:
A Virgin River Hinterland, Clark County, Nevada
University of Utah Anthropological Paper
McGuire, Kelly R. and Hildebrandt, William R., et al.
University of Utah Press 2013

Where Should We Camp Next?: A 50-State Guide to Amazing
Campgrounds and Other Unique Outdoor Accommodations
Puglisi, Stephanie. Sourcebooks 2021

The Overland Journey from Utah to California:
Wagon Travel from The City of Saints to The City of Angels
Lyman, Edward Leo. University of Nevada Press 2004

A Thousand Dead Horses
Miller, Rod. Five Star Publishing 2021

Muddy Valley Reflections: 145 Years of Settlement
Tobiasson, Beezy and Hall, Georgia. Tobiasson 2010

100 Years on the Muddy
Hafner, Arabel Lee. Art City Publishing 1967

The Roll Away Saloon
Rider, Rowland W. Utah State University Press 1985

Firebrand Cave: An Archaic Ceremonial Site in Southern Nevada
Blair, Lynda M. and Winslow, Diane L. University of NV 2006

© Copyright Desert Covenant Books, LLC.   All Rights Reserved.

ABOUT THE AUTHOR

Hailing from Yakima, Washington, Dustin Berg first set foot in Mesquite in 2019, hoping for a new beginning. Life, however, had its own set of plans, and while unexpected twists presented challenges, they also added great passion and depth to his narrative. In his personal life, Dustin proudly takes on multiple roles: a devoted husband, a loving father to two adopted stepdaughters, an avid UTV enthusiast, and a caring guardian to three dogs and a cat.

In the business world, Dustin has gained experience and achieved success in marketing and communications. Throughout a career spanning over 15 years, he has assisted over 500 small business owners, helping their brands reach new heights. He's a skilled businessman, who enjoys making the perfect BBQ brisket and has a natural entrepreneurial spirit.

"**All Around Mesquite**", is a departure from his usual professional pursuits. This heartfelt work is an ode to his desert community. Dustin pays tribute to the resilient spirit of Mesquite's pioneers, and deeply respects their determination. The book becomes a symbol of endurance, both of a land and its inhabitants, and the deep community bonds they share.

At the heart of his Mesquite experiences, and woven throughout his life's tapestry, is Dustin's connection with God in Christ, a quiet anchor amidst the ever-challenging desert sands of life.

I can do all this through Him who gives me strength.
Philippians 4:13

INDEX

13 Mile Loop	*123*
1880 Rock House	*109*
21 Goats Petroglyphs	*109*
Airplane Ridge	*132*
Amelia Earhart	*44*
Anasazi Valley	*157*
Apple Valley Chevron	*157*
Aravada Springs	*109*
Art Coleman	*76*
Ash Springs, Nevada	*132*
Aviation Arrow	*109*
Baker Dam	*157*
Bar 10 Ranch	*138*
Barclay and Pine Park	*157*
Barracks Overlook	*163*
Barracks Trail	*157*
Beaver	*157*
Beaver Dam Lodge	*138*
Beaver Dam Wash	*157*
Bigfoot	*53*
Bill Hall Lookout	*161*
Black Mountain	*157*
BLM Pakoon Basin Airstrip	*138*
Bloomington Cave	*158*
Bloomington Petroglyph Park	*158*
Boundary Peak Survey Marker	*143*
Brian Head, Utah	*158*
Buckskin Gulch Budweiser Fence	*109*
Bullfrog Basin Bunker Pass Rd Burnt Mountain	*158*
Cabin Canyon Road: An Exciting 4wd Route	*110*
Cabin Spring Rock Cabin Castle Cliff Station	*110*
Casto Canyon	*163*
Cedar Breaks	*159*

182

Cedar Canyon	159
Cedar Pocket Sinkhole	143
Choo Choo	110
Clark Gable	50
Cliffs of Insanity	161
Colorado City Red Cliffs	151
Conception Cave	164
Coral Pink Sand Dunes State Park	159
Cottonwood Canyon	161
Crazy Jug Point	161
d.i. Ranch	160
Davidson Memorial Deer Creek	133
Deer Lodge	165
Delamar, Nevada: The Widowmaker	133
Desert Mound Mine	159
Devil's Cove	110
Devil's Throat	111
Diamond Valley	151
Dinosaur Rock	143
Dixie Sugarloaf	160
Double Sammy	166
Drain Tubes	143
Duck Creek	167
East Rim & West Rim	166
Edge of the World	166
Elbow Canyon	144
Elephant Arch	160
Elgin Schoolhouse State Historic Site	133
Enterprise Sinclair Station	160
Fallen	166
Falling Man Petroglyph	111
Fault Line, Lower West Rim	166
Figure 4 Canyon	143
Firebrand Cave	111
Fire Lake	163
Fisherman's Cove	112
Flag Point / Indian Cliff Dwelling & Pit Houses	161
Flat Top Mesa	112
Flintstone House	166
Fredonia Fire Point	161
Frehner Haven Ranch (Cold Springs Ranch)	144

Front Range	166
Garden of Eden Aka Red Rocks (Outcropping)	144
Garden of Eden Slot Canyon:	145
Gibson Jones Ranch	145
Glitter Mine	161
Gold Butte Cistern	113
Gold Butte Townsite	113
Gold Strike, Utah	162
Gooseberry Mesa, Grafton	162
Grand Gulch Mine	145
Great Eastern Mine	113
Grotto	145
Gunlock	162
Gunsight Point	162
Halloween Point	145
Hancock Peak Heart of the Mesa	161
Hell Dive Canyon Petroglyphs	162
Hell Hole Pass	162
Hidden Canyon	164
Hole in the Rock Canyon	167
Honeymoon Trail	166
Howard Hughes	39
House Rock Valley	169
Hump'n'bump Event	123
Hurricane Canal Overlook	164
Hurricane Cliffs	163
Hurricane Mesa	163
Ice Cave	145
Indian Walkway	163
Ivins Reservoir	163
Jackson Spring Petroglyphs	163
Jacob's Well	145
Jenny Mine	165
Johnston Canyon	165
Kanab	163
Kanarraville	164
Key West Mine	114
Keyhole Rock	114
Kit Carson	23
Knife-Blade Cliffs	114
Kolob Terrace	163

Kolob Terrace Road	*163*
La Verkin Canal Overlook	*164*
Lake Mead National Recreation Area	*121*
Lakeside Mine	*123*
Landslide Trail (AZ Strip Overlook)	*167*
Last Chance Canyon	*164*
Ledges	*167*
Leeds	*161*
Limekiln Canyon	*146*
Lion's Mouth Cave & Petroglyphs	*164*
Little Creek Mesa	*164*
Little Finland, Gold Butte	*113*
Little Grand Canyon	*146*
Little Jamaica	*146*
Logandale Trails System	*123*
Lone Mesa	*133*
Lone Pine Arch	*164*
Long Valley Foothills	*164*
Lost City	*124*
Lost Springs Mesa	*164*
Lot's Wife	*115*
Lower & Upper Lime Mountain Wells	*133*
Lower Toquop Rd	*114*
Lytle Ranch	*164*
Maze	*167*
Mesquite Healing Garden/Labyrinth	*114*
Mesquite Medicine Wheel	*115*
Middle Canyon	*146*
Milt's Mile	*166*
Mineral Mtn	*164*
Moapa Navigation Arrow	*125*
Moapa Valley Branch of the Bank of Las Vegas	*124*
Moapa Valley National Wildlife Refuge	*124*
Modina, State Line Mine	*165*
Moquith Mountain	*165*
Mormon Mesa	*124*
Mormon Mountains	*133*
Mountain Man	*144*
MSR	*146*
Mt. Ella	*134*
Mt. Trumbull	*165*

Mud Mountain	*147*
Muddy Mountains Wilderness	*125*
Navajo Lake	*159*
Nephi Twist	*165*
Nickel Creek	*115*
Old Irontown	*165*
Old Tobin Wash Trail	*165*
Orderville Gulch	*165*
Pakoon Basin	*147*
Pakoon Spring	*147*
Panguitch Lake	*161*
Papa Smurf	*166*
Parade Ground Memorial	*166*
Paria Plateau	*169*
Paria River	*169*
Parowan	*165*
Peekabo Slot Canyon	*165*
Pine Canyon Dam	*151*
Pinnacles Trail	*165*
PLAN B	*134*
Poverty Flats	*165*
Quail Hill	*166*
Radio Tower	*165*
Rainbow Canyon	*166*
Razzle Dazzle	*116*
Red Bluff Spring	*134*
Red Butte	*166*
Red Cliffs National Conservation Area	*116*
Red Pocket Mountain	*168*
Red Pocket Spring	*151*
Red Rocks	*147*
Resurrection Trail	*147*
Riverside Ghost Town	*126*
Rock Houses	*166*
Rogers Spring	*116*
Sand Dunes	*135*
Sand Hollow	*126*
Sand Mountain Recreation Area: Second Left Hand Canyon	*166*
Seegmiller Mountain	*165*
Seven Keyholes	*166*
Shedder Trail	*167*

Shinob Kibe	*116*
Shivwits Arch	*123*
Shivwits Brickhouse	*167*
Short Creek Mesa	*147*
Silver Leaf Mine	*167*
Silvestre Vélez de Escalante	*167*
Slats Jacobs	*116*
Sliplock Gulch	*20*
Smith Mesa	*145*
Smith Mesa Loop	*167*
St. Thomas	*26*
St. Thomas Memorial Cemetery	*126*
Strawberry Point	*165*
Sunshine Trail	*168*
Tassi Ranch	*147*
Temple Trail	*168*
The Beaver Dam Wilderness	*151*
The Chute	*166*
The Cookie Cutter Petroglyphs	*168*
The Little a'le'Inn	*135*
The Old Spanish Trail	*117*
The Pyramid	*117*
The Seeps	*117*
The Submarine	*117*
The Three Corners Monument	*135*
Thelma & Louise	*148*
Timbertop	*168*
Tom's Canyon	*168*
Top of the World	*166*
Toquop Wash	*118*
Toroweap	*148*
Triple Seven	*166*
Tusher Mtn	*168*
Tweed Point	*165*
Twin Points	*166*
Unsolved Mysteries	*59*
Valley of Fire State Park	*127*
Vermilion Cliffs Monument	*169*
Vernal Rock Valley	*169*
Veyo	*169*
Virgin Gorge Outlook	*149*

Virgin Mountains	*119*
Virgin River Canyon Recreation Area	*148*
Walter Ray Memorial	*136*
Warm Springs Natural Area	*127*
Warner Valley	*161*
Washington Dam Underpass / The Tanks	*167*
Water Tanks, Staging Area, and Green Gate	*166*
Wayne's World	*166*
Weiser Bowl	*128*
White Dome Nature Preserve	*169*
White Pocket	*149*
White Rock Campground	*118*
Whitney Corral	*118*
Whitney Pocket	*119*
Wolf Hole Valley	*149*
Zion National Park	*169*

IN PART SPONSORED BY...

YOUR LOCAL MOM-AND-POP MORTGAGE TEAM

**NORMAN & LORI UTLEY
LOAN OFFICERS**

Norman's NMLS# 1150450 | Lori's NMLS# 876186
CO NMLS# 160265 | NV LIC #5385
36 W Pioneer Blvd. Ste 105, Mesquite, NV 89027

SUN AMERICAN MORTGAGE

CONTACT US ANYTIME!
(725) 271-6060
theutleys@sunamerican.com

CONVENTIONAL | FHA | VA | USDA LOANS

UNLOCK YOUR ADVENTURE

POLARIS Can-Am HONDA WORLD

MESQUITE, NEVADA
ON-ROAD & OFF ROAD PARTS, SALES & SERVICE

Test Drive Today!
or
Ask About Free Delivery

Find out more by calling or texting
(702) 346 - 5429

Explore our entire inventory online at
PCH-WORLD.COM

Visit us in-store at
991 Hillside Drive, Mesquite, NV

All Around Mesquite Challenge

ACROSS:
4. Unlikely Creature at Pakoon Springs
7. Originally known as Moapa River
9. Desert Tree named after Bible Book
10. Ground Zero of the Bundy Standoff
11. Built by the CCC in Gold Butte
12. Mesa Due North of Mesquite
14. Rare Petroglyph Depiction of Man

DOWN:
1. Nickname of Dixie Red Rock
2. Southern Utah Petroglyphs and Cave
3. Home to Angel's Landing
5. Original County of Mesquite, NV
6. Figure Shown Near Virgin Canyon
8. Endangered Moapa Fish
12. Rock Climbing Sport Canyon in AZ Strip
13. Canyon Trail named after Body Part

IN CASE OF AN EMERGENCY, LOST OR INJURED

Contact the Lincoln County Sheriff's Office By Calling **911** or **(775) 962-5151**

(Note: CELL phone signals are line of sight. Find the highest spot to get a CELL signal. Texting may work when a phone call may not.)

Give Your Name _____

Nature of Emergency _____

GPS Location _____

Other emergency numbers:
Mesquite Police Department **(702) 346-6911**
Mohave County Search & Rescue **(928) 341-4901**

If you need evacuation by medical helicopter call: Mercy Air **(800) 222-3456**

It is preferred that you stay with your vehicle as long as possible to make locating you much easier, especially from the air. If you decide to walk for help, stay on well-traveled roads/trails. Leave information for searchers with the vehicle: where you're heading, the equipment and supplies you're taking, number in your party, when you left, and the color of the clothes you're wearing.

Made in the USA
Monee, IL
17 May 2024

58442722R00109